Gillian (Gill) Angrave

 Born in Leicester in 1945, Gillian was educated at Guthlaxton Grammar School and the Leicester College of Technology. After 3 years working in Leicester as a PA for an architect, an engineering company and The Rank Organisation, she joined P&O as an Assistant Purser in 1967, sailing in CANBERRA and ORIANA until 1974.

After a brief spell ashore, she again got itchy feet and in 1976 joined the Foreign & Commonwealth Office as Ambassador's PA, a position she held (and greatly enjoyed) for 29 years. Her postings took her to the Philippines, Peru, Guatemala, Chile, Mexico and Hungary. She retired from 'The Office' on 16 April 2005, her 60th birthday.

Single (her love of travel somehow always seemed to get in the way of marriage), upon retirement Gillian became a Registrar of Marriages in West Sussex, a job she also loves. Now she marries everyone else!

Hobbies: travel; photography; modern languages; bell-ringing, gardening; golf (1991 Hungarian Ladies Open Champion); and, of course, writing!

To my sister, Sheila,

with much love

Acknowledgements

As with any autobiography, people play a major part. I have had the privilege to know and work with some distinguished, learned and fun colleagues, and my life has been all the richer for it. We have been through many ups and downs together, and whilst an increasing number these days are sadly "crossing the bar", I value so much those who are still with me, especially my very close, life-long friends. This book is dedicated to you all, with more thanks than I can express for making my life so special.

However, there are one or two people to whom I owe a special debt of gratitude for encouraging, advising and supporting me through the writing and publishing of this book.

Firstly, my sincere thanks go to Sir John Birch, my Ambassador in Budapest, who has waded patiently through my drafts and taken on the task of adviser and general critic. I have so valued his input, encouragement and support, as well as that of his wife, Prim. Thank you both. I couldn't have done this without you.

Secondly, I am very much indebted to my graphic designer, Derek Hall, who has done a superb job in putting this book together, as well as giving me valuable advice and guidance with endless patience. I cannot recommend him highly enough. Thank you Derek.

My thanks, also, go to my "oldest" and closest friend, Marie, for her support and advice during the writing of my book, and to my dear friend, Pam. We have been on many adventures together, made all the more real through Marie's shared recollections and Pam's diaries.

And lastly, but by no means least, a huge thank you to my sister, Sheila, family and close friends, who yet again have had to endure my going on endlessly about yet another book. At least it's not Venice this time! As I always say: "keep the faith".

CONTENTS

Preface

I've been so lucky to have had the most wonderful life, including forty years of travelling all over the world doing jobs that I have loved. People have often asked me (yes, they have!) "Why don't you write about your experiences?" I must admit I've been tempted, but it just never seemed the right time somehow.

Until now. For no reason in particular, I've felt the time is right at last to embark on this literary journey and recount all that has happened to me over the years.

Re-living the past has been both rewarding and fun, but it has also been emotional, traumatic and sad. At times I've felt as if I've been assaulted by an army of ghosts, and buried under a cupboard full of skeletons, and trying to deal with these long-hidden feelings has been tough. It has caused a great deal of upheaval for my "little grey cells" which have for so long been happily enjoying a peaceful, stress-free retirement.

Going back over my life has also meant a lot of digging around in the attic for long forgotten photograph albums; looking at letters that I wrote to Mum and Dad so many years ago, and reminiscing with my best friends and former colleagues over shared times gone by. But, despite the many hours it has taken me, it has all been so worthwhile, and cathartic to a degree. My photographs may be showing their age, a bit like me, and may not be of the quality I would really like, but the memories they have resurrected are precious. Looking at them again has been, for me, a reminder of what fantastic friends I have, some of whom are sadly no longer with me, and of all that we have shared together.

PART ONE

HOW IT ALL BEGAN

CHAPTER ONE

THE GYPSY'S PROPHECY

The brass door knocker clanged loudly and persistently. My mother, who was in the back of the house, having gingerly taken the sheets out of the copper (pre-washing machines), was now struggling valiantly to get them to go in a straight line through the mangle rollers (pre-spin dryers). She tutted in exasperation, more at the sheets than being interrupted, and hurried to see what the caller wanted. On peering round the door, she had to look down to see who it was. A pair of dark eyes stared up at her, set in a wizened face that had obviously seen much hardship during its long life. Wrapped in a black shawl, embroidered skirt billowing in the breeze, the diminutive Romany gypsy pushed forward a woven basket containing sprigs of heather on one side, hand-crafted wooden dolly pegs on the other.

"Want to buy, Missus?"

The year was 1948. The end of the war at last. My parents, who were not at all well off, were living in a rented house, 11 Uplands Road, in Oadby, on the outskirts of Leicester, and could only afford to furnish four small rooms. Mum, who had heard many old wives' tales about the magical powers of these travellers, had very little cash to spare, but was reluctant to send the gypsy away lest she put a spell on the family. Such were the beliefs in those days! Looking at the items for sale, Mum didn't really want or need any of them, but feeling rather sorry for the old woman, decided that the dolly pegs would be the more useful (to hang up those horrid sheets!) and so she went to get her purse.

"How much for the pegs?" she asked.

"Thruppence for six would do very nicely, Dear", croaked the reply.

Mum rummaged around for the bronze coin, found easily as there was very little money in her purse. The gypsy took it gratefully and handed Mum the bundle of pegs.

"Shall I read your fortune?" she enquired.

Mum nodded, afraid it might be bad luck if she said "no", but dreading that it might cost more.

"You will have two daughters. One will be musical, and one will go over the seas", was all she said as she turned and trudged wearily back down the path.

"Thank you", Mum called after her, not quite sure what to make of the prophecy. Although she had one daughter, me, I was playing contently, out of sight, in the back garden with my much-loved pot-headed dolly, Dodo. Poor Dodo, not long after, met a tragic end when I slipped and fell on the parquet hall floor and her head shattered into a thousand pieces. I also broke my collarbone, but that didn't matter. Dodo was dead, in a manner of speaking, and I was distraught!

As there was only me, and my sister, Sheila, was not even a twinkle in my parents' eyes, the gypsy's words seemed unimportant at the time and Mum went back to those wayward sheets. Little was I, or my parents, or Sheila, to know, however, just how true this prediction would be. Sheila became a flautist, and I did indeed go over the seas, having had the most wonderful travelling career spanning 40 years (and still counting). Uncanny. Spooky, even!

I only learned all this many years later. Just after Dad died in 1997, as Mum and I were reminiscing about the great times we had had as a family, some phrase must have triggered the memory of the gypsy's prophecy in her mind and she told me then. I was flabbergasted. So was Sheila when I told her. And when Mum realized the significance, she was too. Whatever had

4

prompted this little woman to say such a thing? How I wish I knew. In those early post-war years wider travel for anyone was difficult to say the least, especially for a woman on her own. There had always been music, of course, but it was still fairly uncommon for a female to earn a living by it. However, from that long-forgotten encounter it seemed that destiny had taken a hand. The course of my life (and Sheila's) had been charted, and I was about to embark on a never-ending, wonderful journey of discovery that would indeed take me not only over the seven seas but also to the fascinating and thrilling countries that bordered them. As I was to discover over my forty years of travel, it was indeed a small world, and the more you explored it, the smaller it seemed to get. It was an eerie feeling to hear all this back then, and I felt a shiver come over me.

The Angraves

Grandpa George and Grandma Annie Angrave,
and Dad, aged 3

The Gambles

Grandpa Charles and Grandma Elizabeth (Lizzie) Gamble,
and Mum in her ATS uniform

CHAPTER TWO

MEET THE FAMILY

When you lead an itinerant life as I have done, you soon come to realise just how important family is. To say they are your rock is an understatement. When you are so far away from home and things, perhaps, are not going too well, to know that someone cares and is supporting you, no matter what, gives you the confidence to carry on. I (and Sheila) have been blessed with the most wonderful, loving parents anyone could ever wish for, and although they are no longer around to read this book, it is dedicated to them also. I hope they would approve of what I've written and be pleased at the way my life has turned out.

My Parents

I don't think I ever knew how and when Mum and Dad met, though it was possibly in the middle of 1940, when Mum had come home from the ATS on weekend leave and went to a dance at St Phillip's church hall at Evington. Dad, who had desperately wanted to join the RAF with his great pal, Bruce, at the beginning of the War, was working in a factory making flame throwers, an occupation he hated with a vengeance, not only because of the conditions in which he worked, but also because of the use to which the end product was being put. Having experienced the horrors of World War 1, Grandpa had fought tooth and nail to stop him enlisting, for which I don't think Dad ever quite forgave him. So for Dad to go to a dance must have been a much needed respite, and to meet the woman of his dreams, as he said, was an added bonus.

It wasn't easy to maintain a relationship during those war years, Mum said, but Dad knew she was the girl for him and cycled miles, even to Coventry, where Mum was posted, and back, which was long way from Leicester, to meet her. Their love blossomed and they were married on 16 January 1943 at that same St Phillips Church where they first met. Everything was rationed, of course, during those times, so Mum had to beg or borrow coupons to be able to get her lace wedding dress. From the photo, though, it looked lovely, and they look so happy.

I was born on 16 April 1945, and Mum said she had had a terrible time convincing her Superior Officer that she was pregnant, until eventually, of course, it was obvious that she was. The War then ended not long after I was born, so Mum was able to stay at home and look after me, ably helped by Grandma Annie, Dad's mother, to whom Mum was very close.

My sister, Sheila, was born four years later, on 12 May 1949 and our family was complete.

About Dad. (Robert (Bob) William Angrave, was born on 26 September 1920 in Leicester. He was an only child, and was always a bit shy with strangers, I thought, though once he got to know them he opened up and was great fun. He went to a small school (for boys only, judging by his school photo) just around the corner from where he and Grandpa and Grandma lived, in Herschell Street, and seemed to do quite well. Sport was Dad's great love and I think I still have a little cup he won for running. He was an excellent hurdler too, by all accounts. Later, of course, hockey became his passion and played a large part in his and Mum's social life.

He left school aged 16 and went to the Leicester Technical College to study hosiery design and the maintenance of knitting machinery. Leicester was, and still is to a minor extent, an important hosiery and boot and shoe city, so this seemed the way to go.

On leaving the "Tech", Dad went to work for the large hosiery machine company, G. Stibbe & Co Ltd, a major rival of the world

Mum and Dad on their wedding day,
St Phillips Church

Sheila and me, October 1949

leader, The Bentley Engineering Co Ltd, where he stayed until the early 1950's. After that, Dad longed to put his design skills to use and so he moved to J F Carnell, as chief designer and manager of all their machinery, and stayed there until his retirement at 65. I remember he used to bring pattern samples home to work on, and sometimes, if he had to go in to the factory on a Saturday morning to sort out a problem, he'd take me with him and explain how everything worked. I loved it, especially the click, click, click noise of the machines, and the whizzing around of the spindles as they wove their multi-coloured threads on the needles. I was fascinated by the designs that came out at the end, and was always rather proud that these socks would be sent to Marks & Spencers. My Dad designed those, I would say.

Working in this environment did have its disadvantages, though, the main one being the haze of brightly shining lint fibres that used to dance in the sunlight through the windows if it was a lovely day. These got on Dad's chest, and Mum, Sheila and I always joked about his permanently husky voice, caused, we said, because his lungs and throat had a woolly coat. This wasn't funny though, and in later life the constant inhaling of all the lint caused lasting damage to Dad's chest and he certainly did suffer most of his life.

During his time at Carnell's, Dad also became a part-time lecturer back at the Leicester Technical College where he himself had studied and where I was later to go, taking night school courses in hosiery design and engineering at the end of his normal day's work. I well remember him coming home for his tea, then dashing off on his little moped to his classes. It was tiring after a day in the factory, but he enjoyed the opportunity of being able to pass on his expertise to the students.

On one occasion Carnell's sent Dad to communist Czechoslovakia (as it was then) for six weeks to train the young hosiery operators on the machines they had just exported to that country. Dad didn't enjoy this very much at all: being away from home; not being able to speak the language and having to work through an interpreter all the time (though Dad did like this young man). He was constantly being followed, which unnerved him, and he spent hours on his own in the hotel. We sent him letters and copies of the Leicester Mercury, most of which he never received. He was lonely, homesick, and couldn't wait to leave.

As I said, Dad loved sport, but hockey was his real passion and he was excellent at it. He loved to play centre half, and when I went with him to his matches, as I nearly always used to do when I was young, I watched carefully and learned a lot. He played for the Granville Mixed Hockey Club, attached to our local Granville Tennis Club, but later joined the excellent Leicester Men's Hockey Club, where the standard of play was much higher. Friendships from those days stayed with him, and Mum who got involved in the social side, forever, and I'm still in touch with Jean, the widow of one of their best friends at the Club.

We were devastated when Dad got Parkinsons Disease in 1974. It was so tough for all of us, but especially Mum who, with the help of two very special carers, looked after him until he went into hospital just before he died. I think the worse thing for me was that, despite all that we had shared during my life, he didn't recognize me. Only Mum. He died in Shrewsbury Hospital on 28 May 1996, aged 76, and we were at his bedside almost until the end.

Now a bit about Mum.

[Evelyn] Joyce Gamble ("Slap" - I never did found out why she was called this), was born in Leicester on 11 June 1921, the youngest of three girls (the fourth, Winifred, died soon after birth).

Her school days at the private girls' school, Richmond House, were fun, she always used to say, and she made many friends there with whom she kept in touch all her life. She worked hard, and from there went on to a private Commercial College, eventually becoming a very good secretary and teleprinter operator.

At the outbreak of the War, Mum joined the ATS as a teleprinter operator, whilst her middle sister, Eileen, joined the WAAF, also as a teleprinter operator. Though not strictly speaking allowed, but vital for keeping up the morale of the troops, they used to say, when their night duties coincided, they would send telex messages to each other if there was a lull in operations. They both had great senses of humour, so some of their messages must have been very amusing. I only wish I'd seen them. Mum was so proud of the ATS and what she did. Although it was tough, the great camaraderie amongst the girls saw them through, particularly when they were billeted to Coventry, which was badly bombed.

Meeting Dad, she always used to say, was by far the very best thing that happened to her. They were a devoted couple, and the only time I ever heard raised voices was when Mum damaged the new electric cooker. Dad was not amused.

Once the War was over, Mum went to work for Commercial Services, a secretarial agency, whilst Grandma Annie looked after me during the day, and also Sheila when she was born. By this time, it was becoming more common for women to work outside the home, and Mum enjoyed it, though she said she always felt guilty that I had to come home from school to an empty house and search for the key in the coal shed. But this gave me a degree of responsibility which helped me as I was growing up. Eventually Mum left Commercial Services and went work as Secretary at Sundy Shoes, a little firm in Oadby, owned by a family, the Petcher's, who lived nearby. This little firm made beautiful children's shoes, and again I loved to go into the factory to watch the coloured pieces of leather being stretched

12

Dad and me at a local hostelry
(mine's a lager, Dad, since you're buying)

Mum and me in the garden
at Pontesbury

on the lasts, the stitching machines thumping away, and the little leather bows and straps being put on. The end products were so pretty, and the company did well. Mum stayed there many years, made many friends, and was so sorry to leave when she eventually retired aged 60.

Tennis was Mum's sport, and although she had never had any coaching, she played in the Granville Tennis Club team with much success. Eventually she left there to join the larger Victoria Tennis Club and played in their Club matches too.

After Dad retired in 1986, he and Mum moved from Oadby to the rural village of Pontesbury, near the Long Mynd in Shropshire. I know Mum found it difficult to leave all her friends in Leicester, but Dad had had enough of the grime and noise of cities and longed for the peace of the countryside and open spaces, so off they went. They had driven around the country before Dad retired, seeking out a good place for their retirement, not too far from Sheila and her family, and Pontesbury had fitted the bill perfectly.

They bought a little Sprite caravan, and Dad spent hours practising reversing into the drive, much to Mum's initial consternation when he demolished part of the side hedge on his first attempt. Fortunately, he eventually got the hang of it, and they would go off when the mood took them, touring the valleys of Wales, as well as managing to negotiate the tiny lanes of Devon and Cornwall, not easy at the best of times, but even harder with a caravan. They even took the little van to Brittany one year, but Dad found the driving over there quite a trial ("the French are lunatic drivers"), so they didn't go again.

Eventually, when Dad became ill, they weren't able to go off any more and the little caravan just stood there on the drive, a sad reminder of the wonderful times they had had. After Dad died, there was no sense in keep the Sprite any more, and I well remember Mum sobbing when she sold it to a young couple and they towed it away. Dad had really gone forever.

After Dad's death, Mum soldiered on bravely, though I know she missed him dreadfully (as did we all). She got involved in village activities, joining a local choir and the Women's Institute. She also enrolled in a little art class at the local school, and although she had had no tuition at all, I was amazed at how good an artist she turned out to be. There seems to be an artistic flair within the family, not passed on to me I'm afraid, as Dad was always good at drawing as a result of his design skills, and my cousin Michael was a member of the Royal Institute of Painters in Watercolour. But Mum's expertise was a complete surprise, and I proudly have one of her paintings hanging on my wall at home.

Mum continued to play her tennis, but in the end she started to suffer badly with arthritis and had to give it up, much to her dismay.

Mum died suddenly on 6 February 2003 from an aneurysm. I was working at the Foreign and Commonwealth Office ("The Office") in London at the time and was allowed to ring her each morning to check how she was. On the morning of the 6th I got no reply and so rang her neighbour, who went round to check and found Mum dead on the bed. I will never, ever forget that call. My boss at the time, John Macgregor, an Assistant Under-Secretary of State, with whom I'm still in touch and who, coincidentally, Sheila knows well as they both played in the Leicestershire Schools orchestra together, was so kind and understanding, arranging for a taxi to take me home to pack a few things before driving up to Pontesbury.

I rang Sheila to give her the sad news, and we arranged that she would drive down from Wigan to meet me at Mum's house. Then began the harrowing task of sorting everything out. We were both devastated, but were a great support to each other, for which I will always be so grateful. I will never

15

forget Sheila with her flute standing in the kitchen practicing Pachelbel's Canon, which she was going to play at the funeral. It sounded so haunting and beautiful. I just dissolved in tears. I couldn't have got through those days without her.

Although I was far away for long spells at a time, Mum was assiduous in her letter writing and I used to look forward so much to receiving her news, as she did mine, I know. We remained so close and whilst I know she wished I could have been nearer, nevertheless she was always there if I needed advice, had a grumble, or wanted to share good news. She was a true friend, as well as the best Mum in the world.

And by no means least, my sister, Sheila

By her late teens, Sheila was becoming an accomplished musician, even if the recorder drove me mad on occasions when she was learning (the flute sounded much better). She used to take her music into the loo and stay there for hours so no-one else could go, which drove us all potty (excuse the pun). It seemed that her destiny was also progressing well along the prophecy lines, and she eventually became a flautist, playing for the Leicestershire Schools Youth Orchestra, reckoned by Andre Previn to be the next LSO, as well as the Liverpool Philharmonic. She attended the Royal College of Music and became a peripatetic music teacher, later a junior school teacher when her sons were born. She married Len Chamberlain, a Chemistry teacher, in 1978 but he died suddenly in 1999, leaving her with two teenage sons, Christopher and Jonathan to bring up on her own. I have to say, she did a fantastic job. They are a great credit to her. They excelled at rugby, playing for England and Scotland (by way of a family link) Students, and Sheila became a qualified rugby coach. I am now the proud great aunt of Jackson, Jon's son, aged 6, and Martha Mae (2) and Edith Rose (3 months), Chris and Eleanor's two daughters.

I couldn't end my piece on Sheila without mentioning that her great love is Jon Bon Jovi. That's more than my life is worth. She's a massive fan and has followed him all over the world, making many new friends and seeing places along the way. Just to get my own back, I, on the other hand, am a massive Sir Cliff Richard fan, and follow him too. As you can imagine, music in our house can be very interesting at times. Who will win? It's a bit of a tussle at times.

The Grandparents

On the *Angrave* side, there was Grandpa George and Grandma Annie, gentle people devoted to each other and to us and for whom nothing was too much trouble. During World War 1 Grandpa, aged 28, was sent to the Army Service Corps to be a bare-back dispatch rider, even though he'd never been on a horse before. He was later given a motorbike, but not before he had witnessed the slaughter of many of those beautiful animals. He was wounded in the leg and was invalided out of the Corps, going to work as a Warehouse Foreman for the shoe company, Freeman Hardy and Willis, before he retired. Like so many of his compatriots, he never ever talked to us about his war experiences. Mum only learned this from Grandma later.

Grandpa's pride and joy was his little Ford 8 car, which he loved to drive and in which he taught Dad to drive also, though neither of them ever took a test, which wasn't necessary in those days. He polished that car till it shone and I don't ever recall seeing a speck of dust, nor any rust, on it at all.

He also loved gardening, though more growing fruit and vegetables than flowers. That was Grandma's province.

Grandpa died on 3 December 1963, the day I started work at S. Russell & Sons. Mum went down to check on how he was each day, and on this particular occasion came out to wave me off as I left for work. Little did I realise that she had found Grandpa dead on the floor, having choked to death. She didn't want me to know this before I left so as not to spoil my first day at my new job, so I only found out when I got home that evening. What a Mum.

Grandma Annie was an excellent seamstress, making me some beautiful little outfits until the onset of multiple sclerosis. Grandpa tried so hard to look after her at home, but in the end it became too much and she was admitted in 1958 into the foreboding Hillcrest Hospital (formerly the Work House and where Joseph Merrick, the "Elephant Man" had been a patient), where she died within a week or so of arriving there. Again, our lives were turned upside down, but we looked after Grandpa with much love until he too died.

On the *Gamble* side, I remember little of Grandpa Gamble who worked for the Royal Insurance Company until his death on 1 April 1950. I was five when he died, and my only recollection of him is that he wore round rimmed metal spectacles and seemed a quiet and gentle man.

Grandma, on the other hand, who had been a florist, was a bit or a tartar and, I gather, gave him rather a hard time, hence his quietness no doubt. I know Sheila and I didn't relish going to visit as we weren't allowed to sit on the sofa cushions, play on the lawn or be noisy. But she had one redeeming feature as far as I was concerned: she made the most delicious cucumber, onion and vinegar salad.

Uncle Bernard

Instrumental in me embarking on a sea-going career was Mum's brother-in-law, Bernard, a Marconi Radio Operator who, when he came home on leave, kept my dream of travelling alive with his tales of distant shores, mainly South America. I hung on every word he said, and he was thrilled when I too went to sea. When he had to retire through emphysema, he bought a big Hammerlund radio and would spend hours with his headphones on listening to all the shipping messages, though never divulging their content of course. Mum always knew when I was almost home as he would ring up and say "Gillian's just nearing the Solent. All is well." I missed him a lot when he died in 1974.

The Family Today

Now there is just me (single), Sheila and her family, and my cousins' families. I keep in close touch with them all, although I don't see them as often as I would like. But I value their support and encouragement so much: they can't wait for me to finish this book!

Mum and Dad at their much-loved caravan

Sheila, Chris, Jon and me at Christmas, 2010

Sheila (left) and me in Venice, March 2015

Our family in 1959
for cousin Michael's wedding

Gillian

From the Latin meaning "young child"

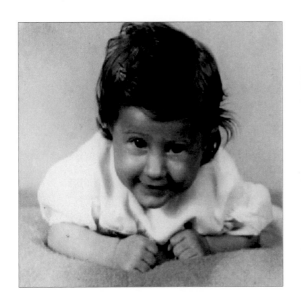

Little Me! October 1945 and October 1948

And with the 72nd Leicester Brownie Pack (I'm holding the flag on the left)

CHAPTER THREE

MY SCHOOL DAYS AND TEENAGE YEARS

'Gillian: a Kind Heart, a Fierce Mind, a Brave Spirit'

This was on a key-ring that was once given to me as a present. Others will be better qualified to judge whether this is me, but I would like to think that it is.

My childhood was full of laughter: A few tears perhaps now and then, but I was so lucky to have such loving parents who would do anything for my sister and me.

The Post-War Years in Oadby

Just before Sheila was born in 1949, we moved from 11 Uplands Road to 58 Grosvenor Crescent, a few doors away from Grandma Annie and Grandpa George, later moving again after Grandpa died to 2 Hermitage Close in 1967, just before I went to sea. No 58 was a nice three-bed semi-detached house with a small garden backing onto the horse box park at Leicester Race Course: we would spend hours watching the trainers trying to get the horses back into their boxes after a race meeting.

We were a very close-knit little community at the Crescent, helping each other when needed and having great times together. I always remember our (not adjoining) neighbours, the Crowden's, having the one thing we coveted most but could only dream about – a TELEVISION! It was a tiny black and white Bush with a 9 inch screen, smaller than today's laptops and some i-pads even, and you really needed to be on top of it to see anything in detail. The first time I ever watched television was at their house when almost the whole Crescent crammed into their small lounge to watch the Coronation in 1953. We children sat on the floor at the front and were all mesmerized by these moving, talking images. The fact that there was no colour didn't seem to matter in the slightest.

It was at the Crescent that I met my two longest-standing friends, Marie Elliott as she was then (now Handyside), and Sue Ross (now Smith). We've been the closest of friends for over 70 years, having played together when I used to visit Grandma and Grandpa before we actually moved there. I can't put a price on what their friendship means to me. They were, and are, such wonderful people: caring, loyal, fun – everything one could ever wish for in a true friend. Thank you both so much for sticking by me for all these years!

Tuppence

Throughout all my life I've had a nickname - "Tuppence". It came about when I started infant school and Mum made me a little royal blue felt purse with a long cord to wear over my shoulder, in which I could put my handkerchief. But I wasn't happy. To me a purse meant MONEY, and I didn't have any, so Mum and Dad gave me a shiny new penny to put in it, hoping that would solve the problem. It didn't. Money made a sound, but I couldn't hear my lonely penny in its little purse. I needed to hear a jingling sound so another bright penny was found which went in the purse as well and at last I was satisfied: I had real money and now I felt important. From that day on I was always known a "Tuppence". All Mum's and Dad's letters to me started off "Dearest Tuppence" or "Dearest Tupp", and they very rarely called me anything else, unless I'd done something wrong (surely not)! How I'd love to hear those words just once more, or receive just one more letter.

My School Days

I've always been fortunate in that I have loved all my school days. Marie and I started at the Sandhurst Street Infants School together in Oadby in 1950, whilst Sue went to Stoneygate

College. Mum always said that the memory of that first day haunted her for a long time. All the other children had gone inside, but I was still there, clinging to the closed school gate, sobbing "Mummy, Mummy, please don't leave me". She couldn't bear to turn around and look at me as she pushed Sheila home in the battered, second-hand Silver Cross pram. Mum said she cried all the way, and for most of the morning too, and she said she was nearly an hour early waiting there for me to come out of school. Finally, my wonderful teacher, Mrs Camp, came out to comfort me and take me inside. Although I was only 5, I remember that day very clearly too, as does Marie.

It took me a little while to settle. In the end Mum had to ask Mrs Camp if I could sit next to Marie who, being smaller, sat at the front whilst I, being tall, sat at the back. That seemed to do the trick and I really enjoyed it after that, even the milk from the fat little silver-topped bottles left outside in the sun!

From the infant school, Marie and I then went to Gartree Junior School, about a two mile walk along the A6 from the Crescent. I liked it there, but as it was in a Victorian building that no longer served its purpose, a new school was built, renamed Langmoor. We all moved there at the end of my second year, but as it was on the edge of large estate on the other side of Oadby, it meant Marie and I had to walk over fields and through the estate itself, about 2 ½ miles: fine in summer, not so good in winter. Being a brand-new school, the facilities at Langmoor were excellent and much better than what we had had before. There were great playing fields for sports, and larger, brighter classrooms, though the size of the classes didn't decrease and there were 58 of us crammed into our classroom during my last year!

It was here that I discovered my love of writing, and dreams of travelling to far off places. I won a Cadbury's National Schools Essay Competition, aged 10, and the subject – Life on a Tropical Island. Of course, I'd never been to one, but that didn't deter me, and my imagination had a field day! My prize – an enormous box containing 3 months' supply of every kind of chocolate you can imagine. I shared some with Sheila and my friends, but ate most of it myself, got sick and was covered in spots. Serves me right.

When I passed the Eleven Plus, I then went to Guthlaxton Grammar (later Comprehensive) at Wigston, a suburb of Leicester. I took the bus most of the time as it was about 7 miles away, but if I was staying late for sport, I would cycle. I missed Marie: she went on to Kibworth Grammar School as her elder sister was there, but we still saw each other a lot after school.

At "Guthie", we had a distinctive uniform, which I loved, though it did have its drawbacks. We wore a purple blazer, and for winter a white blouse, grey skirt, V-neck jumper and a purple and gold tie. During the summer it was a purple and white striped dress. This was fine when we were behaving, as we usually did of course. But we were very identifiable when we did not.

When I started, as a Grammar School there were 240 of us and we were split between a prefabricated hut and a beautiful old house, Abingdon House, converted into "classrooms", about half a mile away. We seemed to spend most of our time dashing between the two, which cut down the lesson time enormously. Not ideal. But when we became Comprehensive after my first year, we moved into a brand new school next door to Abingdon House and the numbers shot up to 1200 overnight! What a shock, but we had no alternative but to adjust which we did, thanks to our Headmaster Lawrence Olivier, Sir Martin Olivier's cousin.

Academically, I was a "slogger". I studied hard, missed out the fourth year, and left as Deputy Head Girl with eight 'O' Levels (Spanish, French, Latin, History, Geography, English Language, English Literature and Biology) and three 'A' Levels (Spanish, French and History) under my belt.

It had not been easy, but all the hard work had paid off, and whilst I never went to University, the qualifications I gained set me up for a fascinating and fulfilling career - one that I wouldn't have missed for the world.

My Hobbies

Brownies and Guides were very popular when I was growing up and I was anxious to join too. I was a Brownie (Kelpie) with the 72nd Leicester (Stoneygate) Pack, and a Guide (Poppy) with the 72nd Leicester (Stoneygate) Patrol. Memories of my Brownie days are of me trundling a large toy mangle (not another one!) on wheels half a mile to catch the Corporation bus, so I could decorate my "Six Home". I nearly lost it en route as the bus swerved and it began to roll towards the open entrance, only being saved in the nick of time by a quick-witted conductor who spotted it starting its journey over the edge.

With the Guides I went camping, sat for hours on my own in a wood to gain my Nature Badge, listening, observing and taking notes. I joined the excellent Leicestershire Guide Choir, and with them travelled around the county and attended civic functions giving much appreciated concerts. It was all fun, and very character-building, for which I'm grateful.

Dancing

In my earlier years, dancing was one of my great loves, which was just as well as I was later to discover. I went to the Adelphi School of Dancing, run by Victor Packer and Vera Dunham, at New Bond Street in Leicester. There I honed my skills, took my IDMA (International Dancing Masters Association) exams, and by the time I left to join P & O, I was the proud possessor of the Statuette for Ballroom and Second Gold Bar for Latin American. I still have them, though the Statuette could do with a bit of a polish! Those were the days. Little was I to know that dancing would play a big part in my future life on board ship!

My School days

1950: Sandhurst Street Infant School, Oadby. Me, 3rd row, 4th left. Marie, 3rd left, 2nd row

Guthlaxton Grammar.
Form VF with Mr Allen, our Form Teacher

Our very successful tennis and First X1 hockey teams

Leaving Day, Guthlaxton School, July 1962
Receiving my Deputy Head Girl's Prize
from the Bishop of Leicester, Dr Williams

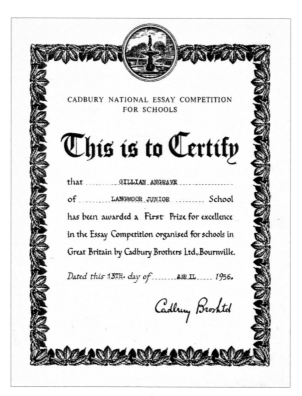

How my love of writing began!

CHAPTER FOUR

FOR THE LOVE OF SPORT

Above all, like Dad, I loved my sport. I still do, though the old bones are somewhat reluctant these days!

Swimming

I learned to swim when I was four (as did Sheila), and joined the little local Brabazon Road Swimming Club at the Oadby Baths above the library. There, we were under the care of Mr. and Mrs Phoenix, a very kind, elderly couple who taught us and looked after us well. Marie joined the club as well, so we would walk the mile and a half or so up there together. Recently we've been trying to calculate exactly how big the pool was (it no longer exists). We could do about ten strokes per width, so maybe 30 feet, and the length must have been about 50 feet. There was also a spring board at one end, which was great fun.

The Club held Swimming Galas now and then and on one occasion I even won a cup for diving. Marie has reminded me that her Grandfather Mandale, who was a prominent jeweller in Workington, Cumbria, donated all the Cups for the Club galas.

Sheila and I remember one particular swimming incident vividly even to this day. Sheila was three. I had gone to the swimming club and Mum and Dad were in the back garden, behind the garage, talking to the Crowden's. When Sheila woke up, she couldn't find Mum and Dad and felt frightened. As she knew I'd gone swimming, she had to find "GinGin" as she called me (nothing to do with my later P & O years, I hasten to add), so, at around 8 pm this little three year old, dressed in pyjamas, no shoes, walked on her own up Oadby Hill, the main A6 road to Market Harborough, through the village till she reached the Baths. How she remembered where to go, neither of us know.

But she did. Instinct, she says. No-one stopped her. She just kept on walking. The first I knew about it was when Mrs Phoenix came rushing into the Baths, waving at me wildly.

"Gillian, Gillian. Get out of the water. Your sister is here."

Dripping wet, I went to the entrance to find Sheila calmly standing on the doorstep, asking for GinGin. I couldn't believe it! While Mrs Phoenix took her in and wrapped her in a towel, Mr. Phoenix got on his bicycle and cycled frantically down to Mum and Dad (we didn't have a telephone in those days). They were horrified and immediately went to borrow Grandpa's Ford 8 to drive up to the Baths to collect us, Mr. Phoenix furiously pedaling some way behind. After profuse thanks to the Phoenix's, we went home. Imagine if that had been today. It just doesn't bear thinking about.

Hockey

I continued to shine at sport at school, captaining our hockey and tennis teams with great success. We were formidable opponents - St Trinian's had nothing on us! I have to confess we occasionally left a trail of bruised ankles behind us, but in fairness, I got some in return.

When I left school, I played hockey for Southfield Ladies, the Leicestershire County, and Midlands B, mainly as centre half, but also as right back. However, it's not easy to play hockey on board ship, so sadly I had to give it up until I finally came ashore. It was only when I was posted to Chile that I was able to take it up again seriously, playing for Craighouse Old Girls, a prestigious Chilean high school, mainly for expatriate children.

Tennis

I wasn't bad at tennis, either. I practised hard, even being in the same coaching class as Mark Cox (one of Britain's Wimbledon players) on one occasion. I got as far as the second round of the County Tennis Tournament and was always grateful to our coach, Dougie Haines (who had played at Wimbledon himself), for his perseverance with me. He was a tough task-master, but very good, and I enjoyed tennis for many years afterwards.

On our doorstep at Oadby was the Granville Tennis Club, more like a social club-cum-community centre than a tennis club, but a facility that was badly needed after the war. It served our estate, and even further afield, well. There were six good hard courts, a verandah, a large wooden clubhouse, and a lawn where we put the deckchairs in the summer and sipped our Vimto's. The Club held good tournaments, and put on parties, dances and treasure hunts. There was even an excellent amateur dramatic group, to which Mum belonged. I'll never forget seeing her in Agatha Christie's "Black Lace", where she was made up to look like an old woman. I was horrified. Even though it was a tennis club, there was also an excellent Mixed Hockey Team for which Dad played (and I did when they were short). We, as a family, and Marie's and Sue's families, spent many happy hours there. It was a much needed lifeline after the austerity of the war years and we made many lasting friends.

For me, Hungary was the best posting for tennis. Our Ambassador and his wife were excellent tennis players and we used to have some fiercely fought Embassy tennis tournaments on courts we hired at Pasareti ut.

Golf

"A good walk spoiled", as my non-golfing friends keep telling me.

My main love was golf, though, which I only learned to play in the Philippines. At all my postings, I played whenever I could, although it wasn't always possible for me to join a local club, either because it was too expensive or too exclusive, so I had to be content with paying a green fee. But at least I could play.

I had some memorable rounds, for unusual reasons. Read on, and you will discover why!

Back home, I've tried to continue with my golf, but hating the cold and being busy with weddings in the summer, I don't get to play all that often these days. However, I do chuckle when I remember all those challenging rounds of golf so long ago. Life seems pretty tame on the course these days!

CHAPTER FIVE

GILLIAN'S WHEELS
(AS OPPOSED TO SHEILA'S WHEELS)

Driving has always been a love of mine and I've covered many thousands of miles during my travelling career.

My first time behind the wheel was "memorable". I was just 17 and was anxious to learn to drive. Dad had gone through the driving theory with me, so I had some idea of what I was supposed to do, but reality is very different from practice! We were on our annual family holiday to Tenby, a beautiful seaside town in Carmarthenshire, South Wales, one August (1962) and, as the weather was nice, Mum and Dad decided we could have a day out at Pendine Sands, just along the coast towards Swansea. Here Dad said I could have my first go at driving (brave man!). In the early 1900's this 7 mile stretch of firm sands was used as a venue for motor cycle and car races. Because of its straightness, it was considered much safer and more suitable for racing than winding roads. In 1924 Malcolm Campbell set a world land speed record of 146.16 mph in his Sunbeam 350HP car, Blue Bird, and between 1924 and 1927 four other record-breaking runs were made: two by Malcolm Campbell and two by the Welshman, J G Parry-Thomas.

I, on the other hand, whilst also in "Bluebird", our so-called, second-hand blue Morris Oxford Mk 2, would be travelling at a slightly more sedate pace (Dad prayed), and for a shorter distance! So, with Mum and Sheila watching from a safe distance in the sand hills, Dad drove onto the beach and I got behind the wheel. It's a good job no-one else was attempting a record that day as my kangaroo-hopping produced great ruts in the pristine sand! Dear Dad was hanging on for dear life, but after about 15 minutes I seemed to get the hang of it a bit better and managed a fairly smooth run. I loved it, but after another 15 minutes Dad decided that his nerves could stand no more, so we went back to pick up Mum and Sheila and headed off to the pub for lunch (more for Dad to have a desperately needed pint than for anything else, I think).

From then on Dad valued his life and his well-being, so he arranged for me to have lessons, at an hourly cost of 17s 6d, with a Mr. Whitehead in his white Ford Anglia. I applied myself diligently to this task and after 7 lessons was considered ready to take my test, which I passed first time, much to Dad's enormous relief, although now he had another problem: "Dad, can I borrow the car, please?".

But from that day onwards, I have never lost my love of driving except, perhaps, through the endless roadworks on the M6 from Birmingham to Wigan, where Sheila now lives. I suspect I'm not the only one they drive mad. Dad loved to drive too, and we would go together to the British Grand Prix at Silverstone in Northamptonshire whenever we could. How I enjoyed those outings with him!

Having passed my test, I now needed a car. I was saving hard to buy one, so we trawled the ads in the Leicester Mercury and eventually Dad spotted a car that might suit - a royal blue, split-windscreen, 1956 Morris Minor, LAY 333. How I loved that little car: how I wish I had kept it! We went to look at it and I just knew it was the car for me. It had been used for rallying and had a large spotlight on the boot (which never worked) and, even more exciting, a short gear lever instead of the usual long, willowy one. I bought it for the princely sum of £75.00 (Mum and Dad putting a bit towards it) and I drove it home with such pride. "Little Car" (not a very original pet name, I know) and I happily travelled many miles together, but it did have its drawbacks. The heater never worked well, so in winter I had to drive with a hot water bottle on my knee. And the semaphore arms got stuck in the out position every time I wanted to turn left or right, so I had to keep stopping to push them back in. But I wouldn't have swapped it for the world, and still look lovingly at my one and only grained photo of her.

Since "Little Car", I've had quite a few, and have enjoyed them all. My next one, when I left P & O was an orange Datsun Cherry, but when I joined the Foreign & Commonwealth Office (FCO), it nearly always meant that I was encourage to "buy British" to fly the flag when abroad which, of course, I was happy to do. If I was taking out a car loan to buy one, which I invariably had to do, then I definitely had to fly the flag, which usually meant buying a Ford Escort, suitable for my grade. I repaid the amount monthly over the duration of my posting, but having it paid for "up front" was a great help.

My cars came in all colours and were mainly 1300 cc.

In the Philippines, my lifelong P & O friend Pam, who by this time was working for British Airways, managed to come out to stay with me twice. We would pack up my little blue escort and set out, swerving to avoid carabao (water buffalo) and jeepneys (a type of colourful passenger jeep) in our quest to reach our destination (Baguio in the north, the Maya Maya Beach Club in the south). We covered some miles, little blue car, Pam and me.

In Peru, I had a bright orange VW Beetle as I wasn't allowed to import a foreign car. It went like the clappers but struggled a bit in the high Andes through lack of oxygen, as did I for that matter, but "the Orange Devil" and I survived.

In Mexico, again where I had to buy locally, I had a silver Nissan Tsuru Dos. This was very luxurious driving after the Beetle and it went some way (just a bit) to compensating for the absolutely mad locals on the road. But little "Silver Cloud" (I wish!) didn't take kindly to rough mountain roads and at times, on my adventures, I wondered whether I would ever make it up or, more importantly, back down again, to civilisation.

In Chile, it was yet another Escort, white this time, and when Pam came out to stay again, our exploits continued as we travelled near and far, across desert areas, and on one occasion loading the car onto the train down to Puerto Montt and driving back to Santiago.

I think my longest journey, however, was when I bought my navy Escort in Denmark (tax free) and Pam drove down with me to Budapest for my posting there. It was a "novel experience", and I couldn't have done it without her navigating.

I was subsequently to drive, alone, to and fro between Hungary and the UK twice - on mid-tour leave and when I finally left that country. That last journey, in a metallic red right-hand drive Rover (bought from the newly-opened Rover dealership in Budapest) was heart-stopping on quite a few occasions. It's so difficult to see the road signs when you're driving on your own, especially in a right-hand drive car in a left-hand drive country, with a car stuffed to the gunnels with a television, record player (no I-pads in those days), pots and pans and umpteen suitcases.

To and from Budapest, I usually overnighted in Passau, home of Adolf Hitler and his family from 1892-94. This picturesque town, on the Austrian/Hungarian border and at the confluence of three rivers, the Danube, the Inn and the Ilz, had the most wonderful Cathedral, St Stephen's, and I was grateful to get out and stretch my legs in such beautiful surroundings. I stopped overnight again as near to the Belgian border as I could get, and then carried on up to Zeebrugge, where I caught the P & O ferry to Hull, and thence on to Mum and Dad at Pontesbury.

Now home, I'm a big Honda fan. I've loved my Civics, but have just had to swap my last 2.2 litre for a higher seated Jazz 1.4 because of spasmodic back muscle problems. How I miss the acceleration of that 2 litre engine, but "Little Red Riding Car" does have her advantages. This is the first automatic I've driven, and whilst I'll always prefer a manual shift, I must say on long journeys I don't find it as tiring as I used to.

Grand Prix, Speed and Me

Since the days when Dad and I used to go to Silverstone, I've always enjoyed Grand Prix Racing. Abroad, I managed to go a few times to the Hermanos Rodriguez circuit in Mexico City with my Mexican doctor boyfriend, Román, who was as big a fanatic as I was. We loved it.

In Budapest, it was the Hungaroring, where I was lucky enough to meet John Watson, Nigel Mansell, and my absolute favourite, Martin Brundle, who was very successful there. I well remember going to Vörösmarty tér, just near the Embassy, when the Hungarians decided to present Nigel Mansell with a racehorse. When they said horse power, I'm not certain that was what he envisaged, but he rode the steed round the Square and seemed very happy. How he was going to get it home was another matter.

When I came back to the UK after Hungary, I immediately joined the Martin Brundle Supporters Club, which I supported until he stopped racing and started commentating and decided it didn't seem right to have a Supporters Club any more. We disagreed, of course, but followed his wishes. Martin was fantastic. Although we weren't a big group, he was most generous with his time and had regular get-togethers with us at Silverstone, where he'd take us round the Pits, give us lunch and then beat us all at go-karting.

How can I ever forget, though, my own modest foray into the world of motor racing? I was in Daytona Beach in 2003, staying with my friend Pat, when the opportunity arose for me to take part in the Richard Petty Racing Experience (cost $135.00) on the Daytona Nascar circuit. Without a second thought, I jumped at it.

There were six of us (I was the only woman), and after an intensive half-hour safety briefing, we were taken to get kitted out and meet our driver (no-one was allowed to drive on their own). Mine was a really nice young man called Kevin, who seemed very happy to have me on board. We set off, two lots of three cars together, and it wasn't long before we reached 172.2 mph. Brilliant. I was amazed at how steep (three storeys high) the banks were at either end, and just how bumpy it was over the surface, but you get a tremendous sling-shot off those banks. I was in my element, and could have easily done another six laps, but sadly that was all we were allowed.

As my nephews said later, "wicked Auntie Gill, wicked". Too true lads. You aren't joking. It was AWESOME!

My "wheels" through the years

My wonderful Morris Minor
("Little Car") 1963

Sheila and our "Bluebird", 1963
(Grandpa George and Grandma Annie's
house is at the bottom on the left)

Foreign "wheels"

The Philippines: My Escort all alone at the Maya Maya Beach Club, Batangas

With the "Orange Devil on the coast road between Lima and Pisco, 1980

Santiago. Putting the car on the train en route to Puerto Montt

Hungary. Taking delivery of my new Escort in Copenhagen

Home at last! Just arrived from Budapest at Mum and Dad's home

Daytona Beach. The Richard Petty Racing Experience, 2003

with Kevin

I'm in the car in the middle

Above: With my hero, Martin Brundle, at Silverstone, testing with Jordan, 1997

Below Left: At the Hungaroring for the Hungarian Grand Prix 1993
Below Right: Nigel Mansell, Budapest

CHAPTER SIX

COLLEGE AND MY FIRST TASTE OF WORK

On leaving school my aim was to get some useful practical skills under my belt, so I attended a year's Commercial Course at the Leicester College of Technology. The College was spread between quite a few buildings and was down by the River Soar, which meant a long bus journey into Leicester, and a long walk from the bus station, again fine in summer, a real pain in winter. My course, however, gave me a good grounding in secretarial skills (and a life-time of loathing for the William Tell Overture which acted as a metronome for our typing sessions!). I left after the year with good qualifications and, aged 18, set out to see what the world had to offer.

Into the Outside World

Once I was mobile, I could drive to and from work. But that was yet to come.

My first job was as Junior Secretary at a firm of well-known architects, Henry Goddard & Partners (specializing in heating cathedrals), in Newton Harcourt, a small village outside Leicester. Group Captain Henry Goddard owned the beautiful Manor House that became my office for six months after leaving college. Apart from Henry and his Partner, Camilla Epps, there were four of us: Sylvia and myself as secretaries; Gordon Punt (a good rugby-playing friend of my cousin, David), and Bertie de Lisle as Junior architect: we became like a little family as we all got on so well.

Henry was a very caring boss too. We went to the local pub (The Greyhound at Great Glen, in the next village) for lunch four days a week and I well remember roaring down the country lanes in Bertie's Triumph Roadster, hanging on for dear life in the dicky seat at the back! However, in those days The Greyhound only served sandwiches and Henry felt we needed a hot meal once a week, so he made arrangements with Emily, an elderly lady in the village, to prepare a hot meal for us on Fridays. All four of us traipsed up there and squashed into the little dining room in her tiny cottage. She was always so pleased to see us, was excellent cook, fed us loads, and we arrived back at the Manor finding it hard not to fall asleep during the afternoon, having had such an "excellent sufficiency", as Mum would say.

The Manor was, and still is I gather, a beautiful old house and I loved it. The architect business occupied one wing and Henry's wife,"Paddy", used to keep us well supplied with tea and coffee when she wasn't out and about. I especially loved the hot summer's days when I could take my little portable typewriter out onto the ha-ha and type away amidst this rural idyll. It was perfect.

But, as much as I loved this job, there were no prospects and so I decided it was time to move on. I answered an advert for a Secretary to the Sales Manager (Jack Radford) at S Russell & Sons (Engineers and Ironfounders) in Bath Lane in Leicester, not far from where Dad worked at Carnell's, and after an interview, got the job.

Russell's was one of the largest engineering firms in Leicester at that time. It was a busy job, but again I enjoyed it, especially when the Foreman took me onto the shop floor to see the molten iron being poured out of the furnaces. So much for health and safety in those days! I stayed with them for three years, eventually becoming Secretary to the Sales Director, Jim Draycott, but again I felt the need to move and in April 1967 I joined Rank Taylor Hobson, off the main London Road in Leicester, a subsidiary of the big Rank Organisation which made the Varotal television camera lenses. There I would be Secretary to the Chief Executive, Joe Higham.

Itchy Feet!

The work at Ranks was fascinating and I think my love of photography must have stemmed from my time there. I used to go into the laboratory now and then with Mr. Higham to watch the enormous, thick lenses being ground, quite unlike anything I had ever seen before and not at all what I had been expecting, having only had a very simple camera myself.

But those itchy little feet just wouldn't stay still and were on the move again. Just before I started at Ranks, I had also applied to join that most prestigious of shipping companies, P & O, The Peninsular and Oriental Steam Navigation Company, as an Assistant Purser. I have to confess that I omitted to tell Mr. Higham this at the time, thinking that I didn't stand a chance of being accepted by P & O as the competition was so fierce. But I applied anyway, and couldn't believe it when a letter arrived about two months later inviting me to go for an interview.

My life of travel was about to begin.

PART TWO

A LIFE ON THE OCEAN WAVES

Woman Assistant Purser
GIllian Angrave

Carrying red roses aboard ORIANA
to give to each lady passenger on Valentine's Day1973
(Sydney Morning Herald)

The Rev Mary Welsh, with whom I stayed in London during my training.
She died on 3rd June 2006. She was very keen on snooker
and was quite a connoisseur. I miss her a lot.

P & O's New Recruit. Gillian Angrave,
Junior Woman Assistant Purser (in
"blues" – 1967)

Woman Assistant Purser
in "whites" tropical gear -
October 1970

CHAPTER ONE

THE START OF A NEW LIFE

And so, in July 1967, I went down to London for my interview and medical. I had all the right qualifications and was hopeful. I was single (a requirement); over 21 (the minimum age P & O would accept); had all the requisite skills: two languages (Spanish and French); good typing and shorthand; and, as my interviewer said, "a friendly and engaging manner" (his words, not mine). My interview went well, and I went back to Leicester full of confidence. In August another letter arrived, this time confirming that I had got the job and was to start in October. I was elated. I handed in my notice at Rank Taylor Hobson and embarked on my new, itinerant life.

But before going anywhere, I had to become a human pin cushion. I've lost count of how many inoculations I've had to have, both for P O and for The Office, but the list is impressive: rabies, yellow fever, Hepatitis A and B, tetanus, polio, Monovalent Typhoid, Normal Human Immunoglobulin, influenza, and a vaccination against ticks for Hungary. And then there was the range of Malaria tablets for tropical climes. I rattled like a tin can sometimes, but I never minded. All these were for my own benefit and I was grateful for the protection they (usually) gave me.

Although I think my parents were sorry that I was leaving home, they realized that I needed to spread my wings, and became proud of my achievements in being accepted for this exciting job.

At the beginning of October, I moved to London for my period of training before actually being allocated a ship. It was so tough saying goodbye to Mum and Dad, as it was throughout the whole of my forty years of travelling, but they understood and were thrilled for me.

The P & O Head Office was situated in Beaufort House, St Botolph Street, E1. Being in London meant I had to stay somewhere, but help was at hand in the guise of Mum's cousin, Mary, who was a Deaconess at the Deaconess Training Centre at Clapham Common. There was a spare room there and, since I would only need it for a maximum of five months or so, which was how long my Purser training was to last (more or less), I was very welcome to stay with them for the duration for a nominal amount for board and lodging.

They were all so kind and Mary and I became very close. Life was fairly spartan and I was expected to attend their Sunday Services whenever I could but, as a church-goer anyway, I was more than happy to do so. I did, however, get into a bit of trouble when I took some of the trainees off one Saturday to watch Fulham play football at Craven Cottage (why Fulham, I've never quite understood). Not the done thing for young aspiring Deaconesses, so it seemed.

I started my P & O training on the same day as my lifelong friend, Pam. We both agree that when we say "training," we use the word advisedly. New Women Assistant Pursers were assigned as Secretaries to various managers until they were allocated a ship and we learned about shipboard life as we went along. I worked for the Marine Superintendent, Captain Sargent, a slightly stern but kind man, and my Personnel Manager was Tommy Atkinson. Pay was minimal and it was a struggle at times to survive. We were given time off for the odd lecture about what to expect once on board, and for fittings for our uniforms. But that was all.

Our uniforms.

Before February 1967 our uniforms had been modelled on that of the Wrens, but in that month P & O changed them to more business-like and fashionable outfits designed by Hardy Amies, designer to The Queen. They cost about £120, which was a fortune in 1967 and which we had to pay for ourselves. For winter/cool weather wear, we had two "blues", that is navy suits with white short-sleeved blouses, with our Stripes (rank and Department) on one breast pocket and language badges (to denote which languages we spoke) on the other. For the tropics we had "whites", that is white cotton dresses with brass buttons down the front and our Stripes and language badges on epaulettes on each shoulder. When I first joined P & O in 1967, our Mess Dress was a short turquoise fitted "creation" with a V-neck back and front. It was OK, but I can't say I was a big fan. Later, the design was changed and we were given long straight black skirts and white *broderie anglaise* long-sleeved blouses with a roll neck. Personally, I much preferred this Mess kit as we matched the men's Mess Dress of black trousers, white Mess jacket and bow tie, much better. We had to provide our own shoes, but to a specific style. Very occasionally, for special evenings like Ladies Night, an exception was made and we were allowed to wear our own long dresses – such a treat.

Our hats were something else, though! I love tricorns, but when I joined P & O they had been replaced by … well, difficult to describe really. A round, high-crowned, navy blue, felt hat, with a rim all around, and with a white thick cotton detachable cover over the crown. I was at constant war with Freddie Fox, the milliner, over mine! I was told I had a small head (?!), but that didn't mean my hat had to look like a pimple on a mountain, which it invariably did (see the photos)! When out on deck in uniform, we always had to wear our hats, even in the Tropics, and in a breeze, I had the devil's own job to hang on to mine so it wouldn't blow off, whereas the other girls could ram theirs down over their ears! The P & O hat badge, which I loved, still have, and wore with pride, featured the quartered flag colours of Spain (red and yellow), Portugal (blue and white), with an anchor and a Rising Sun signifying the Orient. It was, and still is, very distinctive.

Our rank and Department were determined by our gold bars and the colour between them. For the Pursers it was white, Deck and Radio was blue, Medical was red, Engineers was purple, Electricians was green. The number of stripes denoted our rank. As a lowly Junior Woman Assistant Purser (JWAP), I had one thin one: when I became a WAP, I had one that was thicker: and when I reached the dizzy heights of Senior Woman Assistant Purser (the highest we could go in those days), joy of joys, I had two thick ones! I must say we looked very smart and I always felt proud to be part of such a privileged "family" within an historical and illustrious company.

CHAPTER TWO

MY PIER HEAD JUMP

At last I was allocated my own ship: HIMALAYA sailing in February (1968). But before that I had to do a stand-by on ORONSAY over Christmas. This is when a ship returns home and either goes into dry dock, or is moored alongside, and her regular crew go on leave. As a WAP, my job was to do all the secretarial work needed by the Senior Officers and type the Crew Lists in preparation for the ship's departure, normally in about two weeks' time. I was slightly dismayed to find that I had drawn the short straw. ORONSAY was in dry dock. And over Christmas too. Ugh! CANBERRA was also in port, moored further along the quay, and would be sailing on 13 January for a four-month world voyage.

When a ship enters dry dock, it means she is undergoing fairly major inspection and maintenance. I asked whether I could go down into the dry dock at some stage and the Chief Engineer took me when he went on one of his inspections. ORONSAY towered above me. She looked huge, the propellers looked huge, everything looked huge. It was an awesome sight, and I often wonder what it would be like now to stand where I stood with the ships the size they are today. Quite terrifying, I would imagine.

Life on board during stand-by is spartan to say the least. There is little electricity available, so hardly any heating, not much hot water, the galley is practically shut down and there are workmen everywhere. Wires and cables are hanging down from the deckheads, protective sheeting covers the carpets, the loos don't flush properly. Apart from that, it's fine!

There were only a few stand-by Officers and crew permanently on board over this period, and only two of us were female - a telephone operator (Tele-op) and me. I had a passenger cabin not too far from the Bureau (ship's office) but I saw little of the Tele-op, so I don't know where she was. Most of the workmen went home each night, when the ship took on an eerie, ghostly feel. It was so quiet and scary at times. Christmas was a fairly dismal affair. I rang Mum and Dad, who missed me but were happily tucking into turkey, roast potatoes and Christmas pudding, the sherry bottle never far away. I, on the other hand, was cold and lonely, and whilst the stand-by chef had done his best on a few burners, our Christmas meal was rather unappetizing. Alcohol was not allowed, so the men adjourned to the pub after lunch, whilst I went for a walk on my own!

The days ticked by. It was 13 January and I was at last nearing the end of my stand by. I was looking forward to a bit of time off and a trip home having worked continuously for nearly 3 weeks. I was happily typing some letters for the Chief Engineer, when the Bureau door flung open and our Superintendent Purser, Roger Porter, rushed in.

"Right, Gillian", he said. "Stop what you're doing and pack your things. The SWAP on board CANBERRA has just been rushed to hospital with appendicitis so they are one short. That's you. You're sailing in three hours' time."

I remember staring at him in disbelief. (Sadly, he died a short while ago, but whenever we met at our annual P & O Ancient Mariners Reunion lunches in Southampton each May, we always talked about that day. He said I turned quite white. We chuckled then at the memory, but I most certainly didn't chuckle at the time.)

I did a mental calculation: no, it wasn't April Fool's Day. It was 13 January. It was Mum and Dad's Silver Wedding anniversary on the 16th and I had to be home for that. But he was adamant. I

My two "loves" in Vancouver, 1970

ORIANA in Pago Pago, American Samoa

had to go. So, still not quite able to take it all in, zombie-like I put my few belonging (change of underwear, woolly suit, sweater, trousers, socks, gloves, boots, Dad's borrowed transistor radio) into my small case (I was wearing the only uniform, "blues", I had with me), and off I went with him to join CANBERRA for her four month voyage to Australia and back.

I was so shocked at having to leave at such short notice, but I knew Mum and Dad would be even more so. I managed a quick call to wish them Happy Anniversary, promised to write at every port and pointed out that April was not that far away. I tried not to sound upset, but failed dismally. Mum couldn't contain her tears at all, and Dad sounded choked.

I asked if they could get in touch with Pam and go down to Mary's at Clapham Common to pack up my things. She would know what to do and what I needed, and would help them deliver my cases to P & O, who would then forward them on to me at Cape Town. Pam was an absolute brick and Mum and Dad were so grateful for her help and support. So was I. I could not, and cannot, thank her enough for what she did.

CHAPTER THREE

THE PENINSULAR AND ORIENTAL
STEAM NAVIGATION COMPANY

The "Ancient Mariners' Reunions

When you live and work on board ship, it's like acquiring another, extended family. As you spend the majority of your time together, both working and relaxing, for the sake of a happy ship you learn to get on, make compromises and accept your shipmates for who they are. The result is that you make good friends quickly, and some of them remain with you for the rest of your life, as Pam and Tricia have done.

But once you leave the sea, it doesn't necessarily mean that you lose contact with all your shipmates. Whilst I was away and working for The Foreign Office, P & O retirees, both shipmates and shore based, would get together each year to catch up and renew old acquaintances. Now I'm home, I can at last join in and go to our annual Ancient Mariners' Reunion lunch held each May at the Novotel in Southampton. There are about 250 of us still, though sadly our numbers are decreasing each year as former colleagues "cross the bar". Nevertheless, there is much reminiscing to be done, photos come out, a certain amount of alcohol is consumed. I, for one, enjoy these get-togethers immensely.

P & O - A Potted History

Formerly the Peninsular and Oriental Steam Navigation Company, P & O had its beginnings in 1822 when Brodie McGhie Willcox, a London ship broker, and Arthur Anderson, a seaman from the Shetland Isles, formed a partnership to operate a shipping line between England and Spain and Portugal (the

Iberian Peninsula). In 1835 Captain Richard Bourne, a Dublin shipowner, joined the business and the three men began a regular steamer service, using the name Peninsular Steam Navigation Company, between London and Vigo, Oporto, Lisbon and Cadiz. The red and yellow and blue and white of the Iberian Peninsula flags form part of the P & O House Flag today.

In 1837 the company won a contract from the Admiralty to run a mail service to the Iberian Peninsula, and in 1840 this was extended to Alexandria in Egypt. In 1847, shortly after the Opium War in Hong Kong, P & O entered the opium trade and became the Peninsular and Oriental Steam Navigation Company. As the company was incorporated by a Royal Charter in 1840, its name never included Limited or Plc.

P & O's history from then onwards is too detailed to write about here, but the most important event was the merger of P & O with the Orient Line in 1960 to become the P & O-Orient Line.

How things have changed since I joined in 1967! Today, P & O's television adverts depict enormous white floating cities, opportunities for every kind of activity under the sun (or not, as the weather may be), professional entertainment of a high level, Marco Pierre White and his glazed scallops, and Rob Brydon enthusing that "This is the Life"!

In my day, all voyages were considered "main line", that is we took people from A to B, many as £10 immigrants to Australia and New Zealand. It was only after the advent of the jumbo jet in the early 1970's that ships started branching out into cruising as we know it today: once people had the opportunity to reach far-flung destinations quickly by plane, the need for "main line" decreased and eventually stopped altogether. Today long voyages are purely educational or for cruising.

Chapter Four

ALL AT SEA

My Two "Loves"

ss CANBERRA

Nicknamed "The Great White Whale", ss CANBERRA, to my mind was a beautiful ship. Her revolutionary design of both funnels aft made her easily recognizable and gave her a sleekness of her own. She even featured in the James Bond film "Diamonds Are Forever" in 1971 when Mr. Witt and Mr. Kidd tried to kill Bond on board.

Her keel was laid at Harland & Wolff, Belfast, on 23 September 1957 and she was launched on 16 March 1960 at a cost of £17 million. With a gross tonnage of 45,270, she was 820 ft long, her beam was 103 ft, and her draught was 35.5 ft. Between 1961-73 her speed was an average of 27.5 knots, but that dropped to 23.5 knots from 1973-917. For the technical buffs, she was propelled by two Thomson-Houston (AEI) 6,000 volt air-cooled electric motors providing 85,000 hp; power supplied by two 32,000 kW steam turbines, with four auxiliary turbines.

Her passenger complement was 548 First Class, 1,690 Tourist Class, but just before I left she became one class, with1,737 passengers. How different from these enormous liners of today!

She wasn't without problems, though. All her weight was concentrated aft (engine room, funnels, propellers etc), so when she set sail she tended to "plane". This problem was rectified by putting concrete ballast in some of the water tanks in the bow to even her up, but my good friend Malcolm Rushan (ex-Captain) says she never seemed to sail satisfactorily.

She was also designed with a marble fountain in the Tourist foyer aft. This was like a mini-Dancing Waters, a popular aquatic display in those days, with water spouts shooting up all the time. What an absolutely brilliant idea! Who would have thought that during typhoons and rough weather, despite the stabilisers, the water wouldn't go all over the place? Were the marine architects male? Sorry! Needless to say, the fountain didn't last long.

CANBERRA was a very popular ship amongst passengers and her reputation increased in leaps and bounds when she was requisitioned for use as a troop ship for the Falklands conflict on 2 April 1982. I should know – I was posted to Chile at the time.

After a long refit, she was returned to civilian service, but by this time her age and fuel consumption were making her uneconomical to run. A bid for her was made by Premier Cruise Line, but P & O didn't want her sailing under a different flag, so she was taken out of service in September 1997 and sold for scrap to the Gadani ship-breaking yard in Pakistan on 31 October 1997. Because of her deep draught she couldn't be beached near to the shore like most vessels, and so because of that, and due also to her solid construction, the scrapping took nearly a year instead of the normal three months. By the end of 1998 she was razor blades. I couldn't bear it.

We all mourned her loss dreadfully. No other ship could replace her. The Great White Whale was no more.

ss ORIANA

The last of the Orient Steam Navigation Company's (later Orient Line) ocean liners, ORIANA was built a Vickers Armstrong in Barrow-in-Furness, Cumbria (England). Her keel was laid on 18 September 1957, she was launched on 3 November 1959 by Princess Alexandra, and completed in 1960. She cost £12,500,000.

Originally striking with her corn-coloured hull, she remained an Orient Line Ship until 1966, when the company was fully absorbed into the P & O Group. She was painted white in 1964.

Slightly smaller than CANBERRA at 41,910 gross tons, ORIANA was 804 ft long (245.1 m), her moulded beam was 97.1 ft (30.5 m) and her draft was 32 ft. She had two sets of Pametrada steam turbines, twin propellers and four auxiliary steam turbines, each driving a 1,750 KW, 220 V DC generator.

When built, she carried she carried 636 First Class and 1,494 Tourist Class passengers, and when converted to One Class for cruising, she carried 1,750. Her crew initially was 980 and remained the same in 1973.

Faced with increasingly unprofitable around the world passenger routes, she operated as a full-time cruise ship from 1973, just as I was leaving. Between 1981 and her retirement in 1986, she was based in Sydney and sailed around the Pacific and South-East Asia. However, she became surplus to P & O's requirements in 1986 and was sold as a floating hotel and tourist attraction, first to Japan and later to China. As a result of receiving severe storm damage in 1984 whilst in the port of Dalian, ORIANA was finally sold to the local breakers in 2005. Yet another love of my life ended up as razor blades. So sad.

ORIANA's call sign was GVSN.

Ship's Company

As CANBERRA and ORIANA were of a similar size, the composition of Officers and crew was more or less the same, there being less in our smaller sister ships. In CANBERRA, between 1961-73 there were 900 Officers and crew, of whom 21 of us were female.

Each P & O ship is split into Departments: Deck, Radio, Pursers, Medical, Engineers and Electricians.

In my day all the Officers were white and mainly British, with the Deck crew being Indian and the engine room crew Pakistani.

Trying to keep them apart caused us a big headache when the India/Pakistan war was raging. Our wonderful stewards were Goanese.

On the female side, the Officers consisted of Junior Women Assistant Pursers, (JWAPs), Women Assistant Pursers (WAPs), Senior Woman Assistant Purser (SWAP), Children's Hostess, Nursing Sisters and Entertainment Hostesses. Female crew consisted of Telephone Operators, Children's Stewardess, Stewardesses, hairdressers and shop staff.

Deck Department

Above decks, this Department reigned supreme. Well, they liked to think they did, and in fairness, I have to admit that perhaps they did. In charge of navigation, ship's exterior maintenance, stowage of cargo, boat ports, (when a ship has to anchor off as she is too large to go alongside), gangways, maintenance of lifeboats, and all other related responsibilities, their responsibilities are enormous, and although the Captain is in overall charge, he leaves the running of this side of the ship to the Chief Officer and all those junior to him. The Bosun oversees the Indian deck crew who look after the outside of the ship, constantly cleaning, painting and, when we got to Hong Kong, hanging over the side re-touching the white paint.

The Radio Office

Employed by P & O, this consisted of the Chief Radio Officer, First and Second Radio Officer. In CANBERRA the radio room was just outside our accommodation and, because of Uncle Bernard's days as a Marconi radio operator, I used to pop in there quite often to see them at work. On one occasion the Chief, Dick Hawkins, asked if I would like to do the identification announcement to other shipping. A female's voice has a different frequency and is easier to hear, I was told, so I practised, put the headphones on, and recorded the following message:

"This is the British ship CANBERRA, call sign GBVC, calling for radio frequency and station identification."

Well, it seems that I was a big hit! I think Dick rue the day he ever asked me as he kept getting messages from passing cargo ships, probably away for months at a time, saying how wonderful it was to hear a female voice and asking who I was? There was even a Captain Ellison who was asking about me as his ship came into view. As I was off duty and near the Radio Room at the time, Dick came to find me. I went out on deck and waved to the Captain for ages as he steamed by. He reciprocated with great gusto, sent me a really nice message, and Dick let me have a brief conversation with him over the airwaves. I even received a beautiful letter from him which caught up with me a few ports later. Ah – ships that pass in the night! I wonder what happened to him?

The Medical Staff

Consisting of the Surgeon (Doc), Assistant Surgeon (Baby Doc), two nursing sisters and a dispenser (chemist). They were always kind, caring and extremely proficient

Like everyone else on board, I had cause to consult Doc or Baby Doc now and then. My ailments were usually minor - sore throats from the fierce air conditioning and facing passengers over the counter, or stomach upsets – but I did have one stay in the ship's hospital which was memorable.

A Medical Tale

There was one occasion in CANBERRA when I urgently needed the medical staff's help. We had just left Port Everglades en route back to Southampton, when I had appendicitis. Doc Watson (the Surgeon on that trip) didn't want to operate unless really necessary, so he decided to keep me going on drips till we reached port. This meant that I ended up spending the whole of the trans-Atlantic part of our voyage in the ship's hospital, and our Captain Riddelsdell (known as "Woof Woof" because of his gruff voice) was an absolute sweetheart and came down to see me most evenings to check on how I was. Our Deputy Purser (DP) brought down my immigration work for me to do in bed. Thanks, Mike!

On one particular evening, two APs had come down to see how I was (more to see how I was getting on with the work, I suspect). Also in the hospital at that time was the First Engineer, Colin Bauchop ("Pork Chop"), who had fallen down a grating and badly cut his leg. I had been allowed to sit quietly in a wheelchair, still connected to my drip, whilst I struggled to complete the large passengers lists on my knee. "Pork Chop" I gather was also in a wheelchair in his little room nearby. Just then a group of engineers came down to the hospital to see how "Pork Chop" was getting on. Naturally the two lots of lads got together and decided it might be fun to have races up and down the alleyway with us both in wheelchairs. I most definitely thought it would not be fun at all as my appendix was still grumbling, though it hadn't yet reached full protest stage, but despite my vociferous objections they unhooked my drip from its stand, put the bag in my lap, and wheeled me out into the alleyway, where I met up with "Pork Chop".

Fortunately, Doc had heard the commotion in the hospital and came to see what was going on. He was livid. I was quickly put back to bed, as was "Pork Chop" (but not in the same one, I hasten to add) and the APs and engineers were given a right rocket and told to leave the hospital and not come back. Thanks, Doc. I don't know what would have happened if we had got to the Grand Prix stage!

When we arrived at Southampton, I was transferred by ambulance up to Dreadnought, the Seamen's Hospital (as it was then), at Greenwich. It has a fascinating history and continues today under the Dreadnought Unit at St Thomas's Hospital and also the Hospital for Tropical Diseases, part of the University College Hospitals London NHS Trust.

There I was placed under the tender care of the Surgeon, Mr. Higton, who silenced my grumbling appendix once and for all. Marie and her boyfriend came to visit me shortly after I had had the operation, and I was so pleased to see them, as I was Mum and Dad when they came down a day or so later from Leicester to see how I was getting on.

As the only female amongst maybe 100 or so men, I had a room to myself opposite a big ward full of Lascar seamen, moaning and groaning all night. Word soon spread, however, that there was a female in their midst with her own room, and I found myself getting hesitant taps on my door and visitors' heads poking round it unless the DO NOT DISTURB sign was there.

"'Scuse me, Miss. Can I leave these bottles of beer (forbidden) in your wardrobe till I come again?"

I didn't feel well enough to object so, provided it was convenient, men would creep in and out of my room during visiting hours, only staying long enough to ask how I was and stow the beer. In the end I got to enjoy these clandestine visits, welcome breaks from the routine of hospital life. I'm not sure whether the nurses had any idea of what was going on or not, but they never mentioned it, although I'm sure they did.

I remember, too, a lovely, elderly History Professor who had had an operation on both eyes and couldn't see. His room was next to mine, so I used to call for him each morning and lead him by the hand (slowly, as I still had my stitches) up and down from East Wing to West Wing to get some exercise. I'm not sure how he came to be at Dreadnought, but I much enjoyed our time together.

And, as coincidence would have it, when I was landed at Southampton, who came to relieve me but the same SWAP I had relieved when I first set sail. Small world!

My favourite
Captain Riddelsdell

The old Dreadnought Seamen's Hospital as it was then. Today
it is continuing as the Dreadnought Unit of St Thomas's
Hospital (*photo: Barabbas 1312 - Own Work, CC BY-SA 4.0*)

Engineers Department

Below decks, the Engineers reigned supreme without a doubt,
looking after all things mechanical in the engine room under the
steely gaze of the Chief Engineer ("Chief Engines"), First
Engineer and junior Officers. Occasionally the Chief or First
would invite us females on a tour of the engine room, as they
did small passenger groups: not to see the mysterious "Golden
Rivet", I hasten add, though there may have been high hopes in
that direction on the part of some of the younger engineers.
Sorry lads. With my love of engines, I was more interested in
how things worked, and found it all fascinating. Disappointing, I
know, but you can't win them all!

Electricians Department

Although we needed the Engineers to get us from A to B, for
day to day living the Electricians were the ones to chat up. They
were in charge of all things electrical obviously, but included in
their remit were: lifts, laundry, galley, vacuum cleaners, lighting,
passengers' hair dryers and other electrical equipment (though

irons weren't allowed for safety reasons), our office equipment, maintenance of ship's life boat engines, and swimming pool filtering systems, to name but a few. They were invariably rushed off their feet, but I always found them to be very cheerful and helpful, especially after the odd pint or three.

Pursers Department

And then there was - **us.** We reigned supreme somewhere in the middle, but as we held the money, that was our ace card. We were trumps!

Ours was by far the biggest Department. In overall charge was the Purser, followed by the Deputy Purser, with responsibility for victualling, shop staff, galley, and restaurant staff, and accommodation stewards. The Senior Assistant Purser looked after the Bureau staff, assisted by his female equivalent (SWAP). The rest of us did all the work!

The majority of Tourist cabin stewards, waiters and galley staff were Goanese, following the long tradition of recruiting (often from the same family, continuing from father to son) from Portuguese Goa. They were our stewards too and were super: kind, caring, and efficient. But occasionally us females met with a bit of resentment if we had a young steward as it was not the custom in Goa for men to wait on women, rather the other way around. Most of the more senior crew (Leading Hands), First Class stewards, waiters and bar staff were from the UK.

In charge of all the Asian crew was the Chief Pantryman ("Pants"). I can't remember his name, but our "Pants" on board CANBERRA was marvelous. He was extremely handsome, carried himself with such dignity, and was one of the most immaculately dressed men I've ever seen. If there was a problem amongst the Asian crew, the Captain always deferred to him. But, as far as I knew, there rarely was. "Pants" ran a tight ship. So did Captain Riddelsdell, Captain for my first voyages in

CANBERRA: stern but fair, but with a really soft heart underneath. I thought the world of him.

Safety at Sea

One of the biggest fears for any mariner is fire on board. Safety was of paramount importance and was taken very seriously. The Board of Trade required the ship's company to hold regular fire drills ("Fire Stations"), which meant we all had to leave our jobs, put on our life jackets and head immediately to our allocated boat stations. There, a muster was called and if anyone was absent, the head of that Department had to know why. Of course, certain parts of the ship had to be manned at all times, like the Bridge, surgery and engine room, but that didn't include us. Even if we were dealing with passengers at the time, we still had to pull down the counter shutters, stow our gear and head up on deck. Bars had to shut (to the dismay of certain passengers!), and entertainment stopped, although the ship's daily programme had been consulted beforehand so a time could be arranged which would cause the least disruption.

There were also passenger Fire Stations. After each embarkation, no matter how few passengers there were, there was always a fire drill when they had to return to their cabins to collect their life jackets and then go up on deck to their allotted boat station (written down on a notice in their cabins).

I had experience of a fire on board myself when leaving Southampton in ORIANA in 1971. We had just set sail down the Solent when oil-soaked lagging in the Boiler Room caught fire. Smoke was pouring out the funnel, fire tenders rushed to our side and I remember the bulkhead near the Bureau being too hot to touch. Passengers were sent to their boat stations, as were we, but the atmosphere on board remained calm, considering.

It was decided that we would turn around and head back to our berth, where a decision would be made as to what to do next. The engineers must have worked tirelessly in awful conditions to try to put the fire out, which they did initially, but we had two more attempts to sail and the same thing happened each time.

By now this was major news on television and in the newspapers. When we failed to leave for the second time, there was a full-page cartoon in the Daily Express: "The Owners have asked me to remind you, ladies and gentlemen, that this happens to be National Smile Week". Very funny. In the end, it was decided that the passengers should be given the choice: either disembark, be accommodated at hotels in Southampton for however long it took to get us sea-worthy again, and go on shore excursions to pass the time; or accept the company's offer to make alternative onward travel arrangements for those who wished to leave. In the end, most decided to stay, but whatever their choice, it meant a tremendous amount of work for us.

Staff were sent down from London to help us cope, but we had to stay on board, as did most of the Officers and crew as we didn't quite know when we would set sail again. It meant long hours in difficult conditions for everyone; a bit like being on stand-by, but worse. With minimal power the galley couldn't function properly, and I remember the WRVS preparing hot meals for us from a train wagon on the quayside.

It took almost three weeks to fix the problem, and I think we were all a bit nervous as we steamed down the Solent yet again. Thankfully, though, all was well this time, and we completed our voyage safely.

Religious Services

If we were at sea on a Sunday, Services for all denominations were held separately. The Captain took the Service for the passengers and, if a Padre was on board, he would take a Service for the crew. Officers were able to attend the

As a cartoon in the press said,
"The Owners have asked us to remind you,
ladies and gentlemen, that it's national smile week!"

Not so funny when you're on board, believe me!

Fire on board ORIANA, Southampton, August 1970

Below: In Southampton, helping passengers with
their many problems because of the fire

passengers' Service, and one of my favourite hymns, "Eternal Father, Strong to Save" (the seamen's hymn), was normally sung. Each time I sing it now I still pray for "those in peril on the sea". I know Mum and Dad did for me.

If we were in port, passengers were able to attend a local place of worship ashore according to their Faith, but a Missions to Seamen Padre would always come on board to say Mass for our large Catholic (mainly the Goanese) crew. If a Padre was travelling with us, he would be on hand to assist passengers and crew if needed, or spend a few quiet moments with them.

Contrary to popular belief, in those days a Captain was not licensed to marry people on board. Nowadays, he is granted a special Licence to conduct these ceremonies. Now I'm a Registrar, I always fancy doing this on HMS Warrior in Portsmouth, but that is their jealously guarded territory.

Sadness at Sea

Burials

As happens in any community, sadly people die. On board ship was no exception, particularly as we carried a fair number of elderly passengers in First Class. It didn't happen often on the ships I was sailing in, but there were a few deaths, mainly passengers, some of whom I had got to know quite well during the course of the voyage.

The family was always consulted as to burial arrangements. Americans for some reason would always prefer their loved ones' bodies to be repatriated rather than buried at sea. If we were near a port, it was usually decided that the body would be landed there unless there were instructions to the contrary. Until then, the deceased was laid in the Brine Room, part of the engine room, where it was cold, as this was the only place available. Sorry to be so macabre, but this was so. When that happened, there was always a problem with the Pakistani engine room crew who were terrified of approaching that room whilst a body was still in it.

If we were mid-ocean, it was often agreed that the deceased should be buried at sea. As SWAP in ORIANA, I went to three such ceremonies, held at the aft end of the ship out of sight of passengers. They were conducted by the Captain with the maximum amount of respect and reverence, the Death Certificate having been signed by the Surgeon. The family were present if they were on board. Also in attendance were the Surgeon and medical staff, the Purser, and another senior member of the Bureau staff. It was a very moving experience, and I couldn't hold back a tear as the Union Jack draped body slid off the stretcher into its watery grave below.

Stowaways

We had a few and, because of my knowledge of Spanish, I became particularly involved with one such stowaway.

Eduardo Diaz Gonzalez, 43 and single, was a political refugee wanted by the Cuban authorities, who had stowed away on CANBERRA when we left Hong Kong. He gave himself up a day after leaving port and, as he spoke no English and I was the only Spanish-speaking Officer on board, I was delegated to act as interpreter. He was not allowed to mix with anyone and was locked up each night in the ship's "brig".

I spent a lot of time with him, piecing together his story. He was so lonely and frightened, and it was hard not to feel sorry for him.

It seems that he was a Junior Minister for the Castro regime, having spent time in Moscow and Beijing (Peking as it was then). However, he did not want to return to the repressive regime of Cuba, but to live in Australia. He had gone to Hong Kong (he wouldn't say why), where the Cuban Consulate had immediately confiscated his passport. Perhaps they got wind of his desire to defect. He said the Consulate had bought his plane tickets to return to Cuba via Peking and Moscow, but he was terrified that, once there, he would be treated as a traitor and either imprisoned or killed. His father had been killed ten years before, and his mother had died recently.

When he was out one day in Hong Kong with the Consulate driver, he managed to jump out of the car and disappear into the rabbit warren of alleys that make up Hong Kong. As he knew CANBERRA was in port and was going to Australia, he headed for the ship and stowed away.

He kept apologizing for being a bother to the ship. He was willing to go anywhere, but not back to Cuba. Once we arrived in Sydney, he requested permission to stay, but since he hadn't sought political asylum this was denied by the Immigration Department, so he spent the night in a cell in Sydney and was then returned to us on board. The Australian authorities said they would consider his case, but he had to travel with us to Fremantle, where they would let us know what had been decided. Once again, in Melbourne he spent the night in a cell ashore. When we arrived at Fremantle, he was allowed to disembark into the custody of the Australian Immigration Authorities and I heard no more.

All this was reported in the Australian press. I have the cutting, but it's too faded to replicate. I often wonder what happened to him. I hope so much that his asylum request was granted as he seemed such a genuine, kind and sincere man.

Man Overboard

Occasionally, sadly, we would get "jumpers". Who knows why they made such a drastic decision? The sea can have a very hypnotic effect: perhaps they were in a fragile mental state and were just drawn to it.

When the Man Overboard alarm was given, the drill was for someone, anyone, to immediately throw a life jacket into the sea near where the person had jumped. The order was then given from the Bridge to start a Williamson Turn, that is to do a figure of eight back to where the person had gone overboard. This figure of eight was necessary as it took a long time and a great distance for a ship to slow down, let alone turn around.

Meanwhile, the "crash boat" was being prepared for launching. These were fast, covered lifeboats, as opposed to the open, bigger passenger lifeboats, and were used for emergencies. CANBERRA and ORIANA both had two, one port, one starboard, nearly underneath the Bridge.

As soon as we were near the spot where the person had jumped, the "crash boat" was launched to search for him/her. However, the chances of finding anyone who had jumped alive was remote. With a ship travelling at 23 knots or so, and from the height of the deck from which they jumped, their chances of surviving weren't great, particularly if they had jumped aft, near the propellers. But it did happen occasionally, though in my time we never found anyone. If they had relatives on board, they received as much comfort as we were able to give. An entry was made in the Ship's Log, and an Inquest was held at our next port.

A distressing time for us all.

The Weather

During my travelling life there seems to have been an awful lot of it! On board ship it was typhoons: with the Foreign Office it was earthquakes <u>and</u> typhoons.

As well as fire, the "elements" played a vital role in the safety of the ship. September and October were the typhoon months in the Pacific and invariably we encountered at least one when sailing from Honolulu to Yokohama in Japan. It was a weird and, at times, frightening experience. I remember one particular time in CANBERRA when it was impossible to avoid sailing into, and out of, a raging typhoon. The waves broke almost over the Bridge, which was 80 ft high; the wind howled like a pack of wolves all the time; the rain lashed down; and we pitched around like a cork in a bath tub. There was nothing to do but "heave to". Our engines weren't powerful enough to combat the storm and we were going nowhere fast.

Then, for me, the eeriest thing happened. After two days of this battering, without warning we broke through the maelstrom and found ourselves on a sheet of glass, the sun shining brightly, not a cloud in the sky, not a ripple on the water. We had hit the eye of the storm. I've never known anything like it, and can picture the scene as if it were yesterday. We went up on deck and just marveled at this strange phenomenon. All around us, on the horizon, the turbulence continued, and we knew we had to suffer another two days of sailing through this typhoon to reach the other side. But for the six hours or so it took us to pass through the eye of the storm, we caught our breath, spent time in the open air again, and prepared ourselves for what was about to come. In conditions like this, life on board was difficult. Fortunately, I've always been an excellent sailor and bad weather never bothers me physically, apart from a headache now and then. The rougher, the better. But for some it was hell. The medical staff were rushed off their feet with sea-sickness and injuries sustained by falls, and it was a nightmare in the galley, where it was too dangerous to have pans of boiling fat and hot food flying all over the place. The result was that we lived on cold rations for the duration and had the "fiddles" raised on the tables. Few passengers ventured into the restaurant, but the hardy ones amongst us did, so we had the place almost to ourselves.

Working in the Bureau was tricky. We had to lash all the filing cabinets together to stop the drawers from flying out and spewing papers everywhere, and our typewriters had to be put on the deck also for safety, which meant that work ground to a halt as it's not easy to type on the floor! Everything else was stowed away securely. And typhoons en route to Japan were always bad news as this was one of our busiest times preparing the immigration lists for arrival at Yokohama, where the officials were some of the fussiest we encountered. Not able to work properly for four days meant long hours and little sleep to try to catch up.

Sleeping was also difficult and for me it meant putting my bunk mattress on the deck and stowing everything else away. Showering was a nightmare too and we had to hang onto the grab handles for dear life to stay upright.

But I survived the many typhoons and lesser storms I encountered, and have lived to tell the tale.

In complete contrast, sailing through the Sargasso Sea was unforgettable. The stillness was eerie. I felt I was on a ghost ship.

This region in the North Atlantic Ocean is bounded by four currents: the Gulf Stream; the Canary Current; the North Atlantic Equatorial Current; and the North Atlantic Gyre. Unlike other "seas", it has no land boundaries and is distinguished from other parts of the Atlantic by swathes of brown Sargassum seaweed floating in calm blue waters. Sadly, today, after a recent survey a large amount of non-biodegradable plastic was found to have accumulated there, and it is now worryingly called the North Atlantic Garbage Patch. But it wasn't like that when I sailed through it. It was so different from normal oceans, and I spent a long time leaning on the rail taking it all in.

Chapter Five

ACQUIRING A SET OF SEA LEGS

My New Home

But back to me.

At 1600 hours on 13 January 1968 CANBERRA set sail. I missed it all: that first casting off, the Royal Marines playing on the quayside, all the streamers fluttering in the breeze, sailing down the Solent for the first time. Such a shame! I was still slightly numb and was certainly neither use nor ornament the state I was in, so I was sent to the Stadium to help with distributing the flowers. Once that was finished, I was taken down to the Bureau to meet my new "family" for the next four months. I couldn't have wished for a more helpful, friendly set of shipmates. I knew nothing. I'd no idea where I was, where the ship was going, which end of the ship was which, where my cabin was, what public rooms there were. I did have my passport, Seaman's Record and Discharge Book, and ID book as I'd been told to take them with me to ORONSAY, but that was all.

Our Purser, Ross Temple, was a tall white-haired man whom we affectionately nicknamed "Granny". His favourite phrase, if he wanted you, was "Eh, Gillian, gotta minute?", which I'm afraid we mimicked dreadfully. He called me into his office to say hello and then left me in the tender care of the other WAPs, who set about the onerous task of introducing me to shipboard life.

WAP'S Alley!

Our female Officers' accommodation, lovingly referred to as WAP's Alley, was on Sun Deck, near the Radio Room and a door onto the outside deck. There were nine of us, six WAPS, one

Children's Hostess (Chilly Ho!), and two Entertainment Officers (female, naturally!). I had a nice outside cabin which should have been the SWAP's, and was so lucky that the WAP in the cabin next to mine, Patricia (Tricia), was very nice, friendly and helpful. She remains one of my lifelong friends. Facilities were a bit difficult as we shared one bathroom (no shower) and one loo between all of us, which meant it was a mad dash in the evening when we were trying to get ready for dinner and the evening's entertainment all at the same time. But we managed well, and amicably.

One of my main problems was clothes. I hadn't much of anything: only one set of "blues", and no "whites" till my baggage turned up, which meant I had to borrow from the girls nearest to my size, though their dresses never fitted properly, and I felt very conspicuous. I was allowed as a special dispensation to wear my black, and only, shoes, which looked most odd with "whites". It was that or my boots. I had no Mess Dress and, as most of the girls only had one evening outfit and they couldn't lend me one, it meant I couldn't go on deck much till I got my own, which was a real pain. I bought a few toiletries from the ship's shop, but that was it.

The Bureau
The Bureau was the hub of the ship, we always liked to think, though other Departments seldom agreed. But, as I said before, we held all the cash, so we were". We were situated amidships on the Promenade (Prom) Deck (easy to nip out for a quick look when arriving and sailing) and working conditions were good except during typhoons and "inclement weather". But that applied to us all.

Our Pursers Department consisted of seventeen officers and three crew. The Purser was in overall charge, and then came one Deputy Purser (DP in charge of victualling and the hotel side);

one Senior Assistant Purser (SAP, running the Bureau); one SWAP (in charge of us females); six male Assistant Pursers (APs – cashiers and looking after crew matters); six WAPs (us); the Travel Adviser (from Head Office and considered an officer); two male Letter Writers (the ship's Post Office) and our bellboy, who were part of the crew.

"Bells" were the youngest members of the crew at sixteen, and they needed to be fit as they had to dash around like mad things delivering notes, leaflets and whatever else to passengers and other Departments. It was often their first time away from home, so I could well understand their bewilderment. Some were shy, others were home-sick. We in the Bureau had the luxury of having our own "Bells", and I remember my delight when I discovered that, amazingly, he came from my home village of Oadby too. I hadn't known him previously, but knew where he lived and took him under my wing as he seemed so lost at first. I like to think he was grateful for a friendly face and someone who could talk to him about his home.

In most Bureaux, there was a little cubby hole which we called **The Woodshed,** which housed the public address system and from where we made all our information announcements and requests for passengers to call at the Bureau with whatever we needed from them. It was a tiny space and the APs took great delight in turning off the light when we were making the announcement, or locking us in there for a short time. Little swines! We, of course, were far too nice to do the same to them. But if they needed any emergency sewing to be done, forget it!

One particular announcement, usually made from the Bridge but sometimes by us, was a bit tricky, though. "Please do not sit on the ship's side rail". You try saying that! Invariably it came out wrong, to the great amusement of the passengers.

On the whole, though, the APs were a great bunch! We all "had our moments", and tempers got a bit frayed at times,

Life in the Bureau

Our Bureau in ORIANA, 1971

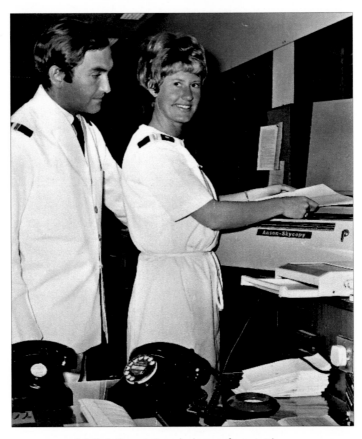

A P & O Promotional photo of me with
our SAP, Dickie Rutter, in CANBERRA, 1969

especially when we were under a lot of pressure, but being part of a ship's company means that, as you're living and working with your colleagues for weeks on end, you have to make a special effort to get on. Compromise and understanding are key. You learn this very fast.

I settled in quickly (you had to) and soon got to know my way around. I spent hours at first going from one end of the ship to the other, learning who did what, where this room was, that room was, and gradually I began to relax and feel at home.

Work (yes, we had to do some!)

Each ship in P & O's fleet was different of course, not only in size and look but also in atmosphere and shipmates. But one thing remained constant: the WAP's work at sea was always the same whichever ship you were on. During the course of my six years at sea, at one stage or another I did all the jobs allotted to us.

On the Counter (Receptionist)

Normally, when we started as JWAPs we were on either the First Class or Tourist Class Counters acting as Receptionist; fount of all knowledge; agony aunt; problem-solver par excellence; recipient of all complaints, whether justified or not; and whatever else our beloved passengers could conjure up. And they were good at conjuring! This was my first job on joining CANBERRA so I needed to know what I was talking about and by necessity it was a rapid learning curve. The other WAP on the counter beside me was one of the Dutch girls employed by P & O for their linguistic abilities. Each ship normally had two. We got on well, though she was very quiet. The two AP's, Mike Staddon and John Keating, on either side of us, though, were a different matter. They were the Tourist cashiers and were not averse to a lot of teasing. One of their favourite tricks was to wind up a little tank and send it across the counter to each other, whirring along in front of us, climbing whatever papers were in its way. This was slightly disconcerting if you were dealing with passengers at the time, but they usually thought it very funny, thank goodness. I'm still in touch with Mike, through our Reunion lunches (and John, if he and wife Linda, with whom I sailed also, attend). Mike nicknamed me "Swilly Gilly", not because I drank a lot, which I didn't and still don't, but it sounded good. He still calls me that to this day. Old habits die hard!

There is one particular incident on board that I remember well, for which those of us on duty got into a lot of trouble (although I was innocent, of course!).

It was evening, we were in port (Nuku'alofa, Tonga) and I was "manning" the First Class counter. Nearly all the passengers had gone ashore to the quite posh International Dateline Hotel, so we had nothing much to do. The boys therefore decided to play rugby with a water melon (as you do!) which had happened to materialize as if by magic. Unfortunately, just as they were executing a particularly swift pass, a smartly-dressed man in tuxedo, and his wife wearing a beautiful long dress, came up to the counter to ask me a question. All of a sudden there was a loud bang as the water melon hit the screen behind me, flew over the top and exploded on the counter in front of us. Water melon went everywhere, but particularly over the elegantly attired passengers and me. We were covered in it and looked an awful sight, me in a pink dress and the gentleman in a two-tone pink tuxedo.

Telling the tale afterwards, this episode seems so funny, but the couple understandably were furious. The Purser came to placate them, agreed to pay for any dry cleaning needed, and gave us all a right rocket, even though I was completely innocent and was only doing my job! We even got a telling off from the Captain, which I thought then, and still do, a bit unfair to lump me with the boys. A few days later the same couple came up to the Counter, warily this time, but I have to say they were very magnanimous about having their evening and attire ruined in such a way. Their forgiveness restored my faith in human nature.

As we got more experienced, we moved up the promotion ladder job-wise. As Juniors, besides being on Reception, we also worked as Crew WAP, typing endless Crew Lists, keeping crew details up to date – all a bit boring really. Then came passenger accommodation responsibilities (known familiarly as the Berthing Queen), always a challenge; and finally, being in charge of Immigration which involved getting passengers from A to B and working with the Immigration Officers of the countries we visited. I found this job really interesting and loved it. Exceptionally, I even did an unscheduled stint as Cashier for one season of Mediterranean cruising as they were short of APs, but as someone who had failed Maths 'O' Level, this gave me many sleepless nights. I'll never know how I got through it and, even more surprisingly, how I managed to balance the books at the end.

Being **Crew WAP** was my least favourite job, and I only did it once, on my third voyage in CANBERRA. Because of our ship's size, there were two Crew APs (John Atkins and David Phillips) instead of one, and we were always busy. I worked in a small side office, isolated from everyone else, at the mercy of the lads, who would tease me constantly and, when they were feeling really mischievous, would sneak up on me as I was typing and bind my hands and legs to my chair with sellotape. I was not amused, as you can imagine, and it really hurt when they ripped it off. If I'd wanted a leg wax, I'd have gone to the beauty salon! It certainly wouldn't be acceptable now, but it was a man's world at sea in those days, so I just had to put up with it.

One of the jobs of the Crew APs was to distribute money to the crew, so for this reason we were always popular. There were no ATMs nor credit cards in those days, so you couldn't just pop ashore and draw out what you wanted when you wanted it. Set times were allocated for crew pay-outs, but back then there was a feeling amongst a few of the older white deck crew that having a woman on board was bad luck, so at times my dealings with them were a bit tricky and I didn't take part in distributing the money. I often wonder whether this superstition is still held in some quarters today. Hopefully not.

On board, we Officers signed for everything and settled our bills at the end of the voyage, but if we needed money to go ashore, we could cash cheques at the Bureau before arrival.

Despite the teasing, I did like John and David. I "forgave them their trespasses" (against my arms and legs), but if ever we should meet in the future, lads, I do feel I have earned a pub lunch out of you as compensation.

"Berthing Queen"

Not at all an elegant title, but that's what we were. Dealing with passenger accommodation was always quite a challenge, especially when you had four unacquainted people sharing the same cabin, as they often did in Tourist Class. One snored, one smoked, one was untidy – and so on. My problem was that normally the ship was full and I had very few cabins and berths to spare to move people around. I felt for them and did what I could to address their concerns, but it was tough and often I bore the brunt of their unhappiness.

In First Class, there were less issues to deal with, but occasionally I would get passengers, even those in suites, who were dissatisfied with their accommodation in one way or another. This was worse, as there were far fewer cabins and berths in First Class to move passengers to, and placating them was an uphill struggle. Again, I did my best: that's all I could do.

Immigration WAP

This was a really busy job involving getting passengers safely through immigration at all our ports. Each country had its own requirements and different ways of processing all the information we had collected. For me, it meant obtaining the personal details of all passengers, which necessitated collecting their passports and vaccination certificates; sorting through the information we had gathered and then transferring it onto the Passenger Manifests. Japan and Panama were the most demanding and I spent hours typing list after list, often well into the night if we were calling at different countries in quick succession. I well recall those horrible Panama Lists which had to be run off on a gestetner machine (forerunner to the photocopier). It needed a special red fluid to work, and I got quite "high" breathing it in. It was awful. And so was the ink, which invariably splodged onto my white uniform dress so that I then had to go cap in hand to the laundry keeper to sort it out. How he loved us!

Being in charge of Immigration also meant that I had to be present on the quayside for embarkation, checking the accommodation lists and passengers' passports and vaccination certificates to see that they were in order.

Things didn't always go smoothly! On one particular occasion, VIP passengers Herb Dimmitt, Vice President of the American department store, J C Penney, and his wife Janee, were embarking at Honolulu, *en route* to Sydney. When I checked their passports, I found that they didn't have the requisite visas to enter Australia and had to break the bad news to them. Herb argued vociferously about this, but I was adamant: they would not be allowed to go ashore at Sydney or anywhere else in Australia, without a visa. In the end, I said I would accompany them to the Australian Consulate in Suva on our route to Sydney, to see if they could obtain a visa there, which they did, thank goodness. They disembarked quite happily and had a wonderful holiday. In the end we became firm friends and often laughed about our unhappy first encounter, although it wasn't funny at the time.

Another reason I enjoyed this job was that I got to meet and work with the Immigration Officers at the ports we visited. On the whole they were a very pleasant and helpful group, and the immigration inspections went well (apart from one visit to Auckland, when a Tongan passenger, slightly the worse for drink, was sick into the box of passports). Sometimes, as for the United States, they would embark at Suva and process all the passengers on board before arrival at Honolulu, which meant more time ashore for the passengers (and us), which was much welcomed. I have special fond memories of one such Immigration Officer who always wore a brightly flowered shirt once on board, and who must have bought shares in the company that produced the men's aftershave, Aramis. The perfume lingered for days after he had disembarked. No names, no pack drill!

C.O.D

My favourite job, however, was Central Office Dolly (COD), a terribly un-PC title these days, but times and attitudes were very different back then, and I for one didn't mind in the least.

Being COD meant working on the Bridge as Secretary to the Captain and Senior Officers, and I had the luxury of a small office all to myself near the Captain's cabin, with a fantastic view when I got time to look out of the porthole. It was an interesting and busy job, but was even more so in port when there were letters to write to Head Office, forms to fill in and Agent's correspondence to deal with. As a result, though, one of the downsides was that I didn't get that much time ashore myself. But I still loved it, even when I had to take a record of Loggings (disciplinary hearings). The language was sometimes very choice, and I often didn't know how to spell the words, but I soon learned. Working as COD did wonders for one's education!

Financial Rewards (ie Pay)

Not enough! But then when was it ever? My Assistant Purser's starting pay in 1967 was just £35.15s.0d per month, rising to £58.15s.0d. after seven years. Of course, we had nothing to pay for board and lodging, and our only expenses were for laundry (we couldn't wash anything ourselves), and bar bills. Booze on board was cheap: 12s for a bottle of gin; as were cigarettes, though I have never smoked. So, what we earned was really just spending money for trips ashore and all those wonderful, though useless, large wooden carvings and baskets from Tonga, which I kept tripping over in my small cabin, as well as wicker "peacock" chairs, linen baskets and tables from Madeira which used to drive the Baggage Master demented!

But I for one never complained. I was just so glad to be doing the job I loved. That was reward enough.

On Board Romances

A very sensitive subject, and one that I won't go into in detail for very personal reasons, and to protect others. Sorry to disappoint!

Suffice it to say that, given the environment and time spent away from home, rightly or wrongly romantic attachments were formed. I was no exception. During the whole of my time at sea I had two great loves (one on board CANBERRA; one on board ORIANA). I cared for them both a lot, and we had great times together. When I left CANBERRA, it was the end of the first relationship. One moves on! When I left ORIANA, it was the saddest of partings, but it was necessary. We always kept in touch, albeit infrequently, as he said he just wanted to know that I was all right. He "crossed the bar" a short while ago. How I miss his voice. How I wish I could have said goodbye.

Some of my favourite passengers

Above left with Janee Dimmit in Los Angeles and right: with Stephen Collier, one of my favourite regular round-world passengers.

Above left: with Janee and William Conrad (Frank Cannon of the American detective series); and right: with Don Cadette, of the popular American Marty O'Conlon Trio (we were an "item" for a time).

Chapter Six

PASSENGERS: OUR BREAD AND BUTTER

Passengers. What would we do without them, and at times what would we do with them?

They came in all shapes and sizes, ages, nationalities, from all walks of life, some travelling on their own, some with their families. Being First Class or Tourist didn't imply that the latter were not as nice as the former: usually they were. They maybe just didn't have as much money to spend.

First Class passengers tended to be either doing a round the world cruise; going out to start an important job abroad (in those days most of our Diplomatic Service members travelled this way to take up their postings); travelling from A to B in style; or were visiting family. They were fantastic on the whole: cultured, well educated, interesting and fun. This may sound rather snobbish, but they were. Occasionally, they were arrogant, rude and a right pain in the derrière. But not often.

I met some wonderful passengers, some of whom I remained in touch with for many years afterwards. Herb and Janee Dimmitt (whom I've mentioned before) from Honolulu, were surely the very best passenger friends I ever had. We became close and I loved to stay with them at their luxurious house on Diamond Head, with its stunning views over Waikiki Beach, enormous swimming pool and lush, tropical gardens. They died quite a little while ago, but I still have such fond memories of them.

Passengers travelling in Tourist Class in the main were emigrating to Australia, New Zealand, and Canada. These were the days of the £10 passage and for many the voyage was an emotional journey into the unknown. They were leaving loved ones behind and were fearful of what the future held in store for them. I, for one, did my best to be as helpful and reassuring as possible, answering any queries they might have as best I could, helping them fill in their immigration and Customs forms. I felt for them, and I like to think they much appreciated a sympathetic approach.

Travelling in Tourist Class were also the tour groups, sports club teams (rugby and football mainly) and passengers seeing the world but on a smaller budget.

The rugby and football teams gave us the most problems! Once we had started a short Pacific cruising season, they were regular travelers, looking forward to a lot of booze, great food and, perhaps, depending on their fellow passengers, great entertainment. ORIANA always had a Master-at-Arms because of the predominantly white crew. In CANBERRA, on such cruises we had two Australian Waterside Police who travelled with us to keep the peace. They were much needed! On one particular cruise it got so bad that we females were banned from going on decks in the evening – to protect ourselves. I well remember one occasion when a rugby player, much the worse for wear, jumped from one deck to the swimming pool on the deck below. Unfortunately, he had forgotten to check that the pool was full of water. It wasn't – it was being cleaned at the time – and he sustained rather serious injuries and had to be landed at the next port.

For the most part, though, all the passengers I met were very nice. I always feel so grateful, and privileged, to have sailed and met such interesting, kind and fun people. They, as well as great shipmates, made my time with P & O so special and worthwhile.

Cocktails Parties

With only a few female Officers, we were much in demand, as

you can imagine! On one particular voyage, I counted that I went to forty-seven "official" cocktail parties! It was enough to drive you to drink. Fortunately, it didn't for me, though it was a major problem for some.

These official receptions were either Captain's Cocktails, held at the beginning of each voyage (one for First Class, one for Tourist Class), or mini-Cocktails, often held in the Captain's cabin, for small numbers of passengers embarking *en route* at the intermediate ports. Everyone got to meet the Captain. Those given by Senior Officers were for selected passengers who sat at their tables or whom they had got to know during the voyage. We were the hostesses. Some of the girls saw them as a chore. Not me. I loved them for the chance it gave me to meet some really interesting people, some of whom became good friends over the years.

"Celebs"

We had a few, but mostly in ORIANA once we had started cruising from the West Coast of America. I remember Charlton Heston used to come with us now and then, and Desi Arnez, Lucille Ball's husband, also. But it was after the US series "Love Boat" took off that there were more "celebs" as it seemed a good way to boost one's profile.

I did meet most of them, briefly, at one time or another, but I do remember William Conrad (Frank Cannon in the US detective series) who was particularly jovial and good fun.

There was one group, though, that used to fill me with despair. In ORIANA we started to run Bridge (the card game) cruises from San Francisco, round the Caribbean and back again. Pretty well all the passengers would be Bridge fanatics (that is nine hundred or so of them), obsessed, competitive almost to the point of physical violence, rude, unfriendly - it was enough to put you off the game for life. On one cruise we had the noted (not to me, he wasn't) Bridge expert, Ernie Rovere, travelling with us and organising all the competitions. He was a large, portly gentleman, somewhat pompous, always dressed in a bright green jacket, but what made him stand out was his lurid bow tie which lit up and whizzed round and round when he pressed a button somewhere on his person. Sadly, or otherwise, I don't have a photo of him, but I can see him now. The Americans worshipped him. I didn't.

"Pour-Outs"

Our own parties were different altogether. Called "pour-outs", they were held whenever we felt like it in our cabins or alleyways, depending on the numbers, and were for fellow Officers and Leading Hands (Senior crew). They could be riotous affairs and I enjoyed most of them, except if they got a bit too out of hand, as they did on occasions.

Tricia and I vividly remember one particular "pour-out". CANBERRA was in Yokohama for three days so we, in WAP's alley, decided it would be a good idea to hold a Sake party on the second day, in the early evening. A few of us slipped ashore on the first day to buy quite a few bottles of Sake, which we surreptitiously brought back on board (which we weren't allowed to do). As Sake should be drunk warm, the next morning we filled our one and only bath with hot water and put all the bottles in it to get them to the right temperature for the party. No baths for us that day. Invitations had already been sent out to those Deck Officers, Engineers, Electricians, and our own boys, who would still be on board. We were all set.

I shall never know to this day whether the Captain had a tip-off or whether it was just our bad luck, but he decided to do "Rounds" (inspection of our quarters) just before the party was due to begin. Maybe the smell was a give-away: it was rather pungent around our Alleyway. Anyway, "Woof Woof" (the

Captain) and Chief Officer turned up unexpectedly, looked in the bathroom and found twenty or so bottles of Sake bobbing away nicely in steaming hot water. We were mortified. He was definitely not amused! The party was cancelled, and we were made to empty all the bottles over the side, which was not an easy thing to do as they were quite hot to carry. Lucky fish: they must have thought all their Christmases had come at once! Tricia and I still laugh about it now, but it wasn't funny at the time. We lost a lot of money that day and didn't do it again.

"Haute Cuisine" on board

All our ships were blessed with their own Marco Pierre White's. The standard of food on board was second to none, as witnessed by our numerous attempts to lose weight. Victualling for such a large number of passengers and ship's company, though, required a tremendous amount of planning, as you can imagine. Making sure sufficient provisions (food and drink) were delivered on board at the right port was a challenge, particularly at some of the smaller ones, and menus were always tailored to what was available where we were. In the tropics we had a lot of exotic fruit; in New Zealand, delicious lamb; in Japan, rice, fish and seafood. Wherever in the world we happened to be, the food was always delicious.

As Officers, we dined First Class: Junior Officers at the Mess tables; Senior Officers having a passenger table of their own (some of them in Tourist). When I became a SWAP I had my own Tourist table of four "down aft" and the Head Waiter had the wonderful knack of allocating the most eligible young male passengers to it. I was for ever grateful!

The majority of our table waiters were Goanese, with the Wine Waiters being British. They were all fantastic: hardworking and courteous, and they were a credit to the Company.

Living this life of gastronomic luxury as we did, though, meant that having three good meals a day in First Class made it all too easy for us to put on the pounds. Not so important for the men, but a disaster for us females. Our Chef in CANBERRA, Sean Kinsella (whom we nicknamed "The Singing Leprechaun" because he had a great voice and was Irish – what else?) was very conscious of this and so tried to accommodate our diet wishes, when the mood took us, which was often. Here was a man of patience!

One particular diet for some reason involved nine eggs a day. It didn't work, and the Bureau was not a nice place to be around, but at least we tried. And we threw ourselves whole-heartedly into as many deck games and dancing as we could, just in case that helped. It did to some extent, but not enough. There were some rather tight-fitting uniforms around.

CHAPTER SEVEN

TREADING THE BOARDS

Unlike today's modern cruising, in those days on the entertainment front, we were **IT**! This is where my love of dancing proved useful! Each ship had an Entertainment Officer and two Entertainment Hostesses, one for First Class, one for Tourist. Occasionally we might have a minor celebrity on board to entertain the passengers, but it was up to the ship's company to keep the passengers amused for the rest of the time. This was, of course, in addition to our main duties which meant long hours as many of the "themed evenings", or other activities, didn't finish until quite late. It wasn't compulsory, but most of us liked to take part and, though I say so myself, we put on some jolly good shows! Did P & O know something we didn't when we went for interview?

As Officers, we weren't allowed to mix socially with the crew or to go into Tourist Class areas. We were strictly "First Class! But entertainment on board CANBERRA took many forms (overseen by the Entertainment Officer), covered both Classes, and gave us a chance to "mingle". There were the Horse and Frog racing evenings, when passengers either wound a handle or pulled a string to move horses and big wooden frogs along tracks. Super exciting! We sold tickets for these not-to-be-missed events.

The evenings which I remember most, though, were when we morphed into Pan's People. "Strictly Come Dancing" had nothing on us!

Bistro Night, as the name implies, was a French evening, with French cuisine on the menu and the bars and lounges turned into Bistros. We Moulin Rouge Can-Can dancers were the star attraction (yes, really), and we weren't half bad - considering! One of our stewardesses (Katie, whom I still see at our Reunion lunches) was a brilliant needlewoman and she made all our costumes from whatever we could find on board. She sewed white doilies onto our black bra's for the top and, having gone ashore to buy the material beforehand, made wonderful black, deep-red frilled Can-Can skirts. With black stockings, suspenders, and black shoes, we definitely looked the part, if perhaps a little more well-endowed than those in France. We practiced often, when time allowed and, believe it or not, I even managed to do "the splits" at the end – well, almost. Ouch!

Roaring Forties Night was, as the name implies, for "flappers"! Again, we learned the Charleston, delivered with much gusto, and wore lovely costumes made by Katie. No need to go to the gym: we got plenty of exercise this way.

Hawaiian Night

Normally put on when we were nearing Hawaii, this was a more gentle affair altogether. We bought grass skirts in Tonga, wore our bikini tops, and learned to dance the "Hukilau" and "Little Grass Shack", which we encouraged passengers to join in. Again, great fun, though I did find those grass skirts very itchy, and on one occasion, when I had a band of scratchy shells round the waist band too, I got awful blisters. I soon got the lawn mower out to <u>that</u> skirt.

London Night.

Our American passengers, in particular, loved this authentically British night. I was either a flower seller or a Suffragette, depending on who else was available, but it was good fun, except when it went a bit wrong, as the photo shows.

Fine dining

Our Officers' Mess table in First Class on Hawaiian Night

My own Tourist passenger table when I became SWAP

Treading the boards
"Bistro Night" - At the Moulin Rouge

CANBERRA (red) and ORIANA (yellow multi).

Above left: No comment! Right: With Le Patron (Staffie Peter Love) .

The CANBERRA Flappers

Hawaiian night

All ready to dance the Hukilau

Winning the Limbo Competition with a passenger.
This was definitely not in my job description!

London Night

As a Suffragette (I'm the upside down one - that wasn't in my Job Description either!)

Olde Tyme Music Hall

"Strolling Through the Park One Day" – what, with that lot!

Roman Night
"A funny thing happened on the way to the forum"

Left: As Scrumptia, one of the Patricians
(well it beat being "Amata Inepta", one of the Vestil Virgins!)
Right: Caesar (Staffie) inspecting the Centurions

The Slave Market, with Syd, Assistant Head Waiter, as the Slave Master
(where did he get that wig and costume?)

A Night at the Forum (or Roman Night)

Funny things certainly did happen on the way to the Forum on Roman Nights in ORIANA, not least the "slave market", when passengers could bid for a slave for the evening (a drink only!). It was great fun, the passengers loved it, and we certainly entered into the spirit of the occasion.

I made my own costume from an old sheet from the laundry locker. The Centurions' tunics came from old sheets as well, their silver armour from rubbish bags, their helmets from a silver paper covered mold from a saucepan (which is why they never fitted very well), kindly lent by the galley; Staffie's toga was also an old sheet. The laundryman was pleased to get rid of so much unwanted and unusable linen. Syd's Slave Master costume - well, heaven knows where he got that from. I doubt that came from the laundry locker, but you never know. However, it came "all right on the night" and we thoroughly enjoyed it.

The **"Olde Tyme Music Halls"** was especially popular with the passengers. It's amazing what talent there is on board amongst Officers and crew. Again, we made our own costumes (Katie helped me with mine), spent hours rehearsing, and the end result was quite a polished performance, much appreciated by the passengers, who would turn up at the Bureau next day full of praise for our efforts. It was for these shows that I was even persuaded to sing "My Old Man Says Follow the Van", was given a birdcage from somewhere, and off I went! I wouldn't have got into the Top 100, but I did my best. I was more or less in tune most of the time (except when, for a joke, someone stole the bird from the birdcage and I only noticed it mid-song, which rather threw me). When I had conquered my nerves, I had a really great time (aided, usually, by a stiff port and brandy beforehand).

But our talents were not just limited to dancing. Oh no.

Parlour Games

"What's My Line", "Twenty Questions" and "Call My Bluff" were very popular radio and television programmes at that time. I had always enjoyed them and took part in them all. Mike Gold, the Second Officer on board CANBERRA, and I made a formidable team and I even became known (forgive the immodesty) for a time as the "Isobel Barnett of P & O", Lady Isobel Barnett being one of the "Parlour Game stars" of that era. The lounges were always full when these were held and we were never short of "helpers" with the answers.

On **Casino Nights,** I sometimes acted as an assistant croupier on one of the roulette tables, helping the Tourist Assistant Head Waiter. We weren't, of course, allowed to take part ourselves. I was never any good anyway, but at least I got the general idea of what is was all about and this proved useful, once, on a subsequent visit to Macao, though only in a minor way!

After calls at Hong Kong, where you could, and I did, get beautiful suits, dresses, and evening wear made up in two days, **Fashion Shows** were a big hit with the ladies. On one call there I treated myself to a beautiful navy and turquoise, paisley print shantung silk dress, with matching knee length silk boots. I felt the "bees' knees" when I wore it and I modelled it with great success at one of the fashion shows. I kept it for ages till, squeeze as I could, I could no longer get into it! Less biscuits, Gillian.

Throughout my life on board, I never realized how versatile I could be, nor how much enjoyment all these new-found skills would give me. You never know until you try.

Crossing the Line

Reaching the Equator was a special moment for most passengers, and the ship's company, Officers and crew, celebrated the occasion by putting on a show for them. It was a messy, slightly inebriated affair involving King Neptune and his court, a drunken sailor, the Staff Captain ("Staffie"), nymphs (us females), and a few willing young passengers.

Those of us who took part (I did many times as long as I wasn't on duty) played our roles with great enthusiasm. We wore our white uniforms, with a bikini underneath. As nymphs, we were made to kneel at the feet of Neptune and were covered from head to foot in foul-smelling thick coloured liquid (whatever the galley had "cooked up" for us). Neptune's courtiers then unceremoniously chucked us in the pool. The passengers loved it and entered into the spirit of things with great gusto. The laundrykeeper didn't! Commemorative certificates were handed out all round and the Officers and crew then retired to Staffie's cabin for a right, well deserved "knees up"! A good time was had by all.

"Staffie", Staff Captain Mike (Sammy) Bradford,
receiving the Order of the Kipper. We then took great pleasure
in throwing him in the pool!

My two certificates (of which I'm rather proud)

FORM 2.
Reg. 53.

FORM M. & M.-2.
(Feb., '64.)

COMMONWEALTH OF AUSTRALIA
Navigation (Examination of Masters and Mates) Regulations No 233

CERTIFICATE OF EFFICIENCY AS LIFEBOATMAN

THIS IS TO CERTIFY that *GILLIAN LINDA ANGRAVE*

has, on the *15TH* day of *OCTOBER*, 19*68*, been
examined at the Port of *SYDNEY* by an examiner appointed under the
abovementioned Regulations and that—

(a) he has proved to the satisfaction of the Examiner that he has been trained in all the operations connected with the launching of lifeboats and the use of oars;

(b) he is acquainted with the practical handling of lifeboats; and

(c) he is capable of understanding and answering orders relating to lifeboat service.

ISSUED at the Port of *SYDNEY*, this *16TH* day of *OCTOBER* 19.*68*.

Delegate of the
Minister of State for Shipping and Transport

Signature of Holder	Date of Birth	Place of Birth
Gillian L. Angrave.	*16/4/1945*	*LEICESTERSHIRE ENGLAND.*

Should this Certificate come into the possession of any person to whom it does not belong, it should be forwarded to the Superintendent of the Mercantile Marine Office at the nearest Capital City Port or handed in at the nearest Police Station.

D. E. WILKINSON, Government Printer, Tasmania.

Exn. 50 G

Steering Certificate

MERCHANT SHIPPING (CERTIFICATES OF COMPETENCY AS A.B.) REGULATIONS, 1959

Surname **ANGRAVE**   Other Names **GILLIAN LINDA**

Discharge Book No. **R 852636**   Rating **FEMALE ASST. PURSER**

Gillian L. Angrave Usual Signature of Seaman

This is to certify that the above-named seaman served as **FEMALE ASST. PURSER** from

11:8:70 to **29:3:71**

in the **S.S. "ORIANA"** *being a ship* (other than a fishing boat) having a gross tonnage

of 100 tons or more and during that time took turns at the wheel in steering the ship (apart from periods of instruction)

for periods amounting in the aggregate to **TEN** hours.
(in words)

*Delete line which is inapplicable.

Date **24:3:71**   Master

N.B.—**Regulation 4(1)(e)** of the above Regulations provides that an applicant for a Certificate of Competency as Able Seaman must, apart from periods of instruction, have taken turns at the wheel in steering a ship (other than a fishing boat) having a gross tonnage of 100 tons or more or a sailing ship having a gross tonnage of 40 tons or more, for periods totalling at least 10 hours.

Regulation 9(1)(b) provides that the above requirement must be complied with before a seaman can take the qualifying examination prescribed by Regulation 4(1)(c) and the First Schedule. (This is the examination for which successful candidates receive an Efficient Deck Hand Certificate).

(4090) D. 183588 3 M. 3/67 P.I. Gp. 889

Chapter Eight

OFF DUTY

Whilst I always looked forward to my free time, there were still goals I set myself and these included gaining my Certificated Lifeboatman and Steering Certificates.

Certificated Lifeboatman
I always think of TITANIC when I think of this.

It was a Ministry of Transport requirement that each ship had to carry a certain amount of Certificated Lifeboatmen (that included women). This was something I was really interested in becoming, much to the Purser's delight, so I took on the challenge with great enthusiasm.

We had many hours of instruction from the Chief Officer on safety drills, equipment, First Aid, and how to lower and take charge of a lifeboat should we have to abandon ship.

When it came to my turn and I was to be examined in Sydney Harbour by the Australian equivalent of our Ministry of Transport examiner, I was nearly guilty of manslaughter.

Sydney Harbour is a busy place, with Manly ferries going backwards and forwards to their terminal opposite our berth at Circular Quay. Not the most suitable of places to launch a ship's lifeboat and take the exam, but there were only certain ports where the examiners were qualified to test us, and Sydney was one. We all climbed into the lifeboat (there were about ten of us), and we were lowered onto the water. It was a lovely sunny, but breezy day as we bobbed up and down. We had to row out into the centre of Circular Quay, where we were then given the order "ship oars", that is stand the oars on end with the blade facing upwards. Ships' oars are very long and heavy. I managed to ship mine satisfactorily, hanging onto them for grim death, but just at that moment a Manly ferry sailed by and its wake caused us to rock violently. I lost control of one of my oars, and it fell forward, missing the examiner by inches. Both he and I were very shaken: me, because I had done it; he, because he had nearly had his head split open. But he knew it was an accident and gave me a "Pass" anyway. Good man!

Steering Certificate

As I love boats, ships and all things maritime, there was another possibility to add to my collection of certificates. ORIANA's Captain, "Adge" Cutler, agreed that I could take my Steering Certificate which would qualify me to take the helm of any ship. I was to be overseen by the Quartermaster on duty all the time, and by the Chief Officer, with the Captain being the final judge as to whether I was competent or not.

The first time I took the helm, I think our Chef could cheerfully have wrung my neck. He rang up to the Bridge to enquire who was the idiot who was steering, as it was pandemonium in the galley, with soup sloshing everywhere and pans falling on the deck. He was not amused. I quickly checked out of the Bridge window. Yes, he was right. The wake looked even worse than a dog's hind leg. It was taking a little while to get the hang of this. It only needed a slight touch on the wheel (not a wheel really, more a handle with grips either end) for the ship to alter course. Finally, to everyone's relief, I progressed, and Captain Cutler thought me ready to take my test at last. Of course, he would pick Curacao, where I was surrounded by enormous oil tankers. But daunting as that was, I gritted my teeth and got on with it. In any case, he and the QM were never far from my shoulder. I did well, he said. ORIANA was still in one piece, and so I passed.

There was one occasion when it came in useful. A virus was going around the ship, as often happened, and most of the QM's were sick. The Captain asked the Purser if he could spare me for one afternoon's 4-8 watch to help out. The Purser agreed and I spent four hours on the Bridge steering ORIANA as we steamed towards Japan. You can't hit much mid-Pacific, fortunately. So, if you have a ship, large or small, and you're a bit short of a helmsman, I'm your woman (though it was 50 years ago, remember, and I haven't had much practice since).

Shipboard "Me" Time

Our time off on board was very limited, but we did manage to snatch a few hours away from passengers and relax on deck if we had a few consecutive days at sea. We would work from 0800 till 1300, have an hour for lunch, and when it was our duty day, return to the Bureau at 1400 to work until 1800. Then began the evening round of cocktails, entertainment duties etc. If it wasn't our duty day, then we had the afternoon off until 1600.

Those of us who were off duty would sometimes get together for deck quoits, but mainly we just sunbathed or swam, anything to re-charge the batteries before we went back to work. We had our own private deck, Sun Deck, where we could chill out without being disturbed by passengers. It was a blissful respite!

When the weather was fine, there was nothing I liked more than catching the sun's rays for half an hour or so, or sitting in a deck chair, feet on the ship's side rail (!), either reading a book or just gazing out to sea. For me there is something mesmerizing and magical about watching the ever-changing shapes of the waves and the horizon.

Now and then there would be dolphins, or an albatross, or whales. They were playful and inquisitive, particularly the dolphins who loved to frolic in the ship's wake. Occasionally the view was not good at all, particularly when we took the (shortest) Southern Great Circle route from Durban to Fremantle, near Van Dieman's Land. Here we would encounter the Japanese whaling fleet, flitting around like midges on a stream, collecting all those beautiful dead whales, big harpoons and flags sticking out of them, to take back to the factory ship, where they would be hauled on board and flensed (cut up). The smell was appalling, and I hated it.

Occasionally there would be other ships in the vicinity, but on our long days at sea we were often completely on our own.

I used to sit there for hours – just looking. And I saw the most incredibly beautiful sunsets. As the sun sank lower over the water, it looked as if the whole world had turned crimson and gold. Puffy little clouds would float gently by and, if you were lucky, you might see a green flash as the sun finally said goodnight and disappeared from view. Pure magic!

Moving House

After two years it was time for me to take my long leave and say goodbye to my beloved CANBERRA. I was much looking forward to a few weeks camping in the South of France, but this was not to be. My CANBERRA relationship ended suddenly, and I was heartbroken. All I could think of was getting back to sea as quickly as possible.

I rang Tommy Atkinson, our Head of Personnel, and asked if I could be allocated a ship quickly. He said I was in luck. There was a vacancy on board ORIANA, sailing in three weeks. Would I like to go there? I jumped at the chance, unpacked the camping gear, got myself ready, and off I went again.

ss ORIANA

Another lovely ship, different in design to CANBERRA, but she had a "homely" feel to her. By this time, I had had a promotion and was a SWAP, though my Discharge Book had me down as a WAP until the day I left P & O.

They were a great crowd on board, in all Departments, and I was welcomed into the Bureau and soon settled down. I had another nice cabin with a porthole that faced forward onto the fore deck. It wasn't big (none of our cabins ever were), but there was a wash basin, drawers-cum-desk, a wardrobe and a day bed which acted as a settee during the day. Into this space I crammed a real rubber tree, record player and, later on, various South Seas wooden carvings. As my bunk this time was "midships", that is it was width-ways on and not length-ways to the ship, in rough weather I had to sleep on deck as I kept rolling out of it with the pitching motion.

The work was the same as it had been in CANBERRA, although this time, because of my minor rise up the seniority scale, I mainly did all the Berthing and Immigration work, which was fine and which, as always, I found interesting and satisfying.

I loved this ship too and have just as many happy memories of my time in her as I do of CANBERRA.

CHAPTER NINE

PORTS OF CALL

Whichever P & O ship you were in, in my day they all called at more or less the same ports at one time or another. Often we moored alongside, although for shallower waters there were the "boat ports", when the ships' lifeboats were used to ferry passenger to and from the shore. Once P & O ventured into the cruising market, there were some new and very welcome additions to our ports of call around the world, but many of these destinations were limited to the smaller ships and so, as CANBERRA's and ORIANA's drafts needed deeper water, even for the "boat ports", we weren't able to visit them.

The itineraries for both CANBERRA and ORIANA were similar, so this meant visiting the same ports many times over. I got to know most of them well and, with few exceptions, loved them all. From 1972, however, ORIANA began to take on more cruising and our ports of call increased to include Pacific islands, the Caribbean and the Mediterranean.

Outward: Cherbourg, Lisbon, Cape Town, Durban, Fremantle, Melbourne, Sydney;

Circle Pacific: Auckland, Suva (Fiji), Nuku'alofa (Tonga), Honolulu, Vancouver, San Francisco, Honolulu, Yokohama, Kobe, Nagasaki, Hong Kong, Sydney;

Homeward: Auckland, Suva, Nuku'alofa, Honolulu, Vancouver, San Francisco, Long Beach (Los Angeles), Acapulco, Panama, Fort Lauderdale (Miami), Nassau, Barbados, Bermuda, Madeira, Lisbon, Cherbourg and Southampton.

I, for one, welcomed the advent of cruising. Although it meant much more work for us as there were many more ports, it also meant that we started to visit more exotic, holiday places such as Curacao, and the US Virgin Islands. We were still too big to enter some of the small ports, which then became "boat ports", but at least we were there.

When in Australia, we undertook Pacific cruising. This was fabulous. Memories of that first school essay I wrote about tropical islands came flooding back. Now I really was visiting them myself!

As well as Suva, Nuku'alofa and Honolulu, which we already called at on our main line voyages, we could also wander along the exotic shores of: Pago Pago (American Samoa); Honiara (Solomon Islands); Noumea (New Caledonia); Rabaul (New Ireland, part of the Bismarck Archipelago); and Port Moresby (Papua and New Guinea). Of course, we passed many other tiny tropical paradises on the way which looked so inviting, but because we were too large to call at most of them, we just had to sail on by - and dream.

When on the West Coast of the States, we now added the Caribbean to our itinerary. This gave us: Antigua, Barbados, Grenada, Martinique, Trinidad, and Charlotte Amelie (US Virgin Islands). Again, it was like being in paradise – and I made certain I made the most of it whenever I could.

This definitely was the life for me!

CHAPTER TEN

DOWN MEMORY LANE

I always consider myself very lucky to have had the chance to visit so many fascinating and exotic places. I'd been to a few on previous holidays, but most of the ports were new to me. Although it's now fifty years ago since I visited many of them, it seems as if it were only yesterday, and part of the joy of writing this book is that it has given me the opportunity to resurrect this wealth of happy memories.

Everyone much looked forward to their precious time ashore. I know I did. As the Bureau had to remain open all the while the ship was in port, this meant that our leave was split in two, but I still managed to see a great deal.

Covering my time in both CANBERRA and ORIANA, I've chosen just a few of my more amusing, fascinating and at times a bit scary, trips shoreside.

Cape Town was my first new port. Seeing Table Mountain for the first time was a memorable experience, and I loved the little steam trains that chuffed along the quayside. However, I must be the only person to go up Table Mountain in the height of summer wearing a wool suit as this was all I had. My baggage had arrived at last, but it was still on the quay. Whoopee! I'd soon be able to wear my own clothes. Or so I thought. Unfortunately, because of my hasty arrival on board, no-one had thought to tell the Baggage Master. He looked at the labels, didn't find my name on his list, and promptly offloaded my cases onto the quay, so I sailed without them. I was not a happy bunny! And I let "Granny" know this. A message was promptly sent to the agents to have my cases sent on to Durban, and we

Down memory lane

Stuck in the Natal Game Reserve
(note lions – they really were – under the trees on the right)

Left: ORIANA at Circular Quay, Sydney   Right: the market in Nuku'alofa

would pick them up there. Miracle of miracles, they actually arrived there in time and were put on board. At last I looked the right size again.

In **Durban**, on another voyage, five of us (Deck and Pursers) decided to hire a dormobile and driver to take us to the Natal Game Reserve. We were a bit disconcerted to see this rather battered vehicle turn up at the quayside, but we all piled in and off we set. We weren't going to break any speed records, but we got there, checked in with the Wardens and were waved through the high metal gates. There was the odd lion and tiger around, and I thought I might have caught a glimpse of an elephant if there were any there, but not much was visible. Things were going well and we were motoring along when all of a sudden the engine stopped. The driver looked perplexed. So did we. Vainly he tried to get it started again, but it just didn't want to go. In those days there were no mobile phones or i-pads, so we couldn't summon for help. There was nothing left but to get out and push. By this time the odd lion could definitely be seen lurking nearby, but we just had to do it. And I just had to take a photo to prove it. Not the most sensible thing I've ever done as this left me away from the group, a likely candidate for lunch, but some photographers will do anything for a photo. I'm one of them.

Eventually the engine started and the dormobile lurched forward. No-one has ever got in a car as quickly as us, I'm sure. Trouble was, we could now only move in first and second gears and we were a long way from Durban. We just had to get back before sailing. If we didn't make it, CANBERRA would have to wait (at great expense and anger from Head Office) till we arrived as it was a ten-day crossing over to Fremantle and we were all needed on board to do our jobs. We made it with half an hour to spare. All the passenger gangways had been taken up and only the gun-port door was open. We were immediately summoned up to the Captain on the Bridge. He was not amused, but realized he had five nervous wrecks standing before him, and so was more lenient than we deserved.

The South Sea Islands and Asia

Tropical islands have a magic all of their own: palm trees waving in a balmy breeze; golden sands littered with colourful shells of all shapes and sizes; the surf breaking over coral reefs, the sea a stunning turquoise within their protective arms, a deep blue beyond; thatched huts; tropical fruit stacked high on tables by the roadside. This was the image I'd carried in my mind ever since I'd written that essay for the Schools' National Essay Competition all those years ago. I was never to tire of visiting paradise.

Nuku'alofa, Tonga

Although similar, each island had its own characteristics. It's difficult to choose which I liked the most.

Tonga was always special. I don't think I've come across a more gentle race. Gentle giants, we used to call them, as nearly all of them were very tall and often quite "substantial". I remember seeing King Tupou IV when he came on board once. Like his mother, Queen Salote, he was quite formidable.

The capital, **Nuku'alofa,** wasn't large when I was there and I suspect it's not that big even today. There were few cars, lots of thatched houses, and a large Catholic College, but the biggest modern attraction was the International Dateline Hotel, with its lush gardens and tempting swimming pool. This is where most of our passengers headed for after they had exhausted the market.

For me, though, and most of us females, it was this market that lured us. Everything tropical you could think of: grass skirts; conch shells; baskets, beaded curtains (I bought one of those too - why?); wooden carvings and bead necklaces. My bank account used to take a minor hit here and I would stagger back to the ship loaded with as much as I could carry, whether it would fit in my cabin or not.

On some of our visits here, the Chief Officer would let a few Officers take one of the ship's lifeboats off to a small atoll nearby. The Chef would prepare barbecue food for us, cold beers would be loaded into cool boxes, and off we'd go. We'd find some drift wood on the beach, light a small fire and cook our sausages. It was heaven! Palms gently swaying in the breeze, the call of exotic birds, snorkeling on the reef – as I keep saying, this most definitely was the life.

It was here at Nuku'alofa that the King's Household versus Ship's Company cricket matches used to take place. They were enthusiastically contested, but the Tongans were big hitters and had the advantage in that they were used to the pitch, a field with an undulating wicket, bounded on one side by the sea, which meant that anyone of our team in the outfield had to wear swimming trunks and stand in the sea to see where the ball went. Whether or not they found it was a different matter. The sixes stacked up against us and we needed a good supply of balls for these matches. Diplomatically, the Household won, which pleased the King immensely. It was great fun for us to watch and a highlight in the Tongan calendar. They enjoyed our cucumber sandwiches immensely (they wanted something traditionally English), but preferred beer to tea.

Next came **Pago Pago** (pronounced Pango Pango), the capital of American Samoa. This was another beautiful island, though I never had time to go too far afield when ashore, normally only to the Intercontinental Hotel near our mooring, or across the Sound in the cable car. I usually chose the cable car ride because of the stunning views you got when you got to the other side.

Leaving this port was always unforgettable. The cable car went to mid-way across the Sound, laden with hibiscus and frangipani flowers, and when we set sail the baskets of flowers were emptied onto our ship as we passed underneath. We all tried to catch as many as we could to take back to our cabins as they floated down on the breeze. Their perfume was beautiful. No photographs I took ever fully captured this magical moment. We sounded our horn to say a huge thank you, and farewell till the next time. The Samoans lined the shore waving, and we waved back. It was fabulous.

Noumea, the capital of New Caledonia, was also a pleasure to visit, with its pale gold beaches and amazing aquarium, the only one in the world then to have tanks full of living coral. It was a reasonably large town with a distinctly French feel to it, but if I remember correctly, it was rather expensive to shop here. There was a downside to us mooring at Noumea, however. Nickel mining was the main industry of the island and we were right opposite the nickel ore loading dock. Invariably the breeze blew our way, which meant that one side of the ship was covered in nickel dust and became distinctly pink. So did we if we stood outside. Unusual to see a two-tone ship! The deck crew went mad. They had to clean it all off.

Rabaul, on New Britain, part of the Bismarck Archipelago near Papua and New Guinea, had an interesting history. It had been a fortification for the Japanese during World War II and the island was littered with rusting gun emplacements and other relics from the war. I often spotted flower pots made out of Japanese metal helmets hanging from the houses. There wasn't a lot to do here but I looked forward to meeting up with my old shipmate, "Daffers" Goldsmith who had left the sea to marry a plantation manager and was living here. The two of them came down to the ship where we normally had a drink on board before heading off

The South Seas – a little bit of "paradise"

Left: **Suva**: The Band of the Royal Fiji Police,
with Viliami Bale, their amazing Musical Director

Right: The Chief and me, in front of his bure (home)

Left: Our fresh water carrier – a WW1 Japanese submarine

Right: At **Rabaul**: Children playing on an old Japanese gun

to the Churchill Club, to which they belonged. That was very exclusive, very colonial, but I had some super meals there.

One odd thing was that the ship took on fresh water brought out in an old, rusting, Japanese submarine. I often wondered what the water was like inside, but as I didn't suffer any ill effects, I presumed it was OK. It was also unusual to see blond curly haired children at Rabaul. I asked about this, and was told that parents used a paste of crushed coral to plaster onto their children's heads, which turned their hair almost white. Perhaps our hairdressers could learn a thing or two. It beats peroxide!

Port Moresby, Papua and New Guinea, was also on our itinerary. Here I took a tour to the village on stilts, but other than that there was not that much to do. Later on in my Diplomatic life, when posted to Manila, I was to play in a golf tournament at Lae, a short drive north of Port Moresby.

Japan (Yokohama, Kobe and Nagasaki), was fascinating to visit, especially at Cherry Blossom time. When the World Trade Fair was taking place in 1970, we stayed for a few days at Kobe, the port of Osaka. From there I went to Kyoto, with its ancient shrine, and I also managed a night in a Riyokan, a Japanese inn with massage facilities and room walls made of thick rice paper. An experience, I have to admit!

Few places in the world can compare with **Hong Kong**. What can I say that hasn't been said already, though I think that now it's part of China, it's lost a lot of its allure and uniqueness. The shopping was amazing and trips on the Star Ferry to Victoria were a must. Other names bring back such happy memories: Kowloon, Sha Tin, Happy Valley, the Aberdeen Typhoon Shelter, Repulse Bay, the Tiger Balm Gardens, the floating restaurant. I couldn't get enough of the oriental atmosphere and was so sad to sail away.

There is a magic in sailing from a port, any port, at night. I used to stand on deck looking at the twinkling lights of the houses, smelling the perfumes and spices that were carried on the breeze. I'd gaze up at the sky and the twinkling lights below were mirrored in the myriad of stars above. As we sailed away and these lights gradually faded and the port became smaller and smaller, I'd pick up the salty scent of the sea. It never failed to make me tingle with delight. Here I could forget the humdrum aspects of work for a moment and lose myself in this watery wonder-world. I used to stay on deck for as long as I could, reluctant to re-enter the real world.

Australia and New Zealand Fremantle (for Perth), Melbourne and Sydney were our ports. I never got much time to go ashore at Fremantle as it was a busy port for us, either the first or last of our visit to Australia. I enjoyed Melbourne, the Garden City even though I had little time off there either. Getting into port, however, was often difficult as crossing Port Philip Bay, which is very large, could be extremely rough at times.

Sydney was always special and a highlight of any voyage. When I first called there, they were just starting to build the Opera House and it was exciting watching it take shape. CANBERRA and ORIANA always had to berth at Circular Quay as we were too big to go under the bridge to Pyrmont. At Sydney I looked forward to meeting my good friends, Eris and Joan White, and their little daughter, Louise, so I would go to Cronulla, where they lived, and spend some time with them. Otherwise, it was off to the Blue Mountains, along the Parramatta River, over to Manly on the ferry, or Taronga Park Zoo to see the koalas. I never failed to have a great time in Sydney.

Auckland, again, was another attractive port. I was busy there with Immigration, but on my first visit Tricia and I managed to get all the time off to visit her parents' very good friends at

Rotorua. We hired a little mini for our 3 hour or so drive down there, and were well looked after when we arrived, being taken to see the geysers and boiling mud pools which, apart from the overwhelming smell of sulphur, were amazing. Then on to a Maori Meeting House, before it was time for our drive back to Auckland. We nearly didn't make it on time as we got stuck behind a mobile home on a low-loader which went for miles at a snail's pace. It was the main road, but only one lane either side, so overtaking was impossible. At last it pulled over and we were able to pass and get a move on back to the ship, but we were so late that we only had time to post the car keys through the door of the car hire firm and make a dash for the ship.

Suva

Fiji, I loved. From about two miles away, you could tell you were getting near by the sweet smell of copra that was carried on the breeze. There was a lot to see here, and I loved to take a trip inland to Nandi.

Also, we had the brilliant Royal Fiji Police Band, under the loving care of Viliami Bale, their Director of Music. What a charming man. So gentle and softly spoken. He took such pride in his band and was overwhelmed when we invited them on board to play for us. These concerts were very special. In their distinctive white *sulus* (special uniform skirts), the musicians were the epitome of smartness. I bought one of their records, which I sadly no longer have, but I can still hear them playing even now.

Canada, Mainland USA, Mexico, Panama and the Caribbean

Honolulu

This was the port we called at most frequently, and the one I always looked forward to. Not only is there the gloriously sandy Waikiki Beach, but travel inland and you're amongst the volcanic

Honolulu

The Arizona War Memorial, Pearl Harbour

Disneyland: "Where the Dream Began".
The wonderful statue of Walt Disney and Mickey Mouse at the entrance

mountains, or follow the coastal plain where you'll find the Del Monte pineapple plantations. Hanauma Bay was also a great place to snorkel and have a beer and groups of us used to hire a car and head straight for that little bit of paradise as soon as we could go ashore.

The history of Pearl Harbour is, of course, legendary and well-documented, but visiting the Arizona War Memorial, hearing the bell tolling to the rhythm sea, and looking down through the glass window onto the wreck of the USS Arizona, with its crew still entombed, is a very moving experience.

Another reason I loved to visit there was to spend time with my great friends, Herb and Janee Dimmitt, at their stunning house on Diamond Head. They always made me so welcome, took me all over the island and, when I spent a week there on leave from the Philippines, even took me on a surprise 3 night stay to the island of Maui, where they had a condominium.

We stayed in touch until they both died in the late 1990s. I miss them.

Vancouver, San Francisco, Los Angeles, Acapulco

They all had their attractions. Each port was memorable, but for different reasons.

In Vancouver, a group of us spent a wonderful three days and nights on the Canadian Pacific Railway going through the Rockies to Banff.

It was February, and the snow was so thick that at one stage a small avalanche had covered the track and the snow plough on the front had a hard time in clearing it. We nearly didn't make it back to the ship on time. I spent most of the journey in the Observation Car, watching in awe as the searchlights lit up the majestic Rockies all around us. When we got to Banff we only had a few hours to spend there before we had to board the train back so we decided to go swimming in the outdoor heated pool at the Banff Hotel – just to be different. We hired swimming costumes and ventured forth! The temperature was well below zero, so this meant you had to hold your breath and swim a little way under water in a tunnel from the hotel to reach the pool. Although I'm a reasonably good swimmer, I found this a bit scary, but it was exhilarating once we reached the steaming pool. The only problem, I found, was that my ears got very cold if my head was above water for long. We didn't linger, but at least we could say that we had done it.

San Francisco

"San Fran" was always popular with us. Arriving here nearly always gave the Captain a heart attack as in both CANBERRA and ORIANA we only just managed to squeeze under the Golden Gate Bridge with a few feet to spare. You relied on the Pilot to make sure we stayed in the deep-water channel in the middle. We'd then make our way to Pier 35 at Fisherman's Wharf, where the jazz band from the Red Garter would be waiting to play us in.

We often spent a night here, and so a trip to A. Sabella's fish restaurant just down the quayside from the ship was a must. The seafood menu has to be one of the best I've ever come across. Then on to the Red Garter pub for a pint or two. I liked to climb up to Coit Tower if there was time; you get a super view of San Francisco Bay from up there. And I did manage to take a trip to Muir Woods to see the giant redwoods, continuing on to the Napa Valley vineyards where, of course, one just had to sample the excellent wine. There was loud snoring on the way back, but the trip was great.

I was back in San Francisco in 2010. How it's changed! I still enjoyed the visit, but I think it has lost a lot of its atmosphere, particularly down near the docks, where it has all been modernized. But that's progress.

San Pedro, Long Beach (for Los Angeles)

It was only a short voyage down the coast to San Pedro at Long Beach, where we berthed for Los Angeles, nearly opposite the old ss Queen Mary.

A little way from our berth was the famous Ports O'Call, a wonderful array of old world, clapboard shops and houses, painted in different, muted colours, and selling a wide range of goods from souvenirs to quite expensive antique furniture. The restaurants were excellent, and if I had time I'd try to go there for lunch.

But Disneyland was, and will always be, a firm favourite of mine. On some trips I was able to fit in a visit, but I never did this wonderland justice with so much to see and so little time to see it. I could never go there without stopping at "It's a Small World". I love it, and I can still hear that emotive theme tune even now. I was thrilled to be able to revisit Disneyland, as well as tour Universal Studios at last, in 2010. The "world of little people" had lost none of its magic for me.

Mexico

From Long Beach it was only an overnight sail to **Mazatlan**, a rather unattractive port I always thought, more commercial than scenic. I think we called there for bunkering and victualling mainly, oil and provisions being cheaper in Mexico than in the States. I never really bothered to go ashore.

But I loved our next port of call, **Puerta Vallarta**, for its true Mexican feel, donkeys in the streets, women doing their washing in the river, chillies hanging from large hooks outside the shops. Liz Taylor even had a house here on the hillside, she must have loved it so much. I made the most of the time I had ashore by just wandering around, having the odd donkey ride and soaking up the atmosphere. *Que bueno*!

On then overnight to **Acapulco**, a beautiful resort I came to know well when I was posted to Mexico. But for now, I had to be content with just a few hours there as this was a boat port, CANBERRA and ORIANA being too big to go alongside, which always cut down our time ashore. But I did learn to water ski here, not brilliantly and the posture was a little suspect, but I could manage to get around the bay without falling off too many times, although it was rather disconcerting to find a dead cat floating inches from my face on one occasion. With true British grit I kept going. I had to, I was half way out in the bay!

The Panama Canal

For me this has to be the most interesting day of any voyage. To date (2019) I've been through the Canal seventeen times, and it has never lost its interest, nor awe at its construction. I commend David McCullough's excellent book "The Path Between The Seas" for anyone wanting to know more.

After Acapulco, we arrived at **Balboa**, the Pacific end port for Panama City, in the early evening and started our arduous immigration formalities. I always felt that, considering the reputation of Panama then, it was a bit rich for the officials to create such a fuss over our paperwork, but we had to produce those dreaded Panama Lists which caused us so much work and which had to give detailed information of all our passengers. Once that was over, a few of us headed out into the delights of Panama City which for me meant the Hilton Hotel to listen to the amazing Wurlitzer Organ there. The men had other ideas. I shall say no more.

It takes eleven and a half hours to transit the Canal, so we set sail at 5 am, having taken on board the Panama Pilot (in my day an American). This is the only waterway in the world where the Pilot can override the Captain, such is the difficulty of navigating the locks and channels. We were all up early and spent as much time on deck as possible, work permitting. The Chef also put on a spectacular deck buffet and barbecue so passengers could spend as much time outside watching our progress as possible.

A brief piece on the Canal itself though. Until 1977 the Canal was owned by the USA, when it then came under joint ownership of Panama and the States. In 1999 it transferred entirely to Panama. Sailing from the Pacific to the Atlantic, there are three sets of locks; Miraflores; Gatun and Cristobal Colon. These raise and lower shipping 85 ft to the Gatun Lake, an artificial lake constructed to cut down on the excavation work needed for the Canal, then back down again to sea level on either side. Each set of locks has two lanes (up and down), but a third wider lane of locks has just been completed to take these enormous super tankers. An engineering feat indeed. The narrowest part of the Canal is called the Culebra Cut and is really only wide enough for one large ship at a time, so you have to wait your turn.

It's the most fascinating experience to sail through the Canal and I was never able to stay inside for long. Fortunately, with most of our work done for Panama, we were allowed to spend time on deck watching the line handlers as they attached our ship to the Mules at either side that guided us through the locks. I really preferred to stay on board, but on one occasion in ORIANA I did get the opportunity to go on one of the overland tours as a Tour Escort, which gave me a completely different perspective of the Canal. It seemed strange to be on the shore watching our majestic ship towering above us as she sailed through the Gatun Locks. We were even given a tour of the lock chambers to see the workings and motors which operate them, which are surprisingly small. There was also a stop at the headquarters of the [American] Panama Canal Company which well documented the history and construction of the Canal. It was hot and steamy wherever you were in Panama, but it seemed worse ashore; and there were alligators and snakes

The Panama Canal

Entering the Culebra Cut.

Our humid early morning start
approaching the Pedro Miguel and Miraflores Locks

The mules that guided the ships through the Locks

lurking where you least expected them, so you had to make sure you didn't stray far from the designated tracks. These were the days of alligator, croc and snakeskin handbags and shoes: it was big business for Panama.

We arrived at Cristobal Colon, on the Atlantic side, in the evening, too late to do much but since it had been a tiring day anyway it was nice just to chill out on deck and contemplate our next ports of call in the colourful and vibrant Caribbean.

But first we had to call at Port Everglades, the port for Miami. There I always looked forward to meeting up with my good friend, Pat (the daughter of Mum and Dad's Best Man, Len), who had gone to work out there, met and married husband, Dan, and had settled down with their four children. It was so good to catch up and see the changes as her family grew up, and she enjoyed this contact not only with me, I think, but also with home. We are still in regular touch.

The Caribbean

I always find this part of the world exciting. There is so much to see and do, and whilst there is a similarity in many ways between the islands with their palm trees, golden beaches and tropical fruit stalls at the side of the road, each has a distinctive character all of its own.

In ORIANA in the early 1970s we started to offer cruises from San Francisco, through the Panama Canal, to the most popular Caribbean destinations such as Trinidad, Martinique, US Virgin Islands, Grenada and Antigua. These were always popular, and we were full to capacity. In CANBERRA, we only called (usually) at Nassau, Barbados and Bermuda on our homeward journey

I think my favourites have to be Grenada, Antigua, and Barbados in particular, though it's hard to choose. Despite some of these being boat ports, we always managed to get a reasonable amount of time off to travel a bit further afield than the capitals.

136

Antigua: The Admiral's House (home of Horatio Nelson for a time), Nelson's Dockyard

My best friend, Marie, at Shelley bay, Bermuda - 1971

Bermuda

Depending on whether we were outbound via the States, or inbound, we nearly always called at Bermuda which, when I was in ORIANA, was a special treat as my "oldest" friend, Marie, had taken up a two year teaching contract there in 1970, so when we called at Hamilton I normally managed to swap duties so I could have all the time off to spend with her. As it was a boat port, she came out, with her friend Pat on one occasion, in one of our lifeboats, had a quick tour round the ship and then lunch, before we both went ashore for a tour around the island in her little car. I loved it, and we chatted non-stop until it was time to head back to the ship for our departure. When she finally came to leave, I spoke nicely to the Baggage Master who allowed me to take her trunk back to Southampton for her, which was a great help.

Murder of the Governor of Bermuda

When I was in ORIANA on our outbound voyage via the States in September 1971, we had the privilege of having on board Sir Richard Sharples, (and Lady Sharples), who was travelling to Bermuda to take up his post there as the new Governor. I was Berthing Queen for this voyage, and I met Sir Richard and his wife early on as there was a problem with their cabin and they needed to move. We were full, but by some judicious juggling I was able to let them have one of our suites. They were very appreciative and invited me to their cocktails parties before we arrived. They were such a nice couple and I liked them a lot.

When we arrived at Bermuda, the very smart Government launch came out to our anchorage to welcome Sir Richard and Lady Sharples and take them back to Hamilton. All the senior Officers were at the gun port door to see them off and I went down too, though I stood unobtrusively in the background out of the way. Sir Richard looked resplendent in his full Diplomatic

Uniform, but he nearly lost his plumed hat when stepping into the launch as it was very breezy. I didn't think he had noticed me, but he had, and came out of his way to shake my hand and say thank you for looking after them so well. I was very touched and wished them both every happiness and success in their new life.

Imagine my absolute horror and sadness when I learned that on 10 March 1973, just six months after travelling with us, Sir Richard and his ADC, Captain Sayers of the Welsh Guards, had been assassinated in the grounds of Government House whilst taking a late-night stroll after a dinner party. Their Great Dane, Horsa, had also been gunned down.

It transpired that the murderers were part of the Black Power Group and their motive was "to seek to make the people, black people, become aware of the evilness and wickedness of the colonialist system in this island." It was also to show that these colonialists were just ordinary people and black people should not be in fear or awe of them.

The two assassins, Tacklyn and Burrows, were arrested and charged with the Governor's murder. Tacklyn was acquitted of that murder, but was convicted in April 1973 of killing a Victor Rigo and Mark Doe at the Shopping Centre supermarket in Hamilton. Both Tacklyn and Burrows were eventually hanged in Casemates Prison on the island. They would be the last people to be executed under British Rule anywhere in the world.

Sir Richard, Captain Sayers, and Horsa, were laid to rest at St Peter's Church in St George's on 16 March 1973. Sir Richard's death seemed to take on an added poignancy once I myself joined the Diplomatic Service. Such a terrible, senseless waste.

As a terrible coincidence, when I was showing Marie (who left Bermuda in 1972) what I had written the other day, she looked up the murder, and found to her shock and sadness that she had lived in a house owned by Victor Rigo, murdered by Tacklyn. It was Mr. Rigo who had taught her to drive her car so as to pass the driving test. She said he was always such a nice man. It's a very strange world sometimes.

Maderia

Madeira is an island of contrasts. There is something to appeal to everyone, from the mountainous rugged interior, to the towering cliffs (some of the highest in the world) along its coast line, the black volcanic sand beaches, and the lush tropical gardens of Funchal. I never fail to enjoy my time in this "Atlantic paradise", even though the capital has grown tremendously since my first visit there in 1968 thanks to the vast sums of EU money that have been provided to improve the infrastructure, making it so much easier to get around. Don't talk to me, though, about wicker furniture and baskets! I could hardly move in my cabin for them, and the Baggage Master nearly went crazy with all the "peacock chairs" that suddenly found their way on board. We must have kept the cane weavers busy for months.

Nearly Home!

From Madeira, we had a few more days at sea until we reached **Lisbon**, another delightful city, where I would take the tram ride along the coast to Estoril, or go in a group to the excellent Bom Jardin restaurant near the centre, where they served the best barbecue chicken I've ever tasted.

We were always very busy on this stretch of the voyage, preparing for our arrival at Southampton, and we often met atrocious weather whilst crossing the Bay of Biscay, but that never mattered as we were nearly home. Only Cherbourg to go, then a short hop over the Channel and we were in the Solent once more.

Once alongside, the "rummagers" (HM Customs) came on board to search our cabins for any contraband. We disembarked our passengers, often saying a very fond farewell with hopes to see them again on another voyage (and some we never wanted to see again - anywhere, ever).

Once all the paperwork was finished, and the standby crew had come on board, we were free to go. Mum and Dad normally came down to the ship to meet me, I gave them a quick tour around, and then we headed home at last. How good it was to be with them again.

Madeira: No wonder our Baggage Master had such a fit when we called here – the temptation was too great!

CHAPTER ELEVEN

"NOW IS THE HOUR"

This haunting Hawaiian song "Now is the hour for me to say goodbye" was always played as we left Honolulu, and despite the sadness of the words, I have always loved it.

As is the way of life, all good things must come to an end at some stage, and I was conscious that, as female Officers had to retire at forty (when we grew two horns and a tail!), and there were no pension arrangements, it was not sensible to consider this a long- term career. I didn't want to leave, and they almost had to drag me kicking and screaming from the ship's side, but I decided to leave P & O at the beginning of 1974 after a wonderful, fascinating and fulfilling life that I knew, or thought I did, could never be repeated.

What Now?

Once ashore, I knew I had to be near my beloved ships, and so rented a flat in Southampton and worked for a yacht company, Fairways Marine at Hamble, for just over a year. In the meantime, I had met a Police Superintendent and things were going well. He was working in Morpeth, so I decided to move up there to be near him to see how things went. After an interview, I was offered a job as PA to the Chief Executive of Winthrop Stearns, which I accepted, and did enjoy for the short time I was there.

I was very fond of Bill, but again those itchy little feet wouldn't let me settle down, and the thoughts of domesticity filled me with horror. Bill knew that I had already applied to the Foreign Office to be a PA a good six months previously, and eventually ("the wheels of Government grind exceeding slow") I received a letter asking me to go down to London for an interview. It was a tough decision, but we agreed that I should go. As soon as I heard what the job entailed, I just knew it was for me. I had all the relevant qualifications, passed all the tests and was accepted immediately, so I packed up my belongings again, said a sad farewell to Bill, who was genuinely pleased for me, he said, and drove down to London to live temporarily in the Civil Service hostel in Gloucester Road as I had nowhere else to go. I think Mum and Dad were proud that I had landed this job, even if it meant me going away again, but I shall always be grateful to Bill for his kindness and understanding. We remained in touch until he finally found someone else and got married.

And so was to begin the next exciting and challenging chapter of my itinerant life.

Time to put away the well-worn Discharge Book - sadly.

PART THREE

ON HER MAJESTY'S
DIPLOMATIC SERVICE

The Foreign and Commonwealth Office, King Charles Street, London SW1

The Foreign Office, as seen from St James's Park in Spring

The Foreign Office's oldest and most tenacious diplomat.
Looking good, Albert.

CHAPTER ONE

SETTING THE SCENE

A Brief Background

The history of Britain and its Empire is complex, controversial and, at times, very colourful, and the Foreign & Commonwealth Office has been at the heart of shaping that history. Whether one agrees with Her Majesty's Government's (HMG's) foreign policy or not, there is no doubt that we have been and still are, though perhaps to a lesser extent these days, a major player on the world stage, and have been a force for good, not always appreciated at the time but vital nonetheless. Much of this work has been carried out in secret, behind closed doors. This is true diplomacy at work. It may seem as if nothing is being done or achieved, but believe me there is a very dedicated and talented team working furiously behind the scenes to achieve our goals. Diplomats are swans par excellence!

It's for this reason that I value so much my time with The Office. I never stopped learning and have had the great privilege and pleasure (mostly) of working for and with some brilliant, inspiring role models. Their command of the English language - both written and verbal - has been truly staggering. They would outshine "Sir Humphrey" any day. I think this is why I've probably been minded to write my books. They have had such an influence on my life, and I like to think that some of their expertise (even a tiny amount) has been passed down to me.

Mind you, when I was typing the Annual Review for the seventh time because of one small mistake (theirs, not mine!), and I was working with eight carbon copies on an old Remington typewriter, then I may have thought differently about the whole thing, but those feeling usually only lasted for a few moments, unless I was having a particularly bad day.

Our London "Home"

As if all this wasn't enough, there is that magnificent building in which I worked when in London, without doubt one of the finest in the world. It occupies the whole of the block from the north side of King Charles Street to Downing Street, with the Treasury on the other side of the street opposite. I only once went into their building. Nice, but nothing like ours, but then "austerity begins at home" I always say. They never missed a chance to point this out to us: now it's my turn. As soon as I walked through the arch into our main quadrangle, my heart never failed to skip a beat with sheer pride and awe, and which foreign Ambassador could not fail to be impressed when walking up the Grand Staircase.

The Foreign Office was originally two offices, the Foreign Office and the India Office, later incorporating the Colonial Office and the Home Office until it moved into its own premises in 1978. The public rooms throughout the whole building are truly stunning: the Locarno Room, the India Office Council Chamber, the Foreign Secretary's room, and the Durbar Court to name but a few.

When I first joined, the beautiful fireplaces (some of them Adam), old fashioned baths (which I used once when going out for the evening), and ancient plumbing, were still in evidence, and you went from the old Colonial part of the building into the Foreign Office part through the "hole in the wall" – just that, only wide enough for one person to pass through at a time. Trying to find it, though, was a Herculean task. There was also an antiquated system of distribution, installed in the 1940s, using Tubes, which whooshed past you at a great rate of knots, landing with a loud thud in your office if the communication was meant for you. Sadly, it's been replaced by emails. Bring back the good old Tubes, I say.

And then there was, and still is, "Albert", that most revered and important member of the Diplomatic Service. Albert, presumably named after Queen Victoria's much-loved husband, is the Diplomatic Anaconda, presented to the Office by a Guyanese Bishop around 1892. I'm not certain I'd be flattered to have a snake named after me, but then "Angrave the Anaconda" doesn't have quite the same ring to it! Albert stretches the whole width of one of the Library end walls and has recently been the centre of some controversy as he's just been re-stuffed at a cost of £10,000. Good for him! He's very long and quite thick (in the physical sense), so personally I wouldn't quibble too much over the price. Value for money, I reckon. Given my fear of snakes, I love him like a hole in the head, but I couldn't bear to see him go. Whenever I went into the Library, I could never sit under him at that end of the Library. However, it was just as bad sitting at the other end, looking at him. I didn't spend much time in the Library!

I was on a home posting when the major refurbishment of the Foreign Office took place between 1986 and 1994. It was difficult at times working with all the mess, but the transformation was remarkable and so many hidden gems came to light, which were a joy to look at. Unknown paintings were revealed beneath other ones, and the cleaning of those already there brought a new vibrancy to the beautiful public areas. It was painstaking work carried out by experts, and they purposely left some bits of the old paint and paper on the walls just to show how dirty and grimy everywhere had become over the decades. The result, however, was reward enough for visiting dignitaries and those of us who worked there.

If you ever get the chance to do the tour, it is definitely worth it.

Chapter Two

EMBASSIES AND HIGH COMMISSIONS

Embassies and High Commissions

As soon as I joined the Diplomatic Service, I had to learn about Embassies and High Commissions. I had to make sure I was *au fait* with what an Embassy actually does, and the difference between a High Commission and an Embassy. The former, headed by a High Commissioner, is the Embassy equivalent in countries of the Commonwealth.

To help in understanding Embassy life, an Embassy is headed by the Ambassador, and then a Minister or Head of Chancery (H of C) or both, depending on the size of the Mission.

There are six sections in a British Embassy.

Chancery, under the Head of Chancery, is the political section and is concerned with increasing British influence abroad and putting over the government of the day's foreign policies.

Next comes **Commercial**, whose aim is to promote British industry abroad, assist British companies in gaining commercial contracts, become involved in trade fairs, and work with the British Chamber of Commerce.

Consular is, perhaps, the best-known section as its aim is to protect and help British subjects abroad, identify and repatriate bodies, and issue visas. I always felt, and still do, that the Foreign Office often gets a bad press in this regard and that expectations of what we can actually do are unrealistic. We are not the "Bank of FCO" as some believe!

Administration Section

Depending on whether Admin would listen to your pleas for

new furniture, a new cooker, or whatever else you required, you either loved or hated this Section in equal measure at different times. It dealt with all the problems associated with a Mission: accommodation, furnishings, customs clearances for baggage and cars; medical problems; servants; leave arrangements etc. It was always very busy and had an invaluable team of locally employed personnel to help navigate the usually unfathomable local customs. There was always a "Mr. Fix It", who often got complaints, but rarely compliments.

Information Section's aim is to promote Britain abroad and aid and encourage tourism to our shores.

The **Defence** Section is involved with the procurement of defence contracts, advising and training foreign military personnel, and putting forward Her Majesty's Government's Defence policies.

In larger posts, like Washington and Paris, all three Services are represented, but in smaller Missions there is a Defence Attaché whose post is rotated amongst the Army, Navy and Air Force. There is also an Assistant Defence Attaché whose rank depends on the grade of the Embassy.

A separate, but important, part of the Foreign Office is the **British Council**, whose job it is to promote British culture and artists abroad, advise on education and provide English teachers. They don't always have an easy time, particularly in Communist countries or countries with repressive régimes, but they do vital work and are a lifeline to some of the world's poorer communities.

And no Embassy, High Commission or British Council could function without that loyal, dedicated, and patient group of people, the **locally employed**. In my time a few of them were ex-pats, but mainly they were nationals of the country in which we were in. They worked tirelessly in every department (except

Chancery) on our behalf, and I know we were all so grateful for their advice and support. We didn't mix socially very much: they had their lives and we had ours. But they became our (and my) friends and I cannot speak highly enough of them.

Diplomatic Wives (now The Diplomatic Service Families Association)

It could not have been easy being a "Dippy Wife" (no disrespect intended: that was just what we called them). They contributed greatly (unpaid) to helping their husband's career and the number of dinner parties and receptions they gave was admirable. Having to send your young children off to boarding school must also have been so hard for both husband and wife.

The wives also got involved in local projects, including, in Manila, secretly helping to run a "centre" at the Anglican church in Forbes Park to educate Filipina women on contraception.

I always had the utmost admiration for the wives and counted them among my good friends at the Embassy, even though their lives were very different to mine.

CHAPTER THREE

MY INTRODUCTION INTO THE DIPLOMATIC SERVICE

Getting to grips with it all

I've come to the conclusion that my life has been one long abbreviation or acronym! It was bad enough with P & O: it was now about to get much worse.

The Foreign and Commonwealth Office, the Foreign Office, the Diplomatic Service or, to me, just The Office. Whatever you wish to call this most prestigious of government departments, being a member of it has provided me with a stimulating, interesting, at times dangerous, and fulfilling career and I always felt a great sense of pride at being part of it.

I was not a diplomat in the true meaning of the word, but a member of the secretarial cadre, providing assistance, support and, at times, a shoulder to cry on, for those who were. I always tried to do my job to the best of my ability, and I hope that those for whom I had the privilege to work will feel that I accomplished this well - with perhaps the odd little hiccough along the way. Even PA's can't be perfect all the time!

I received my comprehensive letter of appointment on 8 June 1976, with instructions to report for duty at Curtis Green Building, Victoria Embankment, at 11 am on Monday 5 July (we no longer have that building). I had already met all the criteria: I was single, over the minimum joining age of 21 ("you're rather old to be joining us at 31", I was told by Miss Lofting, Head of Secretarial Branch, when I turned up): and had the requisite 120 wpm Pitman's Shorthand certificate. However, I was still placed on a three-year probationary period like every new entrant and had to take a very difficult typing tabulation test within days of starting, which I had to pass. I then became an S2 (Secretary 2), and when I had successfully completed the three years, my appointment would be confirmed.

My starting pay per annum (including London Weighting (which was paid because it was more expensive to live in London than elsewhere) was £2495.00, rising to £3125.00 in this Grade. A Supplement to Pay of £313.00 pa was also payable for my secretarial qualifications

Later, I would receive a language allowance for my Spanish and French. This depended on being posted to a Spanish- or French-speaking country. If I was not, my allowance was reduced, and every five years I had to re-sit the Institute of Linguists exam. I qualified at Intermediate level, never being able to pass at Advanced Level, which was really for interpreters, but fortunately most of my postings were Spanish-speaking so I received the full allowance (about £500 p.a. if I remember correctly).

Health

During my Foreign Office years most of my postings were in Third World countries. We had our own (local) Embassy doctors and dentists who were constantly monitored by our Department of Health, and a list of hospitals (private) to which we would go if necessary. Hygiene standards were not always of the highest in these countries, and, inevitably, I succumbed to quite a few "afflictions", but I was always very well looked after and was eternally grateful to those who cared for me.

Positive Vetting

However, all the above would be irrelevant if I did not satisfy the security requirements of Her Majesty's Government, so I had to fill in a lengthy questionnaire which was then investigated. These "checks" were on-going throughout my whole career, and every five years or so I had to return home for an in-depth briefing, never particularly looked forward to, but very necessary. This covered every aspect of my life: home, family, friends, relationships - the whole lot. In my time the interviewer was always a man, which could be a bit embarrassing, but "I'm not here to judge you, Gillian, just to ascertain the facts" was what he usually said.

News of my first Posting

Having completed, and passed, all the necessary checks, it would normally be customary to work for about two years in The Office so you could learn the ropes, so to speak, and Personnel could assess how you were doing. I initially went to work in Financial Relations Department, headed by Humphrey Maud, but after six weeks I was summoned to see Miss Lofting again, who said she had a posting for me. Gosh, already, I thought. This can't be bad. There are definite advantages to being an old entrant.

"We'd like you to go to Antigua for two and a half years, Gillian", she said.

My heart sank. Oh no. Not Antigua. I'd been there so many times with P & O, and whilst I enjoyed my visits, the thought of being stuck on the island for two and a half years did not fill me with glee. I explained this to Miss Lofting, who looked horrified. One NEVER turned down a posting. Meet Gillian, who did. So I returned to my Department and thought "That's done it. Now I'll be here for years".

But not so. I received another call about two weeks later, offering me Manila for three years, arriving in October, working as PA to the Commercial Counsellor, Peter George.

The length of a tour was dictated by the climate and hardship at post: tropical posts were usually three years, with mid-tour leave after eighteen months; "easier" Posts were two and a half years with no home leave; hardship posts were normally just for a year.

POD (Personnel Operations Department) probably thought this would be a "punishment", but I was over the moon to be going back to South East Asia. Excellent. I'd be really happy to go there, much to their surprise and delight, so the wheels were set in motion, medical appointments made, tropical clothes bought at the Army & Navy Stores in Victoria Street, and off I went.

I'm sure Mum and Dad were disappointed that it was so far away, but as ever they were very supportive and proud that I had such a "prestigious" job. "Gillian's going to the Philistines", my Auntie Gladys said. "No, not Philistines, Gladys, Philippines," Mum replied, having studied the atlas at length to see just exactly where I was going.

And so, armed with a new passport, vaccination certificates, enough information to turn the little grey cells even more grey, and filled with a great sense of excitement, I girded my loins, ready to take on the Philistines, who turned out to be anything but.

Getting There

Wherever I've been sent to, and whenever possible, I've tried to take advantage of the outward and homeward journeys to stop off and explore places along the way. This was true of going to the Philippines. I'd never been to the Sub-Continent before, so Richard Thomas, my boss in London, arranged for me to stay, *en route*, a week in New Delhi with a colleague, whom I didn't know. Working for the Foreign Office was like belonging to one big family, and this happened quite often: colleagues were very happy to put you up for a day or so if it was convenient.

During my time in New Delhi I hardly saw my hostess, but she left me lots of literature to help me make the most of my stay. I took days tours, only spending a day at the High Commission when I was struck down with "Delhi belly" and had to go to the Clinic for strong medication. Otherwise, I was off to the Taj Mahal, Fatehpur Sikri, the Red Fort, the Qutub Minar minaret – anywhere of interest within a day's reach. I found it all fascinating, but it only reinforced my feelings that my heart lay in South America and I had no wish to be posted here. The same for Sri Lanka, where I stopped off on my return to Manila after mid-tour leave. Interesting, but not for me.

The sub-continent

Above: At a logging camp in Sri Lanka

Below left: The iconic Taj Mahal, and right:
the Qutub Minar, New Delhi, the tallest brick minaret in the world at 238 ft, built in 1193 by Qutab-ud-din-Albak after the defeat of Delhi's last Hindu kingdom.

PART FOUR

THE PHILIPPINES
1976-1980

Above: The British Embassy, 6th floor, Electra House,Legazpi Village

Below: My new home: 59a Paseo de Roxas, Makati, Manila

Back in South East Asia Again

I was thrilled to be back in this part of the world again. Although I'd never visited the Philippines with P & O, I was eager to see what this country was like, and I was not disappointed.

To give you some idea of the geography of the Philippines, whose land mass is slightly bigger than New Zealand, it is part of a huge mountain backbone stretching from Japan to Indonesia: from north to south it covers 1,140 miles and is up to 690 miles wide. The actual number of islands that make up this country is 7,641, divided into Provinces, though only 1,000 of these are inhabited. The main island is Luzon, on which Manila is situated, and as there is so much to see here, this is where I stayed, only visiting two other islands, Cebu and Marinduque. Mindanao was out of bounds to us all because of the Muslim insurgency, but the Ambassador travelled more extensively in the course of his work.

En route to Manila, my British Airways flight called at Singapore. I'd been here in CANBERRA and ORIANA quite often, but I decided to stop off for two nights just to see how it had changed. And changed it had. Almost beyond recognition, particularly in some areas like Change Alley and Boogie Street. Even the Raffles Hotel had lost part of its lush tropical garden to a main road. I was horrified, but such is progress. Nevertheless, it was so good to be back, and I made the most of my two days there.

The Climate

Having been in this part of the world quite a lot, I knew what to expect, but it was to be very different living in such a humid, tropical environment to sailing around with a bit of a breeze blowing. I did find it very tiring at times, and one of the worst things was that, away from air-conditioning, you just dripped. Fortunately, my little house had air-con, but my car didn't, and I invariably arrived for a function with my smart dress clinging to me and my hair in ringlets.

And then, of course, there were the typhoons. The main season was from about June to September, and they were ferocious. Invariably there were power cuts ("brown outs") for much of the time whilst one was raging and getting around was almost impossible.

There were three categories of typhoon: Storm Force One (heavy rain and a strong breeze); Storm Force Two (a gale blowing, and very heavy rain); and the ultimate, Storm Force Three (dangerous for people and property alike). In Three, you just couldn't stand up, nor could you see where you were going because of the torrential rain. Palm trees were almost bent double; roofs were flying around all over the place; windows were shattered and cars were turned upside down. We were expected to go into work for One, Two if possisble, but for Three we stayed at home and rode it out as best we could. We tried to keep in touch with each other to check that we were all safe, but with no telephones and no personal radios, this was almost impossible. We just had to hope we had all made it in one piece. The devastation afterwards was unbelievable and the clearing up took ages, but we were as supportive as we could be to each other, especially to our locally employed who lived in far less substantial houses than ours and were far more likely than we were to have suffered damage to their property, or even worse still, injury.

Funny how, before any of these storms, the locals went to the supermarkets to stock up with sugar, flour and other staples, whilst the foreigners had baskets full of gin and mix!

From October to May, whilst it was still very hot, the humidity dropped and life became more bearable, so I tried to do most of my travelling then.

Martial Law

The Philippines seems to have been under Martial Law on and off since 1944 when, as a client state of Japan during the Second World War, it declared war on the USA and the United Kingdom.

When I arrived, it was under Martial Law again (from 1972 to 1981) under President Marcos on the pretext of stemming increasing civil unrest and the threat of a Communist take-over. During the day it didn't bother me, nor the Embassy, much, but we were all subject to a curfew from 12 midnight to 4 am so it meant leaving dinner parties and other evening entertainment in good time to be sure we were back home by then.

My Arrival

I arrived in Manila in October, courtesy of British Airways, and the heat hit me as soon as I stepped off the aircraft. I was met by the H of C, Bill Quantrill, who took me to meet my new colleagues at the Embassy. On the way from the airport, I was staggered at the amount of traffic and pollution there was in the city. One of the main culprits was the jeepney, a brightly painted passenger jeep covered with all sorts of silver embellishments, religious figures and streamers, which was one of the main forms of local transport and which was an "experience" to ride in, if you didn't mind getting squashed to a pulp.

I was rather surprised at the Embassy building. Electra House was in a new office block in the heart of Legazpi Village, an up and coming commercial area in the suburb of Makati, which was then still a building site. It didn't look very grand at all and I felt a bit let down. We occupied the sixth floor, and saw very little of the other occupants. Once inside it wasn't too bad and I came to love my own little office adjoining my boss's.

After that, I was taken to the hotel used by the Embassy not far away, where I was to stay until I moved into my own new place of abode.

The Ambassador's Residence

The Ambassador's official Residence was a lovely, colonial style mansion on Roxas Boulevard, surrounded by lush gardens and near the seafront in downtown Manila. It wasn't handy once the

Embassy moved from that area to the new office building in Makati, and it always took an age to get there as the traffic was so bad, but there was also another more pressing, reason why, we suspect, it was decided to move the Residence to Forbes Park, the most prestigious urbanisation in Makati.

In years gone by Roxas Boulevard had been one of the most elegant and affluent parts of Manila, but now the Residence found itself in the heart of the very popular and thriving Red Light District, and right next door to one of the most "up market", well patronised brothels in the area. This invariably caused problems, particularly when the Ambassador was hosting functions and guests were arriving or leaving. It just didn't look good for HMG's Ambassador to be welcoming influential visitors with prostitutes hanging around the entrance drive hoping for customers.

I well remember one occasion in particular, the Queen's Birthday Party (QBP), held on or as near to the Queen's Coronation date (June 2nd) as possible, when all the "great and the good" (and us, but we had to attend) were invited to a large, formal reception in the Residence's beautiful gardens. The prostitutes next door, on hearing all the jollity of a very good party, and no doubt thinking of rich soliciting pickings, climbed over the wall and started to mingle with the guests. We, and the ladies present, looked on, horrified as they started to tout for business. This just wasn't the done thing at such an event. However, the "ladies of the night" were determined to take full advantage of a captive audience and it took our security officers a great deal of trouble trying to evict them. The Ambassador was livid. Some of the guests were affronted, but most took it in good part, and some thought it highly amusing. At least it put our QBP on the map! It was the talk of the diplomatic corps for months afterwards. No other National Day came anywhere near it!

My Own Accommodation

But where was I to live? Not next to a brothel, I sincerely hoped. I was anxious to find out.

Bill had identified a small house for me in a not too savoury part of Manila, or so it seemed. It had a small, high walled yard, no garden, with jagged glass on top (not a good sign), a pipe sticking out of the wall to provide water in the kitchen (don't know where the tap was: hopefully one would be fitted), and the house generally looked to be in not too good a condition. I was aghast. I hadn't travelled 10,728 miles to spend the next three years living in such a house, and I said so. I asked Peter ("you must call me Peter, Gillian, not Mr. George", he said to me when we met for the first time) to come and have a look. He, too, was horrified. "There is no way Gillian is living there" he told an unhappy Bill, and that was that. I must live somewhere else.

I then started the hunt for a new place, which I had to do in the evenings and at lunch time. The estate agent and I trod the streets of Makati, where I wanted to be as most of the ex-patriates (ex-pats) lived there and it was close to the Embassy, and eventually we found 59a Paseo de Roxas, on the edge of Urdaneta Village, one of the urbanisations mainly for ex-pats. It was on a busy road, with wasteland opposite awaiting development, but it wasn't far to walk to the luxurious Mandarin Hotel, where I used to get my bread. My own home was in part of a bungalow split into three. It was small, it only had a parking place and no garage, and was not ideal as the front door was the patio doors, but it was all we could find, was adequate, and was close to the Embassy. I was also delighted to find that my neighbour in the middle part of the bungalow was Lorna Best, the New Zealand Ambassador's PA, who was to become one of my close friends there and with whom I'm still in touch.

Bill came to inspect it, agreed that it would be suitable, that the rent was within the allowance for my Grade (the Embassy paid the rent, I paid the bills), and so, with great relief, I packed up my things and moved out of the hotel into my new home. I took delivery of my air freight, and awaited the arrival of my heavy baggage three weeks later. All I needed now was my car, which was being shipped from the UK and was somewhere on the high seas, and I was all set.

My New Life

I quickly settled into the Embassy and Embassy life. Peter, who was on his last posting, was a kind and caring man to work for, and I liked him and his French wife, Andrée, a lot. I seemed to fit in and got on well with my colleagues, both UK-based and locally employed, which made for a very happy working and social environment.

One of my best friends, though, was to be Ann Douthwaite, the Ambassador's PA (we're still in touch). We were very like-minded, though valuing our space and independence too, and were to go on some exciting excursions "up country" together, which I reminded her about the other day.

Shortly after my arrival, Peter hosted a small welcome reception for me which gave me the chance to get to know a few of the local Filipinos and ex-pat business community with whom I would be in contact on his behalf. This proved invaluable: there is nothing like the personal touch, and it makes such a difference if you've met the person to whom you are speaking on the phone.

Nearly everyone in the Philippines spoke some English, and some of the old Colonial families still spoke Spanish amongst themselves. The main dialect is Tagalog, a Malayo-Polynesian language of the Austronesian group. I picked up some phrases and could put a simple sentence together, but it was all too easy to lapse into English to make myself understood, so I didn't really speak it that well by the time I left.

I'd only been there about two months when the Ambassador (Richard Turpin) retired and we waited with bated breath for the arrival of the new one, William (Bill) Bentley - later Sir William Bentley - and his Danish wife, Karen. The Ambassador was the only person in the Embassy whom we didn't call by his Christian name. He was, variously, Ambassador, HMA or, between ourselves, Ambo.

He proved to be a good Head of Mission and was very popular with the Filipino community. He did, however, have one or two idiosyncrasies (don't we all?), as we were to learn over time, but we could have had much worse.

My Work in the Embassy

As you'll appreciate, there is only so much I can say about this. I am governed – until the day I die - by The Official Secrets Act, which I signed on 5 July 1976.

In Manila, one of the main functions of our Embassy was to encourage inward UK investment to the Philippines and help those companies that were already here. To this end my boss Peter, as Commercial Counsellor, was kept very busy, as was I, with a constant stream of visitors whom I found both friendly and interesting. Dealing with commerce also meant he was out and about a great deal accompanying Board of Trade Ministers from the UK and introducing heads of large British companies to Filipino businesses looking for investment. We were in regular contact with our local Chamber of Commerce representative in Manila and helped with trade fairs and exhibitions to try to wrest contracts from the clutches of our main competitors - Europe, The United States and Japan, with great success.

There were also numerous lunches and receptions for Peter to attend, and I was sometimes invited to the latter, which I greatly enjoyed. As Peter's Social Secretary (in larger Missions an ex-pat or locally employed PA was taken on for this job), I was much involved arranging reciprocal functions hosted by Peter and Andrée. This was a busy part of my job: guests lists to draw up, invitations to be sent out, RSVP's to be noted. I didn't get involved arranging the catering side which was done by Andrée and her servants, but I did attend the receptions and, at times, the dinners if a spare female was needed to make up the numbers. This was fine by me - I loved going.

Other Functions of our Embassy

On the political side, as the country was under Martial Law it was important for the Embassy to closely monitor and report on what was going on. HMG always strove to promote democracy in countries under a dictator. This was not an easy task, and required an enormous amount of tact and diplomacy, whilst at the same time not upsetting the incumbent. A fine line had to be trod.

The Consular Section, under the Consul and Vice-Consul, was always frantic, with Filipinos queuing up outside the Embassy door to get visas to visit, or work, in the UK, the favoured destination (with The States and the Middle East) as English was spoken. A great many Filipinos found it necessary to obtain work abroad in order to send money back to help their families as wages in the Philippines were poor.

Then came the needs of ex-pats: new passports; registering Birth, Marriages and Deaths; repatriation of bodies; help for DBS's (Distressed British Subjects). Although at that time there weren't too many tourists, it seemed never-ending.

The British Council played an important role in the Philippines too, supervising UK English teachers, organizing cultural events, persuading pop stars and the like to perform here. I remember I went to see Rod Stewart, who was fabulous.

Admin had an unenviable job looking after our day to day living needs; clearing our cars and baggage through Customs (always a nightmare); arranging for repairs to property;

obtaining furniture; placing orders for alcohol and English "essentials" with Jardine Matheson in Hong Kong. They were indispensable to us and we helped all we could.

The Defence Section tried to win defence contracts, but with the situation in the Philippines as it was, that wasn't easy.

So, all in all, we were a very busy Embassy, which made any time off we could get, very precious.

Receptions and Dinner Parties

I always used to enjoy the official receptions and dinners I attended. There were a great many of them which meant I met people, both local and visiting, from all walks of life, and I found this not only useful for my work but also interesting and rewarding. At the Residence, both Ann and I were frequently asked to make up the numbers at dinner parties if a VIP or businessman who was invited had travelled out on his own.

I also gave my own dinner parties, too, always for eight as that was all I could seat around my table. Choosing a menu wasn't easy as you couldn't get many of the staple English ingredients, but I managed to produce some quite appetizing meals, so I was told, and we had some riotous evenings.

However, some of my own dinner parties were slightly more memorable than others. I decided to host a lavish Christmas "banquet" for some friends and had hired a cook, Vilma, to help on this occasion so that I too could enjoy the party. She brought out the Christmas pudding and we doused it liberally with brandy. Unsurprisingly, it started to flame alarmingly, nearly setting fire to my house. Before I could stop her, dear Vilma, risking life and limb, had grabbed the platter and run outside to let the brandy run off. I was really concerned, but miraculously she was unscathed. Needless to say, we were all a bit shaken and needed a few more bottles of wine after that to calm our nerves, but the brandy-soaked pud went down a treat!

Filipino Cuisine

Filipino cuisine is a mixture of Asian, American and European food, but with some rather odd combinations to my mind.

Sometimes I would take myself off to the local market at 6 am, before work, to buy chicken and pork and loads of vegetables as these were much cheaper than the supermarkets, but I can't say I liked going there much. Flies, offal, carcasses and other assorted animal parts hanging around wasn't always the best start to my day.

I used to be able to prepare *sinigang,* a thick soup of chicken, prawns, fish and vegetables stewed with tamarind, green mangoes and acidic fruit. In fact, anything I wanted to throw in it really. It wasn't too bad, and was certainly filling, but was an acquired taste.

On the pork front, you had *lechon* (suckling pig stuffed with tamarind leaves and roasted till crispy) and *pork adobo.* But I was never keen on *kinilaw*, which was raw fish or shrimp with ginger, onions and chilli. I was liable to feel rather unwell afterward.

Noodles, known as *pancit*, were very popular, whilst rice came in many forms, but was generally glutinous. Good for sticking your insides together if you were under the weather!

The one thing I absolutely drew the line at, though, was b*alut*. It was a half-formed already fertilized duck egg in its shell and was considered quite a delicacy. Not by me, it wasn't. It was sold at night, warm, and my golf pro, Carlos, loved it. It was considered manly to eat it, and he would happily munch away whilst giving me a lesson. In the end I just couldn't stand it and had to ask if he would mind eating it elsewhere. He couldn't understand why I didn't like them, but happily went to crunch through the tiny beaks and claws with his fellow Filipinos. I can see the eggs now, in their basket covered by a bright cloth. The thought still makes me feel quite sick, though it did provide an excellent source of protein and the Canadian Embassy supported a *balut* farm project for this reason.

The fruit, though, was super: mangoes, papayas, pineapples, bananas, kumquats, calamansi (limes). I couldn't get enough of it.

"Hunting, Shooting and Fishing"

Two of the Ambassador's great passions were fishing, and shooting (not at us, fortunately). I'm not too certain about hunting; he might have done that elsewhere too.

He was in fact a renowned fly fisherman and was so good that he even designed a "fly" which was named after him. He liked nothing better than to take himself off, with his Security Guard, and spend a quiet hour or two catching whatever was on offer in the country concerned.

It was with great sadness that I (and I'm sure all his colleagues) learned that, having retired, he had been fly fishing in the River Esk, been caught by a flash flood, swept away and had drowned. Such a terrible, terrible end. One can only imagine the panic he must have felt. But it was more on the shooting side that we felt the consequences of this passion.

Whenever he went on his shooting trips in the Philippines, he took with him Jeremy Larner, our Assistant Administration Officer, mainly to carry the guns.

Although it was Marital Law, the Ambassador was allowed to keep his gun, but Jeremy had to "borrow" one from the military. On one occasion, he told me, he was given a pump action shotgun with which he wasn't too familiar. He took one shot at a duck and went to reload the gun, but it fell to pieces and he spent ages trying to recover the bits from the lake, much to the Ambassador's annoyance.

The Ambassador was not the most brilliant of shots, and when they went to the wildfowl lakes he always put Jeremy in the wet reeds to flush out the ducks whilst he stayed on the bank in the dry to shoot them. Oh, the privileges of rank!

On one particular occasion I myself got caught up in the preparations for one of these expeditions.

We all, except for the Ambassador and No 2 of the Mission (who was Chargé d'Affaires in the Ambassador's absence), had to take our turn at being on duty out of office hours. This was to cover any emergencies that arose, either locally or in London; to deal with any consular crises; or to receive or send telegrams that were urgent. As there were only a few of us who could attend to the latter, our turn seemed to come around with increasing frequency.

Because of the great time difference between London and Manila, this usually meant being telephoned in the dead of night, getting out of bed and going into a dark, eerily quiet, Embassy to see what needed to be done. Depending on the urgency or nature of the problem, we then had to wake up the diplomat on duty to come into the Embassy as well to deal with it. How we loved our duty weeks!

It was during one of my duty weeks, on a Saturday night, that the Ambassador telephoned me at home at about 9 pm. Oh dear, I thought. Bad news, Gillian.

"Gillian, I'm going shooting tomorrow at 5.30 am. Could you please go into the Embassy and get me five boxes of cartridges. My driver (I forget which one it was), will be there at 5 am to collect them."

"Certainly, Ambassador. No problem."

Hmmm, I thought. This could be a bit tricky. In order to get to the Embassy, open up (which took an absolute age because of all the security measures I had to go through), get the cartridges, close up again and be down in time to meet the driver, this meant I had to leave home at just after 4 am. Fine. All part of a PA's happy lot.

But there was one slight problem. It was Martial Law and there was a curfew. That would mean going through four road blocks, with armed soldiers stationed there, who, even though my little blue car had Embassy number plates, would be suspicious as to what I was doing driving alone in the dead of night. (I must say it was always a rather unnerving experience doing this and one that, though I did it fairly often, I never quite got used to.)

This needed some quick thinking, Gillian. It didn't seem too wise, given the circumstances, to say that I was going into the Embassy to collect five boxes of cartridges. It could be construed that we were starting a mini counter-revolution and may lead to a diplomatic incident, which would upset the Ambassador no end. So I concocted a story that the Ambassador was leaving early that day for an important meeting (vagueness was called for), and needed some important papers to take with him that were still in the Embassy. I rehearsed the story once or twice, and off I set.

Sure enough, I did get stopped, but this explanation seemed to satisfy the guards and I was allowed to proceed on my way. I then had to rouse the janitor of our building who, although we got on well, wasn't too pleased to be woken up in the middle the night either. I gave him the same explanation, sympathised, and all was fine. I collected the boxes (I never realised just how heavy boxes of cartridges could be), met the driver, handed them over, and went home. By this time it was almost 6 am, and since I was supposed to be on the golf course at 8 am, there seemed little point in going back to bed, so I had an early breakfast, got to the range early to practise, and played like a drain!

Christmas in Manila

Who were the recipients of these cartridges? Ducks, mainly, but also poor little innocent snipe. Dozens of them, as we found out one Christmas.

It was the Embassy Christmas party for UK based and locally employed at the Residence.

Filipino food takes some getting used to and, quite frankly, I was getting a bit tired of glutinous rice (nothing like Uncle Ben's), lack of potatoes, and lashings of pork, so the thought of a full Christmas dinner was like manna from Heaven.

The food started to arrive. I looked longingly at each platter as it was brought in, but no turkey, nor roast potatoes. Instead, there was a large dish of little humped back things with a sticky sauce over them.

"Have some snipe, Gillian", the Ambassador offered with enthusiasm.

I looked at these unappetising objects with dismay, but it seemed churlish to refuse, so I took one and bit into it. Immediately I had a mouth full of lead shot which nearly broke a tooth and which I had difficulty getting rid of delicately. I could see everyone else was having the same problem and was trying to spit it out without being seen, but the Ambassador pressed on regardless.

As soon as I could, I sidled off when he wasn't looking to try the next dish, but this looked even more weird.

"Ah, bats' wings Gillian", the Ambassador announced with glee, miraculously appearing at my left shoulder. "Try some – you'll like them."

Oh no! Surely not? Why me? Had I been specially selected as Royal Taster? Although not bitten by a bat as yet, perhaps I'd get secondary Chagas Disease, swell up, and die on the spot. I sincerely hoped not. I sincerely hoped that the Ambassador sincerely hoped not too. It's a devil of a job trying to replace a PA at short notice. Gold dust is a precious commodity!

But bats' wings they were. I gingerly picked up the fattest one, but as you can imagine, there's very little meat on a bat's wing so I took a mouthfull of bones instead. Ugh. It was awful. I headed straight for the bar and took a great swig of wine, imported from Hong Kong at great expense. Who cares? I needed it for medicinal purposes. The meal got no better as there was no Christmas pudding at all. Only gooey and very sweet rice cakes, which weren't bad, but they <u>weren't pudding</u>.

The party continued until quite late. We sang carols and generally had a good time, but I was famished by the time we had to leave, so a few of us quietly decided to head off to a nearby restaurant to find something more substantial to eat, which we did. On leaving, I thanked the Ambassador profusely for giving us such a great time, knowing that he meant well. I was grateful for his hospitality, but felt, personally, that the meal itself lacked a little "*je ne sais quoi!*"

Social Life in the Philippines

We were a very social Embassy and went on some brilliant outings together within a day's journey of Manila. One was a boat trip to Corregidor, the island fortress on the southern tip of the Bataan Peninsula, scene of fierce fighting in World War 11. Another was to the Maya Maya Beach Club in Batangas Province, though this usually involved staying overnight.

There were also guided tours of the historical parts of Manila, which I particularly enjoyed, but it was always a special event to go to downtown Manila in the evenings to watch the very popular **jai alai** matches. Brought from the Basque region of Spain, this incredibly fast game is somewhat similar to squash, but with a much larger court (*fronton*), and the players throw the ball with an elongated basket (*cesta*) attached to their arms. The crowds went wild, and there was much noisy betting on the players. It was a great night out, and difficult not to get caught up in the frenzy.

And then there were the monthly get-togethers of the PA's from the other Embassies in Manila, at one of the Residences kindly offered by the Ambassadors in rotation. These were invaluable as we were often in touch with each other, so it was good to put a face to a name.

The Joys of Golf

It wasn't until I was posted to the Philippines that it was possible for me to learn to play golf. As President Marcos was a golf fanatic, facilities there were excellent, and I took to it like a duck to water, though I had to remember not to swing the club like a hockey stick!

I had lessons from a superb teaching professional, Carlos, at the Fort Bonifacio Golf Club. Ben Arda was the Filipino golfing hero of that time, but whilst Carlos wasn't such a success on the circuit, he was brilliant at instruction and I owe all my modest success to him. He told me on the day I left that I had been his "star" pupil. It was tough to say goodbye.

What helped my golf most, I think, was that Carlos banned me from setting foot on the course for three months, but the hours spent at the Driving Range paid off and I quickly went from a complete beginner to obtaining a handicap of 18. I played in all the local tournaments in Manila, and even went to Papua New Guinea with Carlos to play in a tournament there. I didn't win, but I wasn't bad. Most of my free time in Manila was spent either on the course at Fort Bonifacio, at Wack Wack Golf Club (yes, really!) or, as a special treat if Carlos could arrange it, at the very exclusive Manila Golf Club. I often saw President Marcos, with his host of security men, whilst I was playing, and even got the odd acknowledgements, which surprised me.

On one occasion the World Cup was held in Manila. The organisers were looking for markers, so I volunteered and ended up marking for Bob Byman, a well-known American professional at the time.

My main memory of that tournament, though, was going to the social events at the Base after the rounds and mixing with the pros. I really enjoyed those evenings, particularly meeting two young, up and coming British players, who were great fun. Their names – Nick Faldo and Ken Brown.

Hazards on the Course

The Philippines is the place for *snakes*. I have a great fear of them. It was dusk, and I was in the south of Luzon, the main island on which Manila is situated. I was driving back, alone, to my hotel from a golf tournament, along a single-track road lined with bamboo and sugar canes, at the foot of the Mayon volcano (which erupted recently with sad loss of life) when in the headlights I spotted what looked like a large sugar cane lying across the road. As I couldn't avoid it, I drove over it, but as I did so, it felt a bit "soft" and too late I realized it was an enormous python straddling the road. I nearly had a fit. Amazingly I didn't drive off the road into the cane. But even though I don't like snakes, I wouldn't knowingly hurt one, and I was relieved when I looked out of my rear-view mirror to see that it had gone, so fortunately I didn't kill it.

Again, Carlos and I used to play at a club called Filipinas Golf and Country Club just outside Manila (this course was one of President Marcos's favourites). I wasn't aware that before the war it used to house a cobra farm, but that area was bombed and the farm was more or less destroyed. However, apparently not before a few cobras had made a dash for it.

It was another hot, humid day. Again, bamboo and sugar cane lined the fairways and it was an unwritten rule that if your ball strayed into the rough, you didn't go and look for it. Needless to say, you needed a good supply of balls - just in case. Leading up to the greens were Dapdap trees, with their broad, slightly club-shaped leaves (in the playing cards sense). Some of the leaves had already started to fall, and with the sunlight casting dappled shadows on the fairways, it was difficult to spot your ball near the greens.

I was playing well. In fact, I had just shot an Eagle at the par 5 and even Carlos was impressed. Again, on the next hole, the 9th, par 4, I'd hit a cracking tee shot and only needed a 9 iron to

179

A less hazardous moment on the course

After the golf tournament at Legazpi City, in the southern Legazpi Province, 1979 – before my encounter with the python, which is why I'm looking so relaxed!

reach the green. This was the life, I thought, as I sauntered along the fairway, scuffing up the dead leaves with my metal- spiked shoes, basking in the glory of my brilliance at the last hole (and, hopefully, this one).

But my round was about to be destroyed. Without warning, my caddy grabbed my 9 iron, pushed me to one side and started bashing the leaf-strewn ground in front of me. Dear me! What on earth was the matter with him? I didn't think I was doing that badly! Perhaps he'd got a touch of the sun. But he stopped, scooped up a bloodied cobra with my 9 iron, and handed it to me, smiling broadly at having stopped me from treading on it just in time. Without being dramatic, in all fairness he probably saved my life: I doubt whether cobras take too kindly to having metal spikes stuck into them. I stared in abject horror at this battered, dead reptile dangling from the end of my club. What was I meant to do with it? I was hardly likely to take it home and stuff it. I didn't want an "Albert" of my own, thank you. He had it straight back, with instructions to dispose of it, which he did by throwing it onto the short rough (lucky player following me!), and clean the club, which he did with my lovely new LPGA golf cloth, draping it through the handle of my golf bag afterwards. I couldn't bear to ever wash that cloth so it ended up in the bin – shame, I really liked it. Carlos tried to console me with hugs and encouraging words, but I took a 10 to finish the hole.

For his sake, though, I was determined to carry on, but on the back 9, I was rubbish. In fact, I gave up counting strokes and the balls I lost, I was so awful. But when we got back to the Club House I gave my caddy a very generous tip, and myself a large brandy. I rarely used that 9 iron after that, always preferring my pitching wedge, even though it might not have been the correct club. Oh, the delights of playing golf abroad, I thought!

Non-Hazardous Pastimes!

If I wasn't on the golf course, then I'd be on a tennis court at someone's house, which although more energetic, was much safer. As long as it was sport, I was happy.

For the men, there was the Hash House Harriers, a non-competitive running and social club, first started in Selangor, Malaya, for ex-pats and Colonial officers but now an international organization. Their get-togethers and runs were exceedingly popular and always well attended, despite the humidity.

For relaxation, I had a membership, for a nominal monthly subscription, at the Intercontinental Hotel in Makati which allowed me to use the hotel's facilities, such as their excellent swimming pool, gyms and bars. Most of the diplomatic community, ex-pats and business community belonged, so it was a great place to hang out.

Occasionally a group of us would go to the cinema as most of the (English-speaking) new releases were shown, and there was great excitement when some of the mainly American international stars visited. I loved seeing Gladys Knight and the Pips and Aretha Franklin in particular – fantastic evenings.

Television showed mostly American documentaries, films and serials. Some of them were great. And my trusty record player was much in use to keep me company. The Bee Gees could be heard everywhere.

Pam's Visits

I was thrilled that my close (P & O) friend, Pam was coming out to stay from 11-20 May 1977. As I've discovered, she must be one of the world's best diary-keepers, having done so for decades. She has gone to a lot of trouble to delve into her "archives" and note down our itineraries, some of which I had completely forgotten about, and I've included the most important bits in each section of my postings where she came to stay.

We decided to visit Baguio City, a small town in the

mountains, atop a plateau in the Cordilleras. At an altitude of 4,900 ft, I used to love its cool climate and pine clad hills. Such a change from Manila. Camp John Hay was a much-used American military RNR retreat there, but I gather it's now a housing complex.

Baguio was about four hour's drive from Manila (six if you took the Philippine Rabbit bus service), or just over half an hour's flight. It was a long and dusty drive on a single lane road fraught with carabao (water buffalo), jeepneys, mad Filipino Rabbit bus drivers, and even more mad motor cyclists. I needed my wits about me: carabao are quite substantial animals! When I went on my own, I always stayed at the Ruff Hotel (a slightly unfortunate name) just opposite the tiny airport, which was clean, comfortable, not too expensive and friendly, and so that was where Pam and I headed for. After a bit of sightseeing around the city, next day we left the car at the hotel and Mrs Ruff took us to the bus station to catch the 0745 bus to Sagada, up in the mountains, enduring eight bottom-bruising hours to get there. We toured Sagada and were then taken by two small boys with hurricane lamps on a hike to a huge bat-infested cave. On reflection, we must have been mad. Then next day, back on the bus to Baguio, squashed in with chickens and squealing pigs.

After leaving Baguio, we decided to stop briefly at the Sun Valley Hotel on a beautiful beach in the Province of La Union, so we could relax in the sea before heading back to Manila. There I got out the goggle and flippers and spent a very happy time seeing what lurked within the reef.

Back home, we went to watch a *jai alai* game, and met up with Pam's friend, Rick, who had arrived for a conference. Time then to head off to the airport laden, as I recall, with a fragile Capiz shell lampshade which Pam had in her home for many years. A great visit and I was sorry to see her go.

Exploring Further Afield

Sometimes I just needed to get out of the congestion, smog and stifling atmosphere of Manila and its surrounding areas, so I, and Ann if she was free, would get out the map and plan where to go for an adventure. As it was Martial Law, and as always members of an Embassy were prime targets for kidnapping, we all had to be careful where we went, so whilst keen to explore, I had to be sensible and stick to the most familiar visitor areas.

About two hour's drive from Manila is Taal Volcano, 1,000 feet high, a crater within a lake. It's a bit of a hike up to the rim, and it's still very active so you need to heed the geologists' advice about going up, but once there the view was superb, and I always thought it was worth the exertion.

After my trip into the Cordillera Central with Pam, one place I really wanted to visit was the rice terraces at Banaue. This time I went with Ann on another memorable, if a little hair-raising, bottom-bruising ride deep into the mountains, via Bontoc. Again, the bus ride was an education in itself, being wedged in with pigs, hens, vegetables – anything to keep the villagers going until they could get back to Baguio to re-stock again. Once at Banaue, the 2,000 year old terraces, covering more than 100 square miles and clinging to the mountain-sides, are a sight to behold. I only managed to get up there this once, staying the night at the Youth Hostel, but I will never forget my first view of them.

When Ann and I went together to Baguio, and we had enough time, on the way back we'd stop at the Hundred Islands recreation centre, leaving the car on the mainland and taking the tiny ferry over to Children's Island where we would camp overnight, having hired what we needed from the centre. I slept in the open on the sand, but I kept hearing odd rustling sounds and so never slept well: it might have been snakes! Few places could have been more idyllic, though, with golden sand, swaying palms, turquoise sea. I could have stayed on that little island forever. But we had to get back, so we packed up the car once more and set off for the bustle of Manila.

During my three years in the Philippines, I took every opportunity, when work allowed, to get out and about.

Shooting the rapids at Pagsanjan Falls, near the film set for "Apocalypse Now", was quite challenging, but thrilling nonetheless. I greatly enjoyed my trips with Ann to Legazpi City, at the southern end of Luzon, and to Marinduque, where she had a friend working as a geologist at the copper mine there, accompanied by his family. And I endeavoured to get up to Hong Kong, which I absolutely love. Then there was my visit to Lae and Port Moreby on Papua New Guinea for a golf tournament. I played quite well, coming in fifth but got told off by the elderly ladies running the event for wearing too short a golf skirt, which might "excite" the locals, so I ended up having to wear my long denim skirt, which got in the way of my clubs, was really hot and did nothing at all for my game.

Half-way through my tour Ann was posted elsewhere and was replaced by Diana Armstrong as PA/HMA. I did miss Ann, but Diana and I became, and still are, good friends. I'm sure she will agree with me, though, that she didn't quite have the adventurous spirit that Ann did, so I did most of my travelling from then on alone.

After eighteen months I went home for a month on mid-tour leave, spending a few days with Herb and Janee in Honolulu on the way back. My leave fortunately coincided with Sheila getting married, so I was able to be Matron of Honour and celebrate that with her. Otherwise, I spent every hour I could with Mum and Dad, and it was so hard to leave them when it was time to head off for Sri Lanka on my stop-off to Manila.

Whilst I was away, my bungalow was burgled and I lost nearly everything, apart from clothes. All my electrical items disappeared, and I felt sure it was the custodian of the bungalow, who lived in a tiny room in the underground garage. He knew I was away, had seen what I had in my lounge through the patio windows when he called if I needed anything, could easily have used bolt cutters to take off the padlock, and looked decidedly guilty when I asked if he knew anything about the burglary. But I couldn't prove it: I just had to let it go. It did mean, however, claiming on the insurance and putting in an order to Jardine Matheson's in Hong Kong for a new television and those electrical items I couldn't buy in Manila (like an electric kettle). The rest, I had to get locally, which was difficult and very inconvenient.

Paalam Manila

My time in the Philippines seemed to go by so quickly once I got back from mid tour leave, but I tried to cram in as much as I could in the time I had left, and I think I succeeded.

About two months before I was due to leave, I had notice of my next posting – **Peru**, for two and a half years as PA/HMA. I was over the moon: Spanish-speaking, such a rich culture, and a country I'd been longing to visit for ages. As much as I'd loved the Philippines, it was time to move on to pastures new, and what a new pasture.

Admin Section booked the removal company to pack up my heavy baggage, whilst I sorted out what I wanted to take with me back to the UK as I'd have two weeks or so there before going on to Peru. I had to sell my little blue car to someone who was allowed to buy an imported vehicle; and I also had to decide what could go as air freight, as I was allowed a small trunk to follow. This was delivered to where I was staying whilst in the UK, and I would then pack it up again with what I needed to tide me over till my heavy baggage arrived, and it would be collected, and delivered to Post just after I had arrived.

Peter and the Ambassador held farewell parties for me, to which I was able to invite a few of the friends I had made. I said a tearful farewell to Carlos and his family, thanking him for all his patience and support for my golf. It was so hard to leave all my other friends as well. Peter was just about to retire, so I wished him and Andrée well, with a promise to let him know how I was getting on in Peru.

Having done all this, it was time to say goodbye (*paalam*).

I pulled the patio doors shut for the last time, got into the Embassy car to go to the airport, and boarded the British Airways flight which would take me as far as The Seychelles, where I had decided to have a short holiday at The Reef Hotel.

The Philippines had turned out to be everything I had hoped it would be, and I was so grateful. I knew the memories of my time there would stay with me forever, and they have done.

Not a Philistine in sight, Auntie Gladys.

Out and About in the Philippines

Left: Standing on the rim of the Taal Volcano in Cavite Province.
Right: Waiting for the bus at Baguio to take Pam and me to Sagada

Above Left: A gentle ride on a carabao near Baguio
Above Right: a normal ride (and we think our potholes are bad – try the Philippines!)

Above: Camping at Children's Island (an unguarded moment!)

Below Left: Boarding the flight to Marinduque Island
Below Right: one of the copper mine's enormous ore trucks

Above: An Embassy outing to Corregidor Island.

Above Left: The Foreign Embassy PAs get-together lunch (Diana at the table in green)
Above Right: Shooting the rapids at Pagsanjan Falls

Below: The film set for "Apocalypse Now"

The Seychelles – Just One Last Swing

I still couldn't rid myself of golfing hazards. Now came coconuts! Smaller and slightly less terrifying than snakes (and alligators later), but they could be deadly nonetheless.

On the way back to the UK after my tour had ended, I had booked on a British Airways stop-over holiday of five days at The Reef Hotel in The Seychelles. I felt I deserved a proper treat and it was idyllic: a lovely room at the hotel with patio doors straight onto the golden beach, strewn with shells of all shapes and sizes. How I loved to sit there in the evening, glass of wine in hand, marvelling at the crimson sky as the sun set over the Indian Ocean. What could be better!

To my delight, attached to the hotel was a little 9-hole golf course. Just the job, I thought. I fancy a round. So I paid my green fee, chose a rather battered set of clubs, which cost extra, and made my way on my own onto the course.

On the first tee, prominently displayed, was yet another sign, this time of a golfer being struck on the head by a falling coconut. Nothing to worry about, I thought confidently, as I set off. Wrong, Gillian. As I progressed along the palm-fringed fairways, all I could hear was "thud, thud, thud" as enormous coconuts fell from a great height all around me. I dashed to pick one up. It weighed a ton and would have killed anyone who was unfortunate enough to be hit by it. This called for a different tactic altogether. I did complete the course, but with an 8 or 9 iron nearly all the way round, keeping right in the middle of the fairways. If my ball strayed - tough. Better safe than sorry!

This idyllic holiday soon came to an end. I boarded the British Airways flight back to Heathrow, changed to fly to Birmingham where Mum and Dad would meet me. They were keen to hear about my adventures, so we chatted a lot. I just pottered about for three weeks, and then got ready for my next move to Peru. Life certainly was good!

A quiet round of golf in The Seychelles!

PART FIVE

PERU
1980-1981

Above: The British Embassy,
Lima, Avda Arequipa, 12th and 14th floors.

Below: My apartment block,
Avda Benavides esq La Paz, Miraflores
(my flat was on the 6th floor, to the left)

Yet Another New Home

I arrived in Peru at the beginning of 1980. I couldn't believe that I was on South American soil at last. Ever since I started learning Spanish when I was 12, this Continent had held a special fascination for me, and whilst I enjoyed going to Spain and the Spanish culture, I could visit that country on holiday. South America was where I really wanted to be.

I was arriving at an interesting time. With President Belaunde Terry's election in 1980, Peru had at last returned to democratic government after years of military rule, but there was the continuing problem of the *"Sendero Luminoso"* (Shining Path) Maoist *guerrilla* group, founded in the 1960s by Abimael Guzman, whose aim was to overthrow any government and return the country to peasant farmers. Initially they gained support, but they were brutal in their assassinations and eventually the population turned against them. Because of the threat they posed, whilst I was in Peru it was dangerous to travel to remote areas, particularly in central and southern Peru, so I had to be content with being less adventurous.

First Impressions

We had to travel by British Airways if possible, but as there were no direct flights to Lima in those days, I had to fly to Schipol airport in Holland and change to KLM to make my journey. As with Manila, on these long hauls we were allowed to travel Club Class, which was really comfortable. On shorter flights, we travelled Economy. The Ambassador always travelled First Class.

Flying over Lima was an amazing sight. There was a thick cloud which spread up the valleys like the fingers of a glove, with the snow-capped Andes towering above. Away from the city, the desert stretched along the coast into the distance on either side. It was beautiful.

Climate

Peru has two seasons – wet and dry. I had arrived at the beginning of winter (May to October), when it hardly ever rains in the arid desert along the coast during these months, thanks to the cold Humboldt Current which sucks the moisture out of the air. There could be mist and a light drizzle (called La Garúa), from time to time, but that was all.

Lima, however, was different as I was about to discover. For these seven winter months the city is covered by a thick, grey cloud, hence the fingers of the glove in the valleys. During this time, you would never see the sun at all, and the odours of everyday life would get trapped under this heavy cloud, making the city a rather smelly place to be by October. At times it could be a bit depressing, so the answer was to get out of the city as often as you could.

Introductions

I was met at the airport at Callao and taken straight to the Embassy to meet the Ambassador and my future colleagues. Again, the Embassy building wasn't quite what I had in mind: it was a high-rise office block in Plaza Washington, not far from the Residence of the American Ambassador. We occupied the 12th and 14th floors (there was no 13th – even Peruvians are superstitious) – which was fine when the lift worked, but a real trial when it didn't.

I was introduced to the Ambassador, a small man, who welcomed me warmly. He was half-Spanish, half-Scottish, fluent in Spanish of course, and he very much appreciated my knowledge of Spanish. Things were looking good. He had a Social Secretary, Gladys, whom I met later, along with the rest of the locally employed, but first I was to meet my UK-based colleagues who were very friendly. Grace, the H of C's PA, was just about to retire, so sadly we only had a few weeks together before she left. Her successor, Sheila, who now lives just down the road from me and is a good friend, is a few years younger than me, and when we were in Lima, although we got on well, we had different interests and mixed with a different crowd.

Where was I to live?

Once I'd said hello to everyone, I was taken to the residential area of Miraflores, where my new home, previously occupied by my predecessor, was to be in a residential block on Avenida (Avda) Benavides esquina (esq) La Paz or, in English, at the corner of Benavides Avenue and La Paz Avenue. It was a fifteen-storey block, two flats to each storey, and I was on the sixth floor. It was large, comfortable, and the standard Government furniture was fine, but most of all I loved the layout. It had two bedrooms, an inside bathroom, dining room, kitchen and utility room from where I could catch a glimpse of the sea between the other houses and high rises. Perfect. And my Peruvian neighbours, the family Biber Sherpa, a couple with an older teenage son, were so friendly, as were the other residents whom I happened to meet now and then. I just knew I was going to enjoy this Posting a lot.

Settling In

All I needed now was "wheels". As I couldn't import a British car, I had to buy locally within the allowance for my Grade, so I settled on a bright orange (easy to spot in the mountains) VW Beetle which, although a bit short on luggage space and very noisy, was sturdy and would take me where I wanted to go – up mountains and along rough tracks.

Wherever I am, and whenever I move to a new area, the first thing I always do is buy a map and street plan and just drive around and around, getting lost numerous times, until I've got the hang of where I am. Fortunately, I have a good sense of direction, so this hasn't been too much of a problem and, unwittingly, I've learnt many useful short cuts. I now had to apply myself, quickly, and learn how to get to the Embassy and back. Driving in the Philippines had given me a resilience and toughness that was to stand me in good stead in all my Postings: it was certainly needed in Peru.

Next came how to get to the Residence, the shops, colleagues' houses, the sea, and the golf club, in that order. Once I had mastered these journeys, I was all set and enjoyed driving the "Orange Devil", which went like the wind, especially up mountains, though the lack of oxygen was a problem at times.

The Embassy

I settled in well, though I did find the Ambassador somewhat difficult. I discovered early on that he was rather short-tempered, demanding, and it wasn't wise to voice another opinion. If he took a dislike to you, nothing you did would make the situation any better. This happened to us all at one stage or another, so consequently nearly all of us were in the dog house, and at times it was almost impossible to squeeze anyone else into the kennel it was so full!

But the Ambassador wasn't always difficult. He could be very charming and was a congenial host. His reception and dinner invitations were eagerly sought after, and being fluent in Spanish, of course, he and his extremely kind Guatemalan wife were a great hit with the Peruvians. Although as his PA, I seemed to be in the firing line a fair amount, which often goes with the job, I tried my hardest to please him, even though at times it was nigh impossible. I then I just gritted my teeth and got on with the job as best I could.

Because I was finding life rather stressful, at one stage I was admitted to hospital with nervous exhaustion. As I was just getting over a bout of Brucellosis, (Milk Fever, contracted through eating contaminated yoghurt we think), I wasn't feeling too good anyway, which didn't help. Our Embassy doctor, Dr Zapff, was a tower of strength and I relied on him a lot. I can never thank him enough for his understanding and kindness during this time. However, when I came out of hospital the situation didn't seem to have improved, and I knew that as much as loved this country, I just wouldn't be able to stay.

Our H of C was not having a particularly great time either, but was also a tower of strength to me. He contacted Personnel to try to get me moved, to which eventually they agreed, and I received news that I was to be cross-posted to Guatemala for two and a half years as the PA there was leaving for personal reasons. I was heartbroken at the thought of having to leave Peru as there was still so much I wanted to see and do, but you can't win them all.

Great Times

In the meantime, I was determined to get out and about and enjoy myself in Peru as much as I could.

Bag Runs

During my time with The Office, there were of course no emails, laptops, electronic secure communications, mobile phones, etc. Nothing. It was only in the 1980s that I had an electric typewriter: otherwise, I just plodded along on a Remington manual. I sometimes think that the young people of today don't appreciate what it was like to live without this modern technology. But we managed very well, perhaps much better in some respects.

Because of this lack of communication equipment, the only way to get correspondence back and forth between London and a Mission was via the indispensable Queen's Messenger, (normally an ex Service Officer) who never let the Diplomatic Bag out of his sight wherever he went. The QM's were brilliant, and if you talked to them nicely, they might even slip those much missed and desired items such as a packet of sausages or bacon, into the Bag as well (sssh – don't tell The Office). We only hoped the flight wasn't delayed, as did he. The Bags could have got a bit smelly!

The QM's went to all the major Posts, but normally not the smaller ones (often on account of cost), so it was one of the perks of the job that certain Embassy UK-based personnel took it in turns to take the Bag on to the next small Post. These little trips away were much prized and your turn was jealously guarded.

This was the case in Lima, when I was fortunate enough to take the Bag up to our Embassy at La Paz in Bolivia.

We spent two night in La Paz as going from sea level to 13,000 ft in two and a half hours had its own problem and most of us suffered on arrival at the airport at El Alto from "soroche", or altitude sickness, caused by lack of sufficient red corpuscles to absorb oxygen. Whoever picked us up at the airport had an oxygen cylinder with them for us to use, which I did both times. When I'd been there a day the feeling of sickness wore off, though I always had a headache, but one of the best things to cure this was an infusion of "mate de coca" or cocaine leaves, which you put in a cup and poured boiling water over them! It did help, which is why, I'm sure, that you see people living at altitude chewing coca leaves all the time.

Whilst in La Paz, we always stayed in a nice hotel downtown, though we had the Embassy telephone numbers in case we needed anything, and in the evening we were invited to dinner by the H of C.

I found this country as fascinating as Peru – similar, yet different - and I was keen to see as much as I could whilst I was there. I had a list of tour operators and booked on some tours, particularly to go to Lake Titicaca and around the Altiplano, as the high plateau is called. It was tiring because of the lack of oxygen, but I loved it and relished the opportunity of gaining yet more information on these Andean uplands. The Aymara, as the indigenous people in this area are called, were a little wary, especially of my fair hair, and I had to be very careful when taking photos as they believed that if you took an image of them, it took away their souls. Usually, though, a few pesos got over that problem! But still, I respected their beliefs, and still managed to get some good shots and Super 8 footage too, even if it did mean hiding behind sacks of vegetables most of the time.

Leaving La Paz was tricky. We flew Lufthansa and it was usual for our plane to have quite a few goes at taking off because of lack of oxygen for the jet engines. After the third attempt, one usually got slightly worried, but we always made it in the end. Most passengers then had a stiff drink, generously supplied by the airline.

Back at sea level, it took me a day or so to acclimatize myself, but without the coca leaves this time. I left them behind. One doesn't want to become addicted! Anyway, they weren't like English Breakfast.

What Else Did I Do?

I joined La Planicie Golf Club at Monterrico, a very affluential suburb of Lima, and spent many happy hours on the course there at weekends. Some of my colleagues also belonged, as did many ex-pats, so we would all get together, have a round of golf, then lunch and generally relax.

Whenever the Ambassador was away, I'd take the opportunity to travel as widely as I could, and I managed to see a fair amount of Peru in my shortened time there.

The Amazon Basin

I flew to **Iquitos**, the largest city in the Amazon Basin, there being only air and river access, and spent a fantastic three nights amidst the noise and bustle of this former port. Despite the heat and humidity, I went on tours during the day, a particularly memorable one being a trip on the Amazon River, though I was rather apprehensive as the last thing I wanted to do was to meet some of Albert's relatives, or distant cousins for that matter. Piranhas were fine, and there were plenty of those. Another was a short excursion into the rain forest itself, but in 1980 tourism hadn't taken such a hold as I believe it has today so we didn't venture far. I did, however, manage to catch a glimpse of flamboyant macaws and parrots, and the odd spider monkey swinging amongst the thick tropical vegetation. But no Alberts, fortunately!

And I remember being frightened out of my wits when, looking into a large raised tank, up surfaced the snout of a *paiche* (pronounced pie-chay), the world's largest fresh water fish which can grow to more than 10 feet long and weigh 441 lbs. He was inches from my nose and puffed right into my face. He was very friendly, and looked as if he may belong to the dolphin family. He wasn't dangerous, I was told, but he certainly was BIG.

Macchu Picchu

Who wouldn't want to go to Macchu Picchu? I most certainly did. Having arranged five days off whilst the Ambassador was away, I flew up to Cusco where I would stay before and after my visit to Macchu Picchu. This city, once homeland of the Incas, was an ideal place from where to explore the surrounding areas, and there was so much to see here too. Had I have remained in Peru longer, I would certainly have gone back there again.

I made the most of my stay in Cusco, visiting the majestic Cathedral and museums and exploring the Inca ruins at Sacsayhuamán, the Moray stone circles, and the living Inca town of Ollantaytambo. When it was time to go up to Macchu Picchu, I caught the little train that huffed and puffed as it wound its way up the mountainside, and got off at the tiny station halfway up. With my rucksack, it was a bit of a hike the rest of the way up, but I checked into the Lodge, got myself a guide and went off to explore.

I had booked my room well in advance at the Sanctuary Lodge, which used to be a scientists' hut, and which is the only place to stay at the site itself. Trying to get a room there was like gold dust, and I suppose it's even worse today. It wasn't cheap then, but to get up at 4 am and see the sun strike the "Hitching Post of the Sun", was memorable beyond words. The stillness, the noise of the roaring Urubamba river below, having the whole place to myself apart from the five or six other people staying at the Lodge whom I never saw as they had gone off elsewhere: no other experience comes even close to what I felt then, and because of all the turmoil of Lima, I just sat there and cried. It was so beautiful.

There were so many other places I managed to visit, albeit it briefly, mainly on my own, such as Arequipa, with its stunning Monasterio de Santa Catalina; the Reserva Nacional de Paracas, Peru's largest area of protected coastline teeming with wildlife, particularly seals, and the mountains towns and villages around Lima. But the memories of one trip are very special.

Barbara

One of my best friends in Lima was Barbara, the New Zealand Ambassador's PA. She was a little older than me, but we got on well and were kindred spirits. I could talk to her, and I did, though always being aware that she was from another Mission. When our time off coincided, we would go off on "mini adventures", never too far afield, and I drove most of the time as she didn't like driving much. But we got around.

The opportunity arose for a bigger adventure at the end of January 1981 when we both had a few days off as our respective bosses were travelling up country. We decided we would like to go to see the Nazca Lines, giant drawings in the desert more than 2,000 years old, that still have scientists baffled. We drove down to Ica, the nearest town to the Lines, and booked in at the upmarket hotel, Las Dunas. It was a bit expensive, so we shared a room, which worked out well.

You can only see the Lines from the air, so we chartered a little Cessna plane to take us up. There was no runway to speak of, so we bounced along the desert and eventually took off. I was sitting next to the pilot and had a fantastic view. However, it seemed a bit drafty, and when I looked at the gauges in front of me, to my horror I stared at – holes. There were quite a few gauges missing; fuel, altitude – who knows? I didn't tell Barbara as I knew she would have a fit. We flew over the Lines, which were so interesting, managed to land in one piece, and agreed it had been well worth the trip. Back at the hotel, we treated ourselves to a Pisco Sour, the local drink, had a good meal and retired to our room. When there, Barbara happened to mention that she hadn't been feeling too good during the day, but thought she might have eaten something odd (easy to do in Peru). She was also worried about a mark that had appeared on her upper leg, which she showed me. It didn't look right somehow, so I suggested she should go to the doctors when she got back, just to check it out.

When we got back to Lima we spoke often, but only saw each other again once more because we were both so busy. She said she had gone to the doctors and they were sending her to the hospital for tests as no-one knew quite what was the matter, but she felt a bit better so we started planning our next excursion out of Lima, this time to Monterrey and the Parque Nacional de Huascarán.

At the beginning of March, she was dead. I received a telephone call at home one evening from the New Zealand

Ambassador, who knew we were good friends, telling me the terrible news that she had died of an incurable liver disease (I suspect it was cancer, but don't know). I was devastated. He asked if I would like to sign the Book of Condolence, which I said I would, so I went to the New Zealand Embassy to do so. I didn't go to the airport to pay my respects as her coffin was loaded onto the plane - I felt that was purely for her colleagues. But I was so, so sad and wrote a letter to her brother, who was her next of kin, expressing my sorrow at her parting. How I missed her. Neither of us knew I would be leaving in May, but we could at least have had one more adventure together.

Barbara at Las Dunas Hotel, Ica.
R.I.P. dear friend. I missed you a lot.

Adios Peru

In April I got confirmation of my next posting. I was being cross-posted, that is without home leave, to Guatemala in May for two and a half years. There, I would be PA to Michael Wilmshurst, the Consul General, as the Embassy had been downgraded to a Consulate General after a dispute (one of many) with the Guatemalans over British Honduras, later Belize. The country was now in the midst of a bloody civil war, which didn't sound ideal, but I was very happy to go and have the chance to get to know yet another South American country.

I hated to leave Peru, but there was no way the situation with the Ambassador would get any better, so I arranged for the packers to collect my heavy baggage, sold the little "Orange Devil", sorted out my air freight and was ready to go.

I said a fond but sad farewell to my friends, colleagues and neighbours, and a friendly farewell to the Ambassador. I boarded an Eastern Airlines flight to Miami, where I would stay for two nights before flying down to Guatemala City.

I was full of optimism. This was going to be an interesting experience and I much looked forward to my new assignment. How wrong I was to be.

I did meet the Ambassador once more when I flew up from Santiago to spend a few days in Lima. He couldn't have been nicer, shaking my hand, wanting to know what I'd been doing and how I was getting on. I'm not certain he realized just how awful he had been to me, but it was heartening to see him in such good spirits. I was very pleasant to him too: no point in bearing grudges, and we said goodbye on very friendly terms.

He continued as Ambassador to Peru for another year or so, I believe, and died a few years ago.

Macchu Picchu and the Altiplano in Bolivia

Above: Sitting on the edge of the Urubamba
River gorge at Macchu Picchu, with my "friends".

Below: Macchu Picchu - all to myself!

Above: An Inca family at Ollantaytambo, near Cusco

Below: Lake Titicaca. Chiriqui Island, where they make the totora reed boats used by Thor Heyerdahl: A wary little Uros girl (indigenous to these floating islands)

Above: At El Alto, on the Altiplano
The bowler hats cost the equivalent of £10, which was a lot of money.
When it rained, they put them in plastic bags but still wore them.

Below: Downtown La Paz

PART SIX

GUATEMALA
1981

Above: The Hotel "El Conquistador"
where The Consulate-General occupied the 5th floor suite

Below: The elegant Residence

A Traumatic Posting

I've found this to be the hardest part of my book to write. My time in Guatemala was dangerous and upsetting, and even now at times some of the events come back to haunt me. I don't wish to sound melodramatic: what I write is exactly what happened, so please bear with me on this. This was the other side of diplomacy at work, and it gives you an idea of what life can be like at times for members of the Diplomatic Service. It wasn't all receptions and Ferrero Rocher, that's for sure.

Political Situation

Trying to get my head around the political situation in Guatemala hasn't been easy.

At the centre of this complex, long-running dispute with Britain was Guatemala's claim that Belize was part of their territory. All the school text books and maps showed that it was, and it was a very thorny issue. Strategically Belize was important as it gave Guatemala an outlet to the Caribbean, the US eastern seaboard, and trade across the Atlantic. Otherwise, their ships had to go through the Panama Canal, which was costly and time-consuming.

When I arrived in May 1981, we had no Embassy here, having broken off relations with Guatemala in 1963. Talks had broken down between our two countries over the self-government of British Honduras, later re-named Belize, which was granted in 1964. Diplomatic relations were later re-established between us, but only at Consulate-General level, and since then it had always been a tense relationship requiring sensitive handling.

My Arrival

My friend, Pat, was waiting for me at the airport in Miami and we drove to her house, where I was to stay for two nights before going on to Guatemala. It was good to see her and her family again, and to relax for a short time. We talked a lot, then hit the shopping malls the next day as there were clothes and other odds and ends that I needed to buy for my new posting. It had been difficult to get clothes to fit me in Peru as the women there were generally much smaller, so now was my chance to stock up again. A bit of retail therapy works wonders!

Yet Another New Home

The time came to say goodbye to Pat and take the Eastern Airlines flight down to Guatemala City, where I was met by Gordon, our Admin Officer, and taken straight to the Consulate-General to meet my new boss, Michael, and my other colleagues. We were a tiny Mission, being only seven UK-based, three wives, two children aged 5 and 7, and eight locally-employed, plus the Residence staff. We operated from the 5th floor suite of the Hotel El Conquistador, adequate but not ideal, whilst waiting for new Consulate-General offices to be finished nearby, in September, we hoped.

As seemed often to be the case, we had given up my predecessor's accommodation, and so I was to stay at the Hotel until I had found somewhere to live. She had gone back to the UK for a few months for personal reasons, but would return later I gathered as she had a Guatemalan boyfriend whom I think she hoped to marry. I never met her, but it was agreed that as she was only allowed to sell her tax-free car to someone in a similar position, I would buy her Escort from her. But until all the paperwork ('tramites', in Spanish) was completed, it meant relying on lifts, taxis or our run-about car, if it was available, to get around.

After about a month of hunting around with a friendly travel agent, I eventually found a flat on the 12th floor of a newish block on Avenida La Reforma, not too far from the Residence. It wasn't big, and the owner's furniture was not quite to my taste, but the views were stunning, especially at night; and it was within my rent allowance which was more to the point. I moved in with my air freight and waited for my heavy baggage to arrive, which it did a few weeks later. Then started the familiar task of unpacking and settling in. My neighbours, on learning that I was British, weren't too friendly, so I felt it best to keep to myself most of the time. I didn't want to get into a heated argument over Belize, that was for sure.

Above: My tall block of flats on Avenida La Reforma
(I'm on the 12th floor on the right)
Below: View from my balcony over Guatemala City

Michael proved to be a super boss: kind, considerate, amusing, and I loved working for him. His wife, Mary, was extremely nice too, so all was going well. As his PA, I looked after all his secretarial and social work, but in addition I was in charge of communications contact with London and helped out in other areas when needed. There was another UK-based PA, Jo, with whom I got on very well, who worked in Chancery. We were a great team and got on well together, enjoying each other's company both in the office and socially, with the wives and children.

Living Conditions in Guatemala

A violent civil war was raging when I arrived, and conditions were tough. Bodies of dissidents were regularly to be found in ravines or on waste ground, and as we weren't the most popular foreigners in the country because of Belize, there was a degree of risk for us too so we had to be careful where we went. We were restricted to travelling within a twenty mile radius of Guatemala City, and then only in a group. As someone who loves to go on adventures on her own, I found this a bit difficult at first, but fully understood the necessity of sticking to the rules. No Tikal for me then, sadly.

As I was desperate to get out on the golf course again, I hoped to join a golf club and, if possible, a tennis club too. There didn't appear to be that many courses around the capital, and those there were nestled at the foot of the two very active volcanoes, Agua and Fuego (Water and Fire), which dominated Guatemala City and were prone to spewing out ash fairly often. But no matter. I'd conquered pythons, cobras and coconuts: I wasn't about to let a couple of active volcanoes stop me from playing. Being British, I hoped I could fine somewhere where I would be accepted and fit in, and which wasn't too expensive or exclusive, so I began to make enquiries, both for golf and tennis.

At La Democracia, 1981. The Olmecoid Heads

It was good to get away from the city whenever possible, and the first place I visited was La Democracia, a hot Pacific slope town two hours from Guatemala City. It was slightly outside our radius, but as there would be a group of us, we were allowed to go. I wanted to see the huge basalt sculptures which are crude imitations of those Olmec Heads on Mexico's southern Gulf Coast, carved many centuries before. They were impressive, and I found the visit really interesting and enjoyable. Being eaten alive by mosquitos, less so.

One place I really wanted to go to, though, was Chichicastenango, to the north-west of Guatemala City. Surrounded by mountains and deep valleys, this rather remote town, noted for its narrow, cobbled streets and red tiled roofs, had an atmosphere all of its own, and was noted in particular for its huge, vibrant Thursday and Saturday markets of artefacts and brightly-coloured cloaks, cloth, and wall hangings. This sounded like heaven to me, but around Chichi (as it was called) was bandit territory and there had been some kidnappings in the area recently, so much to my dismay it was definitely out of bounds. I knew I could buy these items at the market in Guatemala City, but they were much more expensive and, some said, inferior. Whatever, it just wasn't the same and I was so disappointed.

It was good to get away at weekends. When we could, a group of us would head off the other way to Lake Amatitlán, about twenty miles south of the capital, where some friends of Chris, one of our UK-based, had a boat. This outing was safe, and do-able, we took a picnic to eat on the shores of the lake: the two children loved it. I enjoyed the trips on the lake itself, particularly when I was invited to take the helm. This was more like it. Although the area lacked the volcanic landscape around Guatemala City and to the west, it was picturesque enough, but those dratted mosquitos were a constant pest and I always came back covered in red bumps.

Above at Antigua: The ruins of La Merced Monastery

Below: The twin volcanoes of Agua y Fuego
(the third, Acatenango, is hidden to the right)

My only other outing before I had to leave was to Antigua with my American hairdresser and his wife. Once a capital of Guatemala and brimming with colonial and ecclesiastical relics, Antigua lay at the foot of the three volcanoes, Agua, Fuego and Acatenango, in a stunning setting. Despite having suffered earthquakes, floods, volcanic eruptions, and even being completely abandoned at one time, it had always bounced back, mainly because of the pride of its inhabitants. I loved it here, especially the ruins of La Merced Monastery, destroyed in an earthquake in 1773. I really hoped to visit often as there was so much to see. But it was not to be.

I only went a few times during the day into the old part of Guatemala City. It looked fascinating, but the military were everywhere and it was considered prudent to keep out of their way.

As with the Philippines, a strict curfew was in force here in Guatemala too, which ruled out any late-night visits to restaurants, cinemas or the theatre. I stayed mostly in the modern residential suburbs which were really quite nice, especially near where I lived. This was where the upper echelons of society lived, and where secluded avenues were lined with very elegant houses, like our Residence, set in lush, tropical gardens. I wasn't far, either, from a relatively modern shopping complex, where I could buy most things if I hunted around. Life was quite good, in fact - considering.

On one occasion, I got a ticket to a fantastic Saturday evening marimba concert held in a small theatre nearby. I love the sound of the marimba, Guatemala's national instrument, which looks like an extended xylophone with large wooden pipes. The earliest instruments used increasingly large gourds to obtain its distinctive sound, but all the modern ones use wood. Apparently, the marimba became very popular in the 1940's, when musicians like Glen Miller used it in his compositions.

The more I got to know the ropes, the better life was

The marimba, Guatemala's national instrument

becoming, but I was still reliant on buses, taxis, other people, or shank's pony to get around, and couldn't wait to get my own "wheels" as soon as possible. Sorting out the paperwork seemed to be taking an age, probably because I was a member of the Consulate-General and the authorities were just being difficult. Who knows? But once I had my car, I could go more or less where I wanted within our radius, taking people with me for a change to repay the favours.

"Mozzies"

Those mosquitos never seemed to be far away, and they seemed to like me in particular, despite smothering myself in repellent and taking anti-malaria tablets.

At the end of August, I began to feel quite unwell and was admitted to the local private clinic, where it was thought I had contracted malaria. One minute I was freezing cold and wrapped up in foil blankets, the other I was boiling hot, steaming and was surrounded by ice packs. It wasn't very pleasant, I have to say, and at one stage I was convinced I was going mad when the doctor came into the room with his trousers rolled up, and the nurse had her uniform tucked into her knickers. Looking down, I saw my slippers floating by under the bed. Very strange! What I didn't know was that there had been a flash flood, and as the ground floor of the hospital, which is where my room was, was down a slope, the whole floor had been flooded. Despite the inconvenience, I was relieved to know I wasn't going completely round the bend after all.

I was in the hospital for six days, during which time I had various unpleasant tests which seemed to point not to malaria but to a serious kidney infection. The doctors prescribed antibiotics and I was discharged, still not completely better, and still not knowing exactly what was the matter with me. To this day I have never found out what had made me so ill as the hospital was supposed to send my medical records to me, but they didn't, so I suppose they were destroyed.

When I got back to the UK, The Office was to send me to the Hospital for Tropical Diseases where, after yet more tests, it was decided that it wasn't malaria after all, and that the hospital diagnosis had probably been correct. But I'll never know for sure.

Not feeling one hundred per cent, but well enough to carry on, I went back to work. My colleagues were very concerned, but I was determined. This is what I wanted and had to do.

All Hell breaks Loose

I had only been back at work a few days when all hell broke loose as Belize declared it would become Independent on 21 September 1981, just three weeks away. The Belizeans and British had hoped, before Belizean Independence Day, to broker a non-aggression pact with Guatemala, under which the Guatemalans would drop their claim to Belize in exchange for access to Belize's Caribbean ports and offshore islands. But talks had broken down in August. Guatemala closed its borders with Belize, shut down its Consulates there, and immediately summoned Michael (this was a fairly regular occurrence) for a meeting with the Guatemalan Foreign Minister. Michael knew he would be in for yet another tongue-lashing, but was resigned to it and off he went.

When he came back, he was ashen.

"Gill, could you please ask all the UK-based to come to my office now", he said.

This I did, and it was then that he broke the news that Guatemala had broken off diplomatic relations with Britain. We were all being expelled, the Consulate-General shut down, the locally-employed dismissed, and we UK-based had just three days in which to do all this as we were to leave Guatemala on 11 September 1981.

It was arranged that the Swiss Embassy, under the Swiss Interests Section, would look after our affairs after we left (for which we paid them). One UK-based officer would be allowed to stay on for a few more days to assist them, but after that it was up to them to sort out our leases, arrange onward transfer of baggage and air freight, sell cars, and generally tidy up all the loose ends.

I remember we just stood there in stunned silence. Neither Michael, nor any of us, had expected this. He then asked if I would get the locally employed staff together as he needed to tell them too, but this he wanted to do on his own. When he came back to his office he was extremely upset. I made him a cup of coffee, shut the door, and left him alone until he felt able to face us all again.

At this time, we also learned that a bomb had been detonated outside our new Consulate-General building, blowing out all the windows. Whether the perpetrator(s) thought we have moved in already, we don't know, but fortunately for us, we hadn't.

Closing Down

The next three days were absolutely dreadful. There was so much to do, details of which I cannot relate, but we UK-based stayed at the Consulate pretty well all of the time, snatching the odd hour of sleep when we could, and living off the meals the hotel sent up to us.

The locally employed went home to their families each evening, even though they wanted to stay. We were particularly concerned about our excellent Commercial Officer, Armando. He was late 50's I guess, had worked for us for many years, and was married to a Guatemalan, but most worrying of all, he was a Belizean Citizen. We just didn't know what was going to happen to him, and I still don't know to this day how he fared after we left.

I can't describe the feelings of gratitude and admiration we all felt for our local staff. They were facing unemployment, uncertainty, difficulty in find new jobs maybe, but they remained loyal to us right up to the end and I would imagine they would have continued to do so for as long as it took. They were absolutely amazing.

When in a Mission abroad, our collective lives were run, to a certain extent, by our beloved DSP (Diplomatic Service Procedure). Whatever query arose, the answer could be found in one of the 21 or so (I forget how many) Volumes, under for example Vol 1, Chapter 11, Section XV, subsection (iii). We were now in uncharted territory, and nearly every aspect of our closure required an answer to our question, but having to look up DSP each time was taking an awfully long time, so I remember Michael, in utter exasperation and desperation, finally being driven to send a curt message to London to the effect that "For goodness sake stop quoting DSP. We don't have time to look it up. You do it, and just send us the answer." This seemed to work a treat, and we were able to press on much more quickly after that.

Thinking out of the box became our motto and on occasions we had to take on some rather unusual tasks. I will never forget standing at the bottom of the Residence garden at 1 am, in the pouring rain (it being the rainy season), trying to light a brazier, with no success whatsoever, as our shredder had broken down. So much for my training in the Guides. I still wasn't feeling very well at all. Perhaps I can add pneumonia to the list, I thought. But I just had to grit my teeth and get on with it.

One of my most frightening moments came, however, when I went to collect some urgent documents for Michael from an office in downtown Guatemala City. I drove one of our cars, collected what I needed, and was just leaving the carpark when I was stopped by a soldier who had recognize the car by the number plate. With his rifle, bayonet attached, pointed at me, he ordered me to get out of the car and stand up against a wall. He then approached me, rested the bayonet on my neck, and started haranguing me over Belize, Britain, us - anything he could think of. I was petrified and at one point really thought he might shoot me, or at least thrust the bayonet into my throat. But I had to keep calm, not show I was afraid, but not be confrontational either, so I just keep quiet and looked at the floor. However, not before I had looked briefly into his eyes. Never have I seen such hatred in a person, nor do I ever want to again. It was terrifying. I don't know how long this lasted: it seemed an eternity, but it could only have been a few minutes. Eventually, he took the rifle away, motioned for me to get back into the car, gave me a hefty shove in the back as I did so, and stood there whilst I drove away. I could see him watching me leave in my mirror.

I was shaking as I drove back to the office. When I told Michael what had happened, he was horrified. We talked it through, but he had enough on his plate and whatever he did would only have made the situation worse, so we agreed we should just let it go. But I can't ever forget it.

Packing Up

The wives were as shocked and upset as we were, but they managed to remain calm and were a rock to us all. Dennis went home now and then to check on his family, as it was important to keep the children safe and unaware of what was happening. The wives got on with packing up as best they could, and I know it was particularly harrowing for Mary as she had to mothball the Residence (which we were keeping) and prepare all her staff, save for the caretaker, for a less than secure future.

We three singles, Gordon, Jo and me, had to manage the best we could on our own.

I was able to get home twice: once for three hours or so to sort out my flat and pack up my air freight and carry-on suitcases; and again, after our farewell reception on our last night. I didn't have time to sort out my other belongings. The Swiss would have to do that. All I could do was get my personal items together and decide what I was taking home with me and what would be sent on to my next posting as air freight, whenever and wherever that would be. Photographs were one of my main priorities. Everything else could be replaced, but these couldn't, so I stuffed packets of transparencies in with everything I would need as soon as I got back to the UK, and had to keep bouncing up and down on my two cases to get them shut.

The car was a bit of a problem. The paperwork still hadn't been completed for me to buy it, so I sent word to my predecessor that the sale was off. She was not pleased, as it meant she now had to look for another suitable buyer, but the situation was beyond my control, so I'm afraid that was the way it had to be.

Above: Frantically packing up (one last photo for the archive)

Below: Putting a brave face on things.
The saddest farewell reception of all. The Consulate-General staff at the Residence
just before our departure (Michael is on the right, I'm third on the right)

The "Silver Greyhound"

The emblem of the Queen's Messengers is a silver greyhound. During Charles 11's exile, he appointed four trusted men to carry messages to Royalist troops in England, and as a sign of their authority, he broke four silver greyhounds off a bowl familiar to royal courtiers, and gave one to each man. From that date, the silver greyhound became the symbol of the Corps of Queen's [King's] Messengers.

Just to explain further. The safe passage of Diplomatic Baggage is guaranteed by the Vienna Convention. The Bag is closed by a special seal and has its own passport. It cannot be X-rayed, opened or weighed, does not go in the hold, and must remain with the QM in the passenger cabin at all times.

By early afternoon on the third day we were all absolutely exhausted, but had more or less completed what we needed to do. The result was nearly 300 kgs of Diplomatic Bags, and Jim Hollis, one of our QM's, was sent out to take it all back to London.

I was tasked with going to the airport to help Jim and Gordon deliver the Bags onto the Eastern Airlines flight to Miami (there were no direct flights to the UK), where it would be transferred onto a British Airways flight to London. We loaded all the Bags into the transit van, piled in ourselves, and off we set.

Normally, the official car was allowed to go up to the aircraft steps as the planes were always parked out on the tarmac, but not this time. When we arrived, the military ordered us to take all the Bags out of the car and carry or drag them, in the heat of the day, the 200 yards or so to the aircraft. As we were doing this, the soldiers lined up and jeered at us. I can't tell you how humiliating this was, and memories of that afternoon have stayed with me all these years. The Bags were so heavy, and I was still fairly weak from being ill but, like Jim and Gordon, I struggled on as best I could. When we eventually got to the aircraft steps, we had to haul all the Bags up into the plane ourselves and, once inside, a soldier told us to put them all on one side. By now the plane was quite delayed, but the Captain was very understanding. He knew the score. When he came into the cabin to see where we had stowed the Bags, though, he said he couldn't fly like that as the plane was lop-sided, so whilst the soldier harangued us even more, we had to re-stow them until it was safe to take off. The passengers, who were mainly American, did their best to try to help us, but were ordered to sit down. Eventually, the weight was distributed evenly and the plane was ready to depart. I hung on to Jim, wishing so much that I could go with him, but Gordon and I had to say goodbye. Jim gave me a big kiss, wished us well, and we went back onto the tarmac, to yet more jeering, and stood watching as his plane disappeared from view. The insults continued as we made our way back to our waiting car, but by that time I don't think either of us cared any more.

Once back at the Consulate General, Michael was furious. Jim was appalled at our treatment, too, and I gather a formal complaint was lodged when he got back to London.

Jim became a very good friend of mine over the years. On occasions he would come out to where I was posted, and we would talk over old times. When I was back in London, if he was there briefly too, and there was time, he'd take me out for a pub lunch. We kept in touch until he died. I can never thank him enough, nor can Gordon I imagine, for all he did for us that day. His strength and calmness got us through that afternoon and from that moment on, I always thought of Jim as my "Silver Greyhound in shining armour."

Michael and Mary wanted to hold a small get-together for us all on our last evening. It was so depressing going to that beautiful Residence and seeing it all under dust sheets. Only one room was uncovered so we could have our drinks there. The locally employed were invited too, of course, with their wives if they wanted to come, but many didn't. I think they were just too upset.

We all strove very hard to put a brave face on things, but inevitably there were tears when we came to say our last goodbyes. After that, we all went home to prepare for our departure the next day.

The Final Humiliation

It had been decided, by London I think, though I may be wrong, that we would leave in convoy with our heads held high, and not just slink away unnoticed. Not much chance of that anyway. It was big news and the press were out in force.

Our suite at the hotel had been shut down, so our Consulate cars came to pick us up from our homes and take us and our luggage to the Residence, from where we would be setting off in close convoy, with the transit van with all the luggage following immediately behind. We all squashed into our official cars and headed off to the airport, the press, who had got wind of our departure, close on our heels.

It was a rather hair-raising drive, but when we arrived the military were there as usual, but this time there was a crowd too, and not all well-wishers. The wives and children were ushered straight through into the departure lounge, but we UK-based were taken aside, with our suitcases, and were ordered to empty the contents into one large pile. The Guatemalan officials then took great delight in rummaging through all our personal belongings, scattering them all over the place so that they were all mixed up. We were then told to repack our cases, which meant we just had to grab the nearest clothes to hand, whether there were ours or not, stuff them in as best we could, and take them to the check-in desk where they were sent to the aircraft. At least we didn't have to carry them out to the aircraft this time, as with the Diplomatic Bags. I for one was thankful for small mercies!

By this time, take-off had been delayed quite a bit. After the fiasco with the Diplomatic Bags, I'm sure Eastern Airlines would have been warned that there was likely to be trouble, but the Captain said he would wait for us, however long it took, which he did. When we climbed aboard, we couldn't believe the reception we got. It seemed nearly all the passengers were American, whether by coincidence or design I don't know: if there were any Guatemalans on board, they wisely kept a very low profile. The passengers cheered, hugged us, clapped us on the back, queued to shake our hands. To a man (and woman), I remember there were tears streaming down all our faces. It was overwhelming, and quite unexpected. The Captain came into the cabin to see how we were, champagne corks popped, nibbles were handed round and we were shown to our seats, which we had together. After we had got settled, we fastened our seat belts and the plane took off. For the rest of the journey, save for the odd friendly remark, the passengers left us alone to come to terms with what had happened.

I didn't look out of the window as we left. I never wanted to see that country again.

Our Stay in Miami

By this time The Office were well aware of the state we were all in, so the powers that be had decided that we could stay for three nights (at Government expense) in a very good hotel on the beach in Miami, before catching our British Airways flight back to Heathrow. I know I was so grateful for this breathing space, as I'm sure were my colleagues too. I'm not certain exactly where we were, but it was lovely. Michael and Mary were booked in separately at the luxury Fontainebleau Hotel not far away, to give them much needed peace and quiet away from everything. They did come to see how we were all settling in, and to get their belongings, but mainly they stayed on their own, which we quite understood.

The first thing we all had to do was sort out the baggage. As we were in rooms next door to each other, we put what we had stuffed in our cases in piles and went from room to room trying to find our own things. No point in being bashful: by the time we'd finished, we knew exactly what each other had! Eventually we ended up with what was ours and could start to relax at last.

I think most of us slept for much of the time, or just lazed around by the pool doing absolutely nothing. I know I did. The family and couples stayed together: we three singles met up for a drink in the evenings. Otherwise, we spent the time on our own, which suited me fine. I needed to get myself together for the journey home.

Cars came to collect us from the hotels on the third day and we headed off to Miami airport for the flight back to London. At Heathrow, I said my goodbyes to the family and wives, who went their separate ways, and went with the others in official cars straight to The Office for a "de-briefing" with my Personnel Officer.

We were home at last.

Sadly, as is often the way with life in the Diplomatic Service, once you leave a Post you never see your colleagues again. They are either posted elsewhere, or their home or mid-tour leave doesn't coincide with yours. No matter how hard you try to keep in touch, it's impossible with so many people. Occasionally you may be lucky enough to bump into someone when back in London, and I've still got a few very close friends from my Foreign Office days, but that is all.

Save for bumping into Gordon once in London, I never saw any of my colleagues again.

Michael Joseph Wilmshurst died on 12 October 2006, a much

loved, respected and admired Head of Mission, both by us UK-based and our locally employed alike.

Would I return to Guatemala? I don't know. The civil war ended in 1996 and the country is different, though still not that safe to what it was then. The question of Belize still rumbles on, a bit like with Spain and Gibraltar. Without doubt the scenery is magnificent and there are some fascinating areas to explore. Were I younger, I think perhaps I would, but I would need to lay a lot of ghosts to rest first.

PART SEVEN

THE GREEN, GREEN GRASS OF HOME

When I got back to The Office, Miss Lofting was waiting to see me. She was concerned to find me in such a state and wanted to know all that had happened. We had a long chat, after which she said I could go straight up to Mum and Dad's in Pontesbury for a week before starting work again.

Before I went, however, there were a few things to sort out. The Department would make an appointment for me at the Hospital for Tropical Diseases to try to find the cause of my illness, but the most pressing problem was that I had nowhere to live now I was back in London, so arrangements were made for me to rent a single room at the Civil Service hostel in Castle Lane, between Victoria Street and Birdcage Walk, until I went on my next posting, which was already being considered.

I said goodbye to Miss Lofting, caught a taxi to Victoria Bus Station, rang Mum and Dad to let them know what time my coach would be arriving at Shrewsbury, and settled down to wait for my bus to turn up. After about half an hour it arrived, my cases were loaded into the luggage section, and off I went.

I can't tell you how glad I was to see Mum and Dad again. I just clung to them, sobbing. They were shocked to see how awful I looked, but once back at Pontesbury, with their loving care and Mum's cooking, I began to feel much better. It was September, lovely weather, and the autumn colours looked a picture. We went out for walks in the countryside, had pub lunches, and did some shopping in Shrewsbury. We just stayed close for that whole week.

It was then time for me to get back on the National coach and head for London. Mum and Dad waved me off from the bus station, with mixed feelings I'm sure, but I promised to come back to see them as often as I could at weekends. I hated to leave them, but knew I had a job to do, and the sooner I got back into the swing of things again, the better.

The Waiting Game

When I arrived at Victoria, I was able to go straight to the hostel and settle into the single room that was waiting for me. The hostel occupied quite a few of the old properties in Castle Lane, and my room was on the second floor of a big house on the corner which was used purely for female Civil Servants. It wasn't large, was a bit of a squash with my suitcases, and meant I shared a bathroom and loo with the other girls on my floor, but it served its purpose. I ate most of my meals in the canteen, for which I paid extra, and occasionally went into the communal lounge, next to the laundry room, but my fellow Civil Servants were curious as to why I was there, and I didn't feel like telling them, so consequently I spent a lot of my time on my own.

The best thing about being in Castle Lane was that it wasn't far from The Office, and the lovely walk across St James's Park each morning set me up for the day. It was also handy for the shops, of course, being just off Victoria Street, but it was a quiet and lonely area once they had closed on a Saturday evening.

I didn't have a permanent job, and so spent my time in the typing pool or being sent to work temporarily for Heads of Department if their PA's were away or ill. I went home often to see Mum and Dad at weekends, caught up with Sheila and family, and met up with my friends, mainly Pam and Marie, whenever I could.

At last, in December, I received news that I was being posted to Chile to work as PA/HMA in February. I was elated. Yet another country I had always wanted to visit. I just loved South America so much, and couldn't wait to get back.

I read up as much as I could about Chile, and saw to my delight that it was a great place for sport. As my golf clubs were in my heavy baggage in Guatemala, I hadn't played for ages, save a round with Dad on the municipal course at Shrewsbury now and then (he was learning), and yearned to be reunited with my clubs once more.

I also saw that you could go skiing in the Andes too. I fancied trying my hand at this, so I booked a course of lessons on the dry ski slope at Woolwich. This wasn't a vast success as I was afraid of falling, but I tried hard, and resolved to crack this sport when I actually got out there. I never did. I turned out to be hopeless: skiing just wasn't for me, I discovered.

February came around quickly, so yet again I found myself caught up in the frenzy of pre-Posting activities. I attended briefings; packed up my airfreight; liaised with The Office over my Chilean Visa; got up to date with vaccinations; took out a Foreign Office Car Loan, which had to be paid back monthly over the duration of my posting, to buy a new Escort which would be shipped out to Chile; purchased skiing equipment (that turned out to be a waste of money!) which meant even less space in my small room; and of course – went on a shopping spree to the Army & Navy. By mid-February, I was ready to leave.

I spent a last weekend with Mum and Dad, and on 17 February 1982 boarded my British Airways flight to Schipol where, yet again as BA didn't fly to that part of South America, I transferred onto a KLM flight bound for Santiago.

I was on the move again!

PART EIGHT

CHILE
1982-1985

Above: 1982. The British Embassy, Avenida La Concepcion, Providencia, with our guards outside

Below: The Residence at Las Condes

Above: My flat, Apartamento 62 (6th floor),
Avda Suecia 879, Providencia

Below: Not long after I had arrived! At Cerro San Cristobal,
Parque Metropolitano, Providencia, Santiago

My Arrival

Of all my postings, Chile has to be my favourite. The other countries have each had their special memories (good and bad), wonderful scenery, fascinating culture, amazing chances to explore, but for me Chile beats them all. I've found this chapter hard to write too, but for completely different, happy reasons. I did so much: travel, activities, photography – it's been hard to know what to put in and what to leave out. I just hope I've got the balance right.

Ring of Fire

Flying into Santiago over the Andes was breathtaking. The sun glistened on the snow-capped mountain peaks, which appeared to go on forever. Volcanoes seemed to be dotted everywhere, and the narrow coastal plain, with its deserts to the north and fertile valleys to the south, edged the lower darkness of that immense mountain range like a gold and green ribbon meandering into the distance.

When I knew I was coming to Chile, one of my first thoughts was that I'd be within the Ring of Fire again, as my three previous postings had been. I love geography, and this enormous, horseshoe shaped Pacific basin, with its continuous tectonic plate movements, fascinates me.

In the Philippines, Peru and Guatemala, I'd experienced minor earthquakes, nothing too major, and been surrounded by active, or not quite so active, volcanoes. I wondered what would happen here. Chile still holds the record for the largest earthquake ever recorded – in Valdivia in 1960. Time would tell. As it did.

But for now, I was spellbound by what I saw from the air, and just knew (and prayed too), that the next two and half (three as it turned out) years were going to be so different from what I'd just been through.

The Pinochet Regime

I'd read all I could about Chile before I left London. I would be there during the time of General Augusto Pinochet Ugarte and, yet again, there was martial law, and a curfew. A bit like Guatemala, really, I thought, and standing at the airport, although this was Chile and not the country next door, I felt like Paddington Bear with a luggage label round my neck saying "To be delivered to an Undemocratic, Unstable Country". However, I hoped it would be nowhere near as bad as Guatemala and, if it was, then I felt I was better prepared to cope.

I tried to understand what it would be like living in Chile under the Pinochet regime. Forewarned is forearmed, I felt, though I wouldn't really know till I got there.

From what I'd learned, Pinochet, a relatively unknown army officer, barely three weeks after the President Salvador Allende had appointed him Commander-in-Chief of the armed forces, led a brutal coup on 11 September (that date again) 1973 that overthrew the President, who committed suicide as the air force attacked the presidential palace. During the following months the armed forces became even more barbaric as they put the country in lock-down, banned political parties, imprisoned political dissidents, and executed and tortured many activists, particularly during General Sergio Arellano Stark's Caravan of Death, when at least 3000 died or disappeared. Trying to ascertain the whereabouts or fate of *Los Desaparecidos* occupied our minds greatly.

Pinochet had no qualms about increasing his personal power and bank balance, despite trying to portray himself as incorruptible, but he also tried to re-shape Chilean society. He believed in free-market capitalism, and completely transformed the economy, getting rid of government regulations, encouraging foreign investment, selling off most of the state companies and privatizing health and pensions plans. When I was in Peru on one occasion, I did hear a comment "how we wish we had a Pinochet here", alluding to the economic success Chile was having at the time.

After I left Chile, a powerful vote against him forced Pinochet to hand over power to Patricio Aylwin, but at the same time ensuring that former Presidents, like himself, could continue in a congressional role which would also give them immunity against prosecution.

Firmly believing in this immunity, Pinochet travelled widely, even coming to London for back surgery in October 1998 and meeting Margaret Thatcher, who firmly believed Britain owed Chile a great debt of gratitude over the Falklands. I shall nail my colours to the mast and say I agree.

However, he subsequently found himself under house arrest on 16 October 1998 at 20 Devonshire Place, Marylebone, in London, on the orders of the Spanish judge, Báltazar Garzón, who sought his extradition to Spain as part of an investigation into Spain's *Desaparecidos* during the 1973 coup. The British courts rejected Pinochet's claims to immunity and ruled that he could be extradited to Spain, but things never reached that point as, because of his poor health, Jack Straw allowed him to return to Chile after 503 days of arrest

Pinochet died in 2006.

As I was about to discover, the Chileans and British got on very well, mainly because of our shared ancestry. In the 1800's a great many Europeans – notably, English, Scottish, Irish, Italians and Germans – settled in Chile and played an important role in shaping her into the country she is today. The Scottish in particular, who came over as engineers, left their mark and there was a thriving Caledonian Society throughout the whole country. We Brits seemed to be much liked, and as members of the British Embassy, life for us in Chile under Pinochet was safe, comfortable, and enjoyable. We could move around the country freely (which I did), and there was an excellent social and cultural scene, with very good theatres, museums, art galleries and an Opera House. I remember a superb evening when I went there to see a concert given by the Three Tenors, which was magical. I enjoyed strolling through the beautiful parks and exploring the downtown areas, and I just knew that this time I would be lucky and would have a fantastic posting.

From an official point of view, however, the Embassy's role was slightly tricky as HMG wanted to maintain a good working relationship with the Chileans, but at the same time not appear too friendly, which would have given legitimacy to the Pinochet regime. A fine line had to be trod.

The Embassy

I was met on arrival by our Admin Officer and taken straight to the Embassy to meet my colleagues and my Ambassador, John Moore Heath. He was an expert on engravings, loved to collect stamps, and he and his wife, Patricia, proved to be a most engaging couple. He was a great person to work for, quiet, unassuming and considerate, and I was sorry that he was on the verge of retirement and we would only have a month or so together.

Here in Chile, although ours was considered a medium-sized Embassy, there was much to do, and all sections were very busy. We got on well, and I liked Alison, the young Chancery PA, who proved to be a good friend.

I can't comment on the actual work I did, as you already know, save in very general terms, but suffice it to say I found it interesting, exciting and fulfilling, all at the same time. I had a nice office to myself, adjoining that of the Ambassador's, at the back of the Embassy. I bought a large pot plant to put on top of my filing cabinet (to soothe my nerves if needed), and soon got the place ship-shape. With a busy job like mine, I couldn't bear, nor can I still, to work in a mess! A sign of great inefficiency, I always feel.

Again, I had to find my own accommodation and so I stayed for three weeks at the Hotel Orly, not far from the Embassy, whilst I was looking. It was very comfortable, but I needed to have a place of my own. Luckily, with the help of Diana in Admin, it didn't take me long to find the most superb flat on the 6th floor of a relatively modern, well-constructed block in Avenida Suecia, in the affluent suburb of Providencia, not quite so exclusive as Las Condes, but desirable nonetheless, and only fifteen minutes' drive from the Embassy.

There were four flats to each floor. Mine was at the back on the right-hand side, and I had superb views up the valley to the ski slopes of El Colorado one way, and over Providencia to downtown Santiago the other. The layout was ideal, with a large lounge-diner, two bedrooms, a good bathroom, smallish kitchen with a utility area off it, but what thrilled me most of all was the terrace, which was the whole width of the flat and which had a rattan screen I could pull across when it got too hot. I spent hours there and loved it. My neighbours were friendly, although I never got to know them well, but the two Chilean *porteros* (janitors) were so kind and helpful, and would do anything for me. I found it hard to understand their dialect at times as Chileans tend to eat the end of their words, but we had many a laugh together.

My air freight from the UK arrived, but I never saw the air freight I had packed in Guatemala. It just disappeared, which meant I lost all the new clothes I had bought in Miami with Pat, plus a lot of other prized possessions. Enquiries were made of the Swiss, who had definitely delivered the cases to the carrier, but after that – nothing. I was fearful for my heavy baggage, but that arrived unscathed and I was reunited once more with my precious golf clubs. I didn't have long to wait either before my car was delivered, shiny and new with, miraculously, no dents or scratches after its long sea journey. I was really enjoying work and was getting to know my way around Santiago reasonably well in such a short time. Life was definitely looking rosy.

I Don't Believe It!

I'm a great fan of Victor Meldrew in "One foot In The Grave". I think he's a brilliant character and I have used his famous uttering quite a few times, mostly in my Venice books. It just seems to sum up some of the situations I find myself in somehow.

All was going swimmingly when, just over six weeks after I had arrived – **The Falklands Conflict** started on 2 April 1982 (not a war, as war was never officially declared).

I don't believe it, I thought. Shades of Guatemala and Belize all over again. Disputes seemed to be following me around wherever I went. But this time it was different. Again, I can't say anything about what I did, but being involved in the Falklands conflict proved to be one of the most interesting, challenging and personally satisfying chapters of my whole career with the Diplomatic Service. Despite the gravity of the situation, I was in my element.

From a general perspective, overnight Britain, and by extension us in the Embassy, became the <u>very, very</u> best thing since all the sliced bread in the <u>whole wide world</u>. Chile and Argentina had not always been the best of friends, and if we could give them a bloody nose, good for us.

Working in the Embassy was like working for a pop star (would that my beloved Cliff were there too!). Sacks of mail kept arriving, filled with letters of support, small coins, 5 peso or larger notes, and offers of help from every quarter. There was even a queue outside the Embassy gates of Chileans wanting to join our Forces in the Falklands. It was unbelievable, and very, very touching. All the newspapers and television programmes were full of the conflict, and the media were kept abreast of what was happening through the press releases that we handed out.

On a personal note, I was particularly concerned as the love of my life from ORIANA was now in CANBERRA and was down in the Falklands too. I feared for his safety, but we managed to exchange a few, very short messages just to reassure each other that we were safe.

In the Embassy, we worked away steadily long into the night until the conflict ended with the Argentine surrender on 14 June 1982, returning the Falkland Islands (or Malvinas as the Argentines called them) to British control once more. We all heaved a sigh of relief, and began picking up where we had left off, both at work and in our personal lives. Slowly things got back to normal at last.

My Ambassador could now continue planning for his retirement, which had been curtailed because of the conflict. He would be leaving in July, and his successor, who was to be John Hickman, would arrive in September.

Plans were made and farewell receptions and parties abounded. The Ambassador here had a social secretary, Elspeth Errazzuriz, with whom I got on brilliantly, so we worked side by side on guest lists, sending out invitations, receiving acceptances, making endless telephone calls, and in the end it was all a great success and John and Patricia Heath left in style.

Time then to welcome our new Ambassador, John Hickman, and his wife Jennifer. He was a different character entirely to John Heath, but we got on well and I liked he and his wife.

He did, however, have one rather unusual habit: he took snuff and, it seemed, particularly when I was taking dictation. He would tip a small amount of snuff into "nature's snuff box" (between thumb and first knuckle) and snort away, blowing the residue straight over me, which would then cause

My Two Ambassadors

Above: John Moore Heath, CMG

Below: John Hickman presenting his Letters of Credence
(Credentials) to General Augusto Pinochet

me to have a violent fit of sneezing. The snuff also went over my clothes, and try as I might, sometimes the stain just wouldn't come out. His handkerchiefs were something else, but I tried not to look. I suppose it was fortunate that I quite liked the sweet aroma of the spices he used, but I never became enamoured of this habit. I just got on with my work and bought lots of tissues.

The Ambassador was also writing a book at the time he arrived in Santiago: "The Enchanted Islands: The Galapagos Discovered", which he finished just as I was leaving. His previous posting had been as Ambassador to Ecuador and these islands were a subject close to his heart. He asked me soon after he arrived if I would type a chapter of his book for him, to which I readily agreed. I found the subject fascinating, but as I had a busy job, I had to do this after work. That was fine, but when chapter after chapter kept appearing, I realized I was about to type his whole book for him - free. However, there were other things I wanted to do after work rather than type his book, and so in the end I asked him if Elspeth could do it. She agreed, but only if he payed her the going rate, which didn't go down too well at all. Never mind. Such is life! His shock didn't last long, and she finished the book for him. He was grateful for what I had done, though, and I received a signed copy, which I still have. It is a lovely book. Now I'm writing myself, how glad I am that I can type! Think of all the money I save!

The Ambassador and I got on well together, and I enjoyed working for him.

Sport

Now I had my golf clubs, I could at last get down to the important task of playing again and getting to know another course. How I'd missed it!

I applied immediately to join the prestigious Prince of Wales Golf and Country Club (POW) at Las Arañas, which nestled in the foothills of the Andes on the outskirts of Santiago. This was where most of the ex-pats went, and there were pitches for hockey, rugby and cricket, superb clay tennis courts, a large swimming pool and excellent bar and restaurant. After a brief interview with the Club Secretary (it was that sort of Club), I was accepted, and my sporting life began again in earnest. I can't remember the exact fees, but even though I got a small diplomatic discount, it was still rather expensive. However, for me membership was worth its weight in gold, and I spent many a happy hour there.

It was quite a long, picturesque course, with aromatic bushes and tall trees lining the fairways. I had another fantastic pro, Juan, and under him my golf continued to improve in leaps and bounds, so much so that I ended up winning most of the Club tournaments.

Being a Member of the POW also gave me the chance to play tennis and hockey once again. Craighouse School, an independent co-educational school with Chilean and British traditions, also had an Old Girls hockey team which played at the POW. I asked if I could join and they readily agreed, even though, at 37, I was older than the rest of the team. I should have been an ex-pupil or a relative of one to qualify, so I became a "temporary aunt", though no-one ever asked. We had an excellent coach, Rodrigo Hernandez, who worked us hard. We toured most winter weekends and were very successful, even winning the First League during my second year. Sadly, though, one place I couldn't go to with the team was Argentina, for obvious reasons. I gnashed my teeth, but it couldn't be helped.

A Busy Social Scene

Socially, life was hectic: Embassy lunches, outings, barbecues, dinners, official receptions, trips to the Club Hípico for an evening at the races, pints after work in the Irish pub near the

Embassy (excellent location!). It was hard to keep up at times and it's been difficult choosing what to write about, and what to leave out. I've had boyfriends at all my postings, but when you lead an itinerant life as I did, and they do too on some occasions, we were just "ships that passed in the night", so I won't go into details. Sorry!

One thing I loved to do was to leave the Embassy at 4.30 pm in our mini-bus, with one of our locally employed drivers, and those of us UK-based who could get away, and travel the two and a half hours to Valparaiso for the cocktail party held on board **HMS Endurance**, the British Arctic Survey ship, whenever she came into that port. The Ambassador and his wife travelled down in his official car. The ship called there every few months for RNR, and we were always invited. These receptions, usually held mid-week, were for Chilean Naval high-ranking Officers, the Mayor of Valparaiso, other civic dignitaries, and influential businessmen, and they were always wonderful occasions. We didn't normally get back to Santiago till the early hours, but since we didn't have to drive, and could therefore have the odd glass of bubbly or excellent Chilean wine, it didn't matter. Most of us snored all the way back and work next day was definitely a bit of a trial.

I became very involved with the Caledonian Society in Santiago, and much looked forward to their memorable Burns Night dinners, dances and various other get-togethers. It was a thriving Society, but I always found it somewhat strange to meet members with very Scottish surnames (McDonalds, McEwans, McGregors) who couldn't speak a word of English. Our First Secretary Commercial, Dennis Amy, and his wife Helen, were excellent Scottish dancers, so they formed a Scottish Dancing Team, of which I was a member as I'd done a fair amount of Scottish dancing in the past and loved it. I was partnered by Warwick Crampton, Second Secretary at the Australian Embassy, and we had such fun. We practiced hard, travelled down to Viña del Mar, near Valparaiso, to take part in their Burns Night, and were even invited to

The Prince of Wales Golf and Country Club

Above: the elegant Clubhouse entrance

Below: Craighouse Old Girls Hockey team, with coach Rodrigo Hernandez
(I'm far right, front row)

Above: Our Scottish Dancing Display Team (Warwick is on my left)

Below: In the glider, preparing for "lift off".

Enjoying time with my colleagues

Above: Christmas Day at our H of C's house, after a "proper" Christmas lunch, this time – no snipe or bats' wings here!

Below: Shopping near Valparaiso. Who could resist? Not me!

give a demonstration of Scottish Dancing at the International Dancing Competition in Santiago, which was very well received.

Ross, our Second Secretary Admin, was learning to be a glider pilot at post, so once he had obtained his Licence, I went up with him a few times. We only ventured into the foothills of the Andes, where the thermal currents were more gentle, but the silence, and soaring over this beautiful scenery like the condors in the distance, was both exhilarating and magical.

I had trips to the Concha y Toro vineyards every so often, and up to the ski slopes at Chillán, where I spent the majority of the time on my derrière!

There was a short spell in the Clínica Las Condes, for a minor operation under the excellent care of my surgeon, Dr Leontic, and my Embassy GP, Dr Juan-Pablo Vicuña, but otherwise I was well. I got to thinking, though, that if I had a signature tune it would have to be "I Left My heart in San Francisco". There are bits of me all over the place!

Mv Skorpios 1

When I was in Chile there was a wonderful little ship, **Skorpios 1**, which used to sail from Puerto Montt, through the Chilean fjords and down to the glacier San Rafael. Launched in 1978, she was only 164ft 1ins long (I'm not sure how they got the one inch), had two engines, four decks, maximum speed 10 knots, and could take 68 passengers. She had a simple wooden interior, and the cabins were basic. Copper plates covered her wooden hull as protection against the ice. It was difficult to get a cabin, but at Christmas 1984 I was lucky as the Ambassador was going away, and I could take a week's leave, so I immediately rang to see if there was a vacancy. There was, so I flew down to Puerto Montt and eagerly stepped on board. I will never, ever forget this trip. It was one of the most thrilling and enjoyable I've ever done. My fellow passengers were great, as was Captain Kochifas and his crew, who only spoke Spanish. The Chilean Lake District is stunning, and for one week we sailed in and out of tiny coves between the Isla Grande de Chiloé, which sheltered the fjords from the might of the Pacific Ocean, and mainland Chile. We moored at Chiloé and Castro and explored these two small towns; swam in thermal baths; and eventually arrived at the Laguna San Rafael, at the foot of the enormous glacier. There, we got into the two lifeboats to get closer to the foot of the it, which I must say was a bit hairy at one stage when huge chunks of ice kept breaking away, causing big waves which rocked our small lifeboats furiously. And when the mist came down, brought in with the changing tide, it nearly trapped us in pack ice. So much for health and safety! By this time we needed the celebratory glass of whisky on "2000 year old rocks"; before returning to the welcome decks of **Skorpios**. The barbecues on deck, consisting of huge *choros zapatos* (mussels), oysters and steak, were much looked forward to, as was the sumptuous buffet and riotous party on Christmas Day. I could have stayed there forever.

One thing that used to fascinate me was how we took on water and got the mussels. We would sail right up to a waterfall, extend a sort of metal bucket, and catch the water as it cascaded down; and to get the mussels, we would sail up to a cliff face, where the crew scraped them off with long rakes. A far cry from CANBERRA and ORIANA!

Captain Kochifas was interested in my former Merchant Navy career, and was quite willing to let me take the helm now and then in the wider channels. I was as happy as a sand boy, and didn't hit a single thing!

I see now that she was laid up in 2008, and from a very sad photo, is rotting against the shore at Puerto Montt. Now there is Skorpios 111, but I doubt she is anywhere near as intimate as her oldest sister.

Above: mv SKORPIOS

Below: Captain Kochifas holding court (me on right)

Above Left: Supernumerary First Mate Gillian Angrave taking the helm
Above Right: the seafood stall on the shore at Chiloé

Below: a novel way of taking on water

Above: Nearing the foot of the San Rafael glacier

Below: Hmmm. Getting a bit tricky.

Above: Preparing the oysters and mussels
for our mouth-watering barbecue

Below: Angrave of the Antarctic – well sort of!

My Travels Around South America

I'm a keen photographer, and whenever I got the chance, I was up and away, often on my own, indulging my passion for it. I managed to take some wonderful photographs (well I think so), and going through them again has brought back such happy memories. I'd love to describe in detail all my adventures, most of which I can still remember vividly, but there are far too many to describe here, so I've just picked out a few of the most memorable and enjoyable.

I flew up to Arica in the north of Chile, from where I went with a small tour group to the Parque Lauca, near the border with Bolivia. We got as far as the Lago Chungará, the highest lake in the world at 15,000 ft, but I suffered very badly with *soroche* and so we had to drop down a few thousand feet very quickly.

From Arica, I went by bus through the Atacama Desert, the driest in the world, to Iquique, then on to Calama and San Pedro de Atacama. The Ambassador had kindly arranged for me to visit the Chuquicamata copper mine, the world's largest open pit quarry, and be taken around by one of the managers there. The mine is vast: 2 miles wide, 3 miles long and 2,300 feet deep. It was such a great privilege, as well as being so interesting, to visit this single biggest contributor to Chile's finances. After that, a night at Calama and then on to the thermal hot springs and geysers at El Tatio, eventually catching the bus back to Santiago.

I went to **Rio de Janeiro** on a Bag run: and had a few days in Asunción, from where I spent two nights at the Iguazu Falls. Absolutely spectacular, if not a little frightening with the roar of all that water pouring into the gorge below.

I had a few days back in **Lima**, catching up with old friends, colleagues, and Dr Zapff, who was pleased to see me looking so much better and enjoying Chile. I even met the Ambassador, who was still there though coming to the end of his posting. As

I've said before, he was keen to know how I was and what I'd been doing, so we had a good chat.

I also paid a visit to **Ecuador**, staying with my opposite number in the Embassy in Quito, whom I didn't know and with whom I got on very well, who very kindly took me out and about on the weekend I was there. Unfortunately, there was no time to visit the Galapagos, but once back in Chile my Ambassador was keen to know how I'd got on.

Pam's Visits

Again, I've really enjoyed reading her diary summaries of her two visits to stay with me in Santiago.

On her first visit, she arrived on 25 February 1983, and her first two days were spent relaxing and I enjoyed showing her around the Prince of Wales Country Club, which she loved.

Our next adventure was to head down south. I'd managed to get eleven days leave as the Ambassador was away, so we decided to make the most of it. Early on 28 February, we loaded the car onto the overnight train down to Puerto Montt, the port where the Lake District meets the Pacific Ocean. Founded in 1853, it was an important port for the shipment of grains and the *alerce* (larch) timber, but these industries have moved elsewhere and now it's a transit port for southbound cruise ships and ferries.

We arrived at Puerto Montt just after mid-day the next day, after a pretty slow and noisy journey. I don't know how old the train was, but it was beautiful inside – just like travelling in Agatha Christie's day. All the woodwork was mahogany, with shiny brass fittings, and the bunks, though narrow, were fairly comfortable. Once we had off-loaded the car, we headed for the Vicente Perez Rosales Hotel, where we stayed one night before leaving the car in Puerto Montt and flying down to Punta Arenas (even now it isn't possible to drive all the way down there from Santiago). Established in 1848 as a penal colony and disciplinary centre for the military, in the late 19th and early 20th centuries Punta Arenas attracted thousands of Europeans fleeing from the horrors of World War 1 and trying to make their fortunes by sheep farming, gold and coal mining, and shipping.

We stayed only one night at the *Los Navegantes* Hotel before embarking on a four and a half hour bus ride to Puerto Natales, which is the starting off point for the Parque Nacional Torres del Paine. We negotiated a price for a driver to take us there the next day, but this meant we had to stay the night at the only lodging available, the Hotel Eberhard, a rather odd little place with no electricity or hot water, which made life a bit difficult. However, in true pioneering spirit, we soldiered on. Our driver collected us early from the hotel and off we set, two spare tyres lashed firmly to the roof of the car as the road was rough and treacherous and we would be miles from anywhere. We weren't fortunate enough to see the *Torres* in all their majesty because of the mist, but just being in such stunning surroundings was enough, our only companions being condors, *guanacos*, and now and then a *huemul* (the endangered South Andean deer).

Then back again to Punta Arenas, a night there before flying up to Puerto Montt to pick up the car and a drive back to Santiago. This took us five days, but we travelled through some beautiful scenery in Chile's Lake District, passing the Volcanoes Osorno and Villarica, and stopping off in Frutillar, Valdivia, Pucán and Chillán on the way.

Once home, we chilled out, went down to the coast, and shopped (what a surprise). I returned to work and Pam flew back on 15 March, after what we both agreed had been a fantastic trip.

Pam managed another, shorter, visit, arriving on 12 January 1985. This time we planned to go north as the Ambassador had arranged for us to visit Cerro Tololo, the AURA Inter-American

Above: Overnight train to Puerto Montt

Below: Travelling in style:
Pam and the luxurious interior.

Above: the colourful town of Punta Arenas

Below: The Monumento de Hernando de Magallanes in the main plaza. I'm following the tradition of kissing the foot, now worn shiny, to ensure I will return to Punta Arena. I haven't so far, but there's still time!

Above: Pam and me in the Parque Nacional Torres del Paine,
with the Torres sadly shrouded in mist

Below: With my new found guanaco friend (there are four camelids: in order of
size - llama, alpaca, guanaco and vicuña)

Above: The remote and inhospitable mountain road to reach the Observatorio.

Below: Cerro Tololo. The AURA Interamericano Observatorio

Observatorio high up in the Andes. We set off on the long, hot drive (I did all the driving) to La Serena, where we stayed the night before winding our way on dirt roads through the mountains and up to the Observatory.

We were welcomed warmly by one of the astrologers when we arrived, who gave us a most fascinating and comprehensive tour, explaining everything in great detail as we went around. I think he was pleased to see two new faces! We thanked him profusely, said goodbye, and began our descent of the mountains.

On the way down, we had just stopped in the tiny village of Rivadavia to get something to eat when we heard a terrible rumble and the mountains started to move around us. Yet another earthquake, which we later found out had been Force 8 on the Richter Scale. I'd been in a few before, but this was the most terrifying. The shop shelves started to fall down and there were tins flying everywhere. I knew we just had to get out of there and get down to the bottom of the mountains to safety as fast as we could. We leapt into the car and started our descent. The loose scree on the mountain-sides was sliding down all around us, and the air was filled with so much dust that I could hardly see where I was driving. Poor Pam hung on for dear life as we careered down the dirt road, round hairpin bends, at full speed. Well done, little Escort. You held up well in the circumstances. So did you, Pam!

We were nervous wrecks when we finally made it to the bottom of the mountains, but at least the tremors had stopped. We headed for the Hotel Yachting at Tongoy, where we were booked in. We needed a stiff drink, and certainly had one! But the hotel was awful, so we decided to stay only one night and make our way back to Santiago a bit earlier than planned.

Once home, we chose to take the bus down to Valparaiso for the day to give me a break from driving. Our Consul there, Clem

Kenrick, had broken his hip, so we paid him a brief visit in hospital, had a look around the port, and caught the bus back.

Back in Santiago, the tremors continued, but nothing major. On 26 January Pam flew home after yet another exciting stay.

Earthquakes

I was to be caught up in another strong earthquake in Santiago a few months later. We were always experiencing minor tremors, but this one was much stronger. I was having a lie-in one Sunday when the earth started to shake. By this time, I had a little budgie, Pablo Perez, and I always knew when a quake was about to happen as he went berserk in his cage. Animals can sense these things much sooner than humans.

I looked out the window and saw the buildings in front of me moving about three feet in either direction. It is the law that high-rise structures, in particular, are built to withstand earthquakes, though as has been proved in the past, this hasn't always been the case, through corruption, incompetence, short-cuts – whatever. But the fact that my apartment block was still standing was a good sign.

I leapt out of bed, snatched up the budgie's cage, quickly found my "grab bag" and went under the table. Wherever I've been on my postings, we've always had to have a "grab bag" which we keep replenished with a bottle of water, dry muesli bars or such like, torch, transistor radio and lots of spare batteries. No mobile phones in those days. The quake must only have lasted a few minutes, but I stayed where I was for quite a while. Had it have gone on for longer, I'd have made a dash for the stairs. It really is a frightening experience swaying back and forth with no way to stop it.

Fortunately, the telephones were still working, so we all rang each other to make sure we were safe. When I got to the Embassy the next day there was a crack on the outside wall. But at least it was still standing too and was safe to occupy, so back to work as usual.

All Good Things Must Come to an End

And so it was with Chile. I'd been in this beautiful country three years instead of my original two and a half, as I'd been asked to extend for six months to fit in with leave, new arrivals, and the Ambassador's travel plans, to which I readily agreed.

The one big downside, though, was that I hadn't seen Mum and Dad in all this time. There was no mid-tour leave in Chile, although we all felt that because of the distance from the UK, and the psychological barrier of the Andes, tours should have been two eighteen months with home leave in between. I'd written to them every week, except when travelling, and Mum, with Dad's bit on the end, had written to me each week too. Our personal and Unclassified mail, both to and from London, went in sealed Diplomatic Bags also, but in the aircraft hold and not with the Queen's Messenger. Our Admin Officer took them to, or collected them from, the airport, and we couldn't wait for our own letters to arrive. The Embassy became a very silent place when that happened!

Mum, Dad and I had had a few telephone conversations, usually at Christmas and birthdays, but that was our only personal contact, and I missed them so much.

By this time, it was just after Christmas, 1985. I began to make arrangements to come back to the UK as I knew it was to be a home posting this time. I'd been away from the Foreign Office in London since 1976, and we all had to go back for a spell in "head office" every ten years or so. I wouldn't find out until I arrived back exactly for whom I would be working, but I knew I'd be in London for at least the next two years.

I had a fantastic send-off, with the Ambassador hosting a lunch for me at the Residence, a lot of parties given by my friends and colleagues, a farewell lunch which I gave at the POW, and an Embassy farewell lunch at the Cocha y Toro vineyard. By the time I'd finished, I felt I was going to "explode"!

It was a fabulous end to a fabulous posting, and with such sadness and tears, I eventually took my leave of Chile in February 1985 for pastures new. Maybe one day I'll go back, but as time marches on - who knows? It's a long way away, but how I would love to be back in that unforgettable country again. Just once.

Above: My farewell lunch at the Concha y Toro vineyard

Re-living some South American memories

Above: Parque Nacional Lauca in Chile's altiplano wilderness. With a group of rather bewildered Aymara Indian children at Parinacota

Below: On the shores of Lago Chungará, with the Volcán Parinacota, 20,762 ft, in the background. (After this photo I collapsed with soroche and we had to descend quickly as the driver had no oxygen cylinders)

Above: Iguazu Falls, on the Paraguayan side. I stood on the end of that walkway.
Absolutely petrifying.

Below: Ecuador. Two tiny Cotocachi Indians. They were so hospitable and trusting,
even though I couldn't understand a word they said

Above: At the Equator at Catequilla, Ecuador 1983

Below: We three "singles" at the Embassy: Alison, Claire and me
(we practiced what we preached!)

PART NINE

HOME AGAIN - TEMPORARILY

Back in London

Mum and Dad were there at Birmingham airport to meet me, and what a reunion it was. We hugged and kissed, talked non-stop for days, and just enjoyed being together again at last. But I had to go to work, and after a fortnight I made my way back down to London yet again.

I bought a second-hand Escort, but the most pressing problem was that I had to find somewhere to live. Despite my travels, I'd saved up hard and now had enough money to put down a deposit on a flat of my own. I knew more or less where I wanted to be in London, and Pam and her Mum very kindly offered to put me up whilst I was looking, so when I got home from work each evening, I'd scan the local papers for suitable properties and set up viewing appointments for the weekends. If Pam was free, she came with me too, and after only two weeks I had found exactly what I was looking for in Wallington, near Sutton: a two-bed, medium sized flat with nice views on the third floor in a complex of four apartment blocks. 53 Fairlawnes, Maldon Road, Wallington, was to be my UK home until 2004, when I moved to West Sussex. The paperwork went through fairly quickly and I collected the keys at the beginning of May 1985, with Mum and Dad coming down from Pontesbury to help me decorate and get my new home all shipshape.

In the Foreign Office Again

My first job in the Office was as PA to [Dame] Pauline Neville-Jones, a brilliant woman with an insatiable appetite for work. I loved it, even if Pauline could be a little "intense" at times, and I spent a very happy eighteen months working for her

After that, I went to work for Andrew Burns, later High Commissioner to Canada, in South Asia Department. This was a very busy job, with late hours, but again it was interesting and rewarding. I loved it, and Andrew (and his wife, Sarah) were super.

It was when I was working for Andrew, in July 1987, that I was given my next posting – Mexico for three years. I was over the moon again, and so happy to be going back to that part of the world. I had to re-take my Intermediate Spanish Institute of

Linguists exam, which I needed to do every five years to continue receiving the Language Allowance. I passed, and could now look forward to being back in a Spanish-speaking environment once more. My knowledge of Spanish was invaluable to Ambassadors in South America, and they were keen to have me as their PA, which is why I continued to be sent to that Continent. Anything to oblige! I didn't mind at all!

Time to pack up again, only now I had the added task of arranging for my flat to be rented out whilst I was away. I hated the thought of anyone else living there, but I couldn't leave it empty, and in any case the rent would help to pay for the mortgage. As I couldn't import a car into Mexico this time and would have to purchase one locally, buying another Escort here in the UK was one thing that I didn't have to worry about, so all I needed to do was sort out my air freight and suitcases once again.

I said yet another tearful farewell to Mum and Dad, promising to write every week as usual, then a quick call to Sheila, and my friends, whom I'd so enjoyed catching up with whilst I'd been home, and I was ready to leave.

Of course, I would have chosen 17 October, the day after Michael Fish's famous "hurricane that wasn't" prediction (in fact it was an extratropical cyclone apparently). Everything was in turmoil, flights were grounded, mine included, with no actual time being given as to when it would be re-scheduled. I made a hasty phone call to Pam, who kindly said I could stay with her and her Mum in Horley until I knew.

Eventually I heard I was on a flight on 19 October, so on 18 October Pam, her Mum and I had time for a quick visit to Wakehurst Place to see the devastation there, which was terrible.

On 19 October 1987, all packed up, I headed for Gatwick and boarded a British Airways flight to Schipol, as usual, from where I travelled with KLM to Mexico City.

South America, here I come again! Back to what seemed like my second home. I couldn't wait!

PART TEN

MEXICO
1987-1991

Above: The British Embassy, Rio Lerma 71, Zona Rose, Mexico City

Below: the gardens and the Consular Section partly visible behind.

Above: The Residence, Avda. Virreyes, Lomas

Below: My fantastic bungalow, Sierra Amatepec, Lomas de Chapultepec

"South of the Border, Down Mexico Way"

As I flew into the Benito Suarez airport, I couldn't have felt happier, even though my Paddington Bear label now said "Please send to a country still within the Ring of Fire, and a city at altitude". Mum had kept my letters from Mexico, and I've been reading with much amusement the accounts of my first few days here:

"Heavens, the smog is bad here. It's like walking around in a room previously occupied by cigar-smoking exclusive Club members! All caused by these thermal inversions (upside down thermals), so it seems, which trap the dirt, dust, smoke and everything else, over the city. But never mind. At least everyone else here is suffering from the same bad throats, bad chests, bronchitis, and pneumonia, so you quickly feel quite at home."

Nothing like putting your mother's fears to rest straightaway!

Mexico, and Living in Mexico City

Known as the DF (Distrito Federal), Mexico City is built on "jelly" in a vast valley at an altitude of 7,000 feet, surrounded by a ring of volcanoes. Its foundations lie in the soft earth of an island in what used to be Lago Tenochtitlán, which is why, during earthquakes, structures are prone to wobbling and so much damage is caused during the stongest ones, even though building regulations should ensure that they are safe. The majority of us lived in the more stable area of Lomas, to the west of the city, which is in the foothills of the mountains encircling the vast valley below. Properties here have their foundations set in rock, which provides a greater degree of protection from the devastation of tectonic movement, though our houses were by no means immune from damage, as I was to find out.

Because of the altitude, it really did get cold here, which is not the tourists' image of Mexico at all. In winter the night-time temperature fell below zero, and reached 75° F during the next

287

day, so dressing was more a question of a well-gauged striptease to cope with the extremes.

It took a little while for me to get acclimatised to living at such a height. I'd suffered from *soroche* before, but then at altitudes of around 12,000 ft or higher. The DF was much lower, of course, but I still needed time to "manufacture" more red corpuscles to be able to absorb oxygen (people born at high altitudes already have more of them). After a time I managed to cope fairly well, although eating was a problem as food took much longer to digest, so it was best to try to avoid late night meals. This wasn't always possible, of course, and you were then in for a fairly sleepless night.

Mexico has a rich culture. After a few centuries of intermingling between Aztec and Catholic cultures after *Los Conquistadores* brutally overran the country and imposed their religion and rule on the indigenous population, Mexico began to forge its own identity once it gained independence from Spain in the 19th century. There's too much to write about here, but its history is extremely interesting – to me at least.

Economically, when I arrived Mexico was in a bit of a mess. The Economic Solidarity Pact was in operation, which meant that the price of gas was up by 80%, petrol by 85%, telephone charges by 35%, hotels (bad news for us) by 20%, internal airfares (again not good for us) by 20%, and so on. The list was endless, and all this to try to curb inflation which was running at around 148½%. The President and Government Officials were exempt from these increases, of course, and although we were constantly being reassured that there was light at the end of the tunnel, we weren't exactly sure which one that was.

When I was there from 1987-91, although not the safest of places to live from a personal security point of view, I was able to move about freely within reason, though fair-haired females like me had to be a bit wary. There were some areas, though, where none of us went.

Today it is definitely not a safe place to travel around, which saddens me greatly. Now it is in the grip of the drugs barons and cartels and, what with US President Trump's anti-Mexico policies and his determination to build that wall along the entire border, it's difficult to see a way forward for such a culturally rich and geographically fascinating country. I really do fear for Mexico's future.

My Arrival in Mexico

I was met at the airport by the Assistant Admin. Officer, Alistair Dent, and taken to meet the Ambassador, John Morgan, and my colleagues at the Embassy, which occupies an elegant building on the street just known as Rio Lerma. The staircase leading up to the first (my) floor of the Embassy was lined with beautiful blue and white Delft stye tiles, creating a very cheerful and welcoming impression. I had a small, but quite adequate, office adjoining the Ambassador's, with the middle window over-looking the porch onto the street. An excellent start.

The Ambassador welcomed me warmly, as did both the UK-based and locally employed, and I instantly felt a part of the team. The other UK-based PA, Jane Silverwood, was terrific, and I knew we would get along like a house on fire, which we did, and still do.

Yet Another New Home

After the introductions, it was time for me to be taken to my own rented house, which turned out to be the most perfect little bungalow I could have imagined. I did take this one over from my predecessor, and I was grateful to her for having left it in such good condition.

128a, Sierra Amatepec, Lomas de Chapultepec, was perched on the edge of a deep ravine (*barranca*) overlooking prosperous houses in the suburb of Tecamachalco on the other side There was a small, two-storey apartment block with four flats, and our car park, fronting Sierra Amatapec, and I had to walk through an arch and down the back garden path to my own little house at the bottom, which was completely secluded and quiet, with its own small garden and patio. Accommodation-wise, it had two bedrooms, a large lounge/diner with an open fire and enormous sliding windows leading onto my patio overlooking the *barranca*, a reasonable kitchen and bathroom, and a small yard for laundry at the back. This was, without doubt, the best place I had lived in so far, though there were one or two slight drawbacks, as I was soon to discover.

Apart from the kitchen and bathroom, the whole bungalow was carpeted with white (?) shag pile carpet. This was wonderful, and so cosy in winter. But it was a devil of a job trying to extricate the scorpions from it! I discovered early on that there was a nest of them under the patio step, and I regulary had "visitors", so I had to buy a thick pair of industrial rubber gloves and gingerly picked them out, dead or alive, from the shag pile. However, I soon got tired of doing this, so I consulted my *portero,* Cándido, who mixed a bit of cement and blocked up the hole. Eureka! That did the trick. Now I only had snakes (the *barranca* seemed to be a great place for them, much to my dismay), and geckos to deal with. These little lizards stuck like glue to the walls and ceilings, except at night so it seemed, when the little blighters plopped onto my bed whilst I was asleep and frightened me to death.

But there was one addition to my "ménage" that gave me endless enjoyment, and that was the hummingbirds. There were quite a few around my bungalow, so I bought two hummingbird feeders, filled them up with special sweet liquid, and hung them on the tree on my patio. I rarely looked out of my windows without seeing these beautiful little birds, wings whirring away, having a great time getting high on the nectar.

The garden was a bit overgrown so, keen on gardening, I asked my landlady if I could cut back some of the bushes and plant bourgainvillea, hibiscus and other suitable shrubs. She readily agreed, and was delighted with the result, as were Cándido and I.

Above: Cándido clearing the leaves from the top of my roof
Below: My baggage at last, with Cándido on the right to supervise the unloading

However, when I say "I", I use the term loosely. My indispensable, kind and helpful *portero*, Cándido, whom I "inherited", loved gardening too and was equally thrilled at having some to do, so we tackled the transformation together with great gusto. We'd go down to the market garden at Xochimilco on a Saturday and return with a car full of bushes which Cándido had chosen. This was as much his project as mine, and I wanted to be sure he was fully involved and took credit for the transformation too.

We did have a terrifying experience together on one occasion, when the whole *barranca* caught fire and the flames were lapping at the fence at the bottom of my garden. We fought to beat them back for a short while, but the heat was so intense that we had to move further away. Fortunately, the *bomberos* (firemen) arrived in the nick of time, ran their enormous hose through my garden and started dousing the flames. At that point I dashed inside my house, grabbed my passport and other important papers, and went with Cándido and my neighbours from the flats to wait on the road. The *bomberos* did an amazing job and the flames were extinguished quickly, but it was close thing. I bet that gave the snakes a scare!

Cándido's family lived in a small village way out in the country. He didn't go home often, and missed them a lot, I think, but the money he earned was vital and helped with his children's education. On occasions he would go on "benders", so I wouldn't see him for a day or so. At first I got very worried, but he always bounced back. *"No se preocupe, Señorita Gill. Estoy bien"* ("don't worry , Señorita Gill, I'm fine"), he would always say when he came back to the land of the living. I helped him when I could, reading out documents or instructions he might have as he could neither read nor write, and I gave him things for the family, but I didn't give him money in case he went off to buy another bottle of booze.

Car and Baggage

The start to my posting proved to be a bit fraught, as I was about to find out.

On the advice of our Admin Section, I settled on a locally manufactured silver Nissan Tsuru II for my next car. It was by far the most comfortable car I had had, but it did have a temperamental temperature gauge which worked perfectly for the garage, but not for me – as they do. Again, I took out an FCO car loan to pay for it.

My heavy baggage, however, was another matter. I've been reading what I wrote to Mum and Dad, and it all comes flooding back. It sounds funny now, but it wasn't at the time, believe me.

"My heavy baggage was lost, according to the Customs, but I was undeterred. It had to be somewhere. So, clad in jeans and sneakers, I spent two days of my Christmas holiday on my own grovelling around the railways sidings and Customs sheds searching for it. Lo and behold: there they were – two large wooden crates clearly marked ANGRAVE. However, dealing with Mexican Customs officials (all in Spanish) needs more than one's fair share of patience. When the official who was dealing with my importation checked my documents against the ones he had, they didn't tally. My crates had the wrong numbers on. I handed him my passport as proof of who I was, but again he said there was a problem: my passport (all beautifully stamped with Mexican visas, entry permits etc) said nothing about me being a member of the British Embassy. Oh no. Yet more "discussion" followed until he finally accepted the invoice for my car purchase as proof that I was indeed a member of the Embassy.

"I was then sent to present myself to the *Administrador* so that he could see that I was who my photo said I was. This was not easy as at the time I was sporting a rather fetching eye patch (read on). Four and a half hours later, he eventually signed the release papers for my crates. Things were definitely looking up.

"Right, *señorita*, he said (in Spanish of course). Now go and find a lorry. What? You never said anything about a lorry. How do you think you're going to take the crates away, he replied in exasperation? Good point. So off I went to negotiate a lorry, not easy on New Year's Eve when everyone had visions of knocking off early. But when word got around that the Embassy was paying, I was inundated with offers (of lorries!). I could see lots of little cash registers dancing before the drivers' eyes as they hastily calculated by just how much they could inflate their charges. Finally I made my choice: a quiet, shy young man who had been elbowed out of the way by the more vociferous ones. He was absolutely thrilled: the others less so. Shouting at me will not get you my business, *señores*!

"I took him round to where my crates were. But you need a forklift truck, *señorita*. Yes, I can see that now, but I thought you could arrange that for me. "*Pues no*". Sorry! Off I go again to find a forklift truck, which I did, but whose driver was asleep and didn't take kindly to being woken up. Not the best of starts to our brief relationship!

"I showed him where the crates were, and off we trundled with the forklift truck. I then watched in horror as, whether by accident or design, he deftly managed to put the fork right through the middle of the first crate, with a great tinkling sound. There goes my television, I thought! He backed off and manoeuvred the fork underneath the crate, but this time it was lopsided. After another go, it was loaded correctly onto the fork, albeit upside down, and was finally put onto the lorry.

"Now the same had to be done with the bigger second crate, but this was about 30 yards away, behind some pieces of machinery. The driver weaved his way between these, picked up my crate and, with the truck's back wheels precariously close to the edge of the loading bay, raised my crate as high as it would go to take it over the machinery to the lorry. I couldn't bear to watch. I did suggest backing the lorry up to the bay where my crate was rather than taking the crate to the lorry, but a look of disbelief appeared on his face. What a stupid idea! My crate wobbled and promptly fell off the fork, by which time my hands were itching to get round the throats of everyone who happened to be nearby. Finally, the second crate, badly dented, joined the first on the lorry and I waved them off as they left the Customs yard. I remember collapsing in a heap, wondering whether I would ever see the lorry again? But I did – the next day. Well done, my shy young man."

When I reported all this to the Admin Section they smiled, shrugged their shoulders and said "Well, this is Mexico – what did you expect?" That summed it up in a nutshell. My insurance claim for damage was quite high, but I did manage to salvage a few things, though not the television and most of my beautiful Noritake dinner service. Welcome to the life of a member of the Diplomatic Service!

The Exploding Christmas Pudding (Not Flaming Puddings Again!)

As I said before, when I was at the Customs yard I was sporting a rather elegant white eye patch.

The British Council Rep and his wife had kindly invited me to have Christmas lunch with them, and visiting friends and relations. I readily accepted their invitation, and we were having a great time. A proper Christmas lunch again. Snipe were now a distant memory.

At last, in came the flaming Christmas pudding, which was paraded round the table with great ceremony. Just as it got to me, though, some bright spark (forgive the pun) who shall remain nameless, decided to add some rum as well and so sprinkled a liberal amount over the already flaming pudding, with the result that it exploded right into my face, burning my eyes. This wasn't at all funny. I couldn't see, my face was burning, and to cap it all, in the turmoil someone knocked a bottle of the best Champers all over me, so I was sopping wet as well. The outcome was that I was hastily taken to the hospital to find an eye specialist (not easy on Christmas Day), who fortunately was able to give me some drops and ointment to relieve the pain, and put a patch over one eye which I was to wear for a week. I was definitely shaken, not stirred, but I'm glad to say no lasting damage was done. Not easy driving and typing with one eye, though.

Shades of Manila again, I thought. Christmas puddings and I seem to have a strange affinity for one another!

Life in the Embassy

My job was busy, with a constant stream of visitors to see the Ambassador, and a lot of correspondence to deal with too. There was a Social Secretary here also, but I seemed to be getting most of the entertaining work to do as well, which was very time-consuming. However, I just worked on steadily and was managing to keep on top of things. The Ambassador and I were getting on well, and I liked his wife, Angela too, so life was good.

VIP Visitors

One of my favourite visitors to the Embassy was my "hero", Sir David Attenborough, who came out twice when I was there to see the amazing phenomenon of the Monarch butterflies. The Ambassador always held a reception and/or dinner for these VIPs, to which I was often invited. I managed to have quite a chat with Sir David about the butterflies, and as we both came from Leicester, we talked about that as well. What an absolutely charming and amazing man.

The Duke of Edinburgh, as President of the WWF, also visited to see the butterflies just after I arrived. All Royal visits generate a tremendous amount of work, and in the end we were flying around more than the butterflies would have done when they woke up. But everything went well and HRH was pleased with the reception we gave him.

A bit briefly about the butterflies. Their annual migration starts off from the northern parts of North America in early autumn. At this time, a special generation hatches, whose lives last about nine months, and these migrate south to avoid the cold winter. Their flimsy, red and black patterned little wings fly about 190 miles a day until, after a month, they reach the *oyamel* fir forests in central Mexico, where they stay for the winter. In Spring they mate and head off north again. On the journey the females lay about 500 eggs each and then die. These offspring continue the journey north to arrive back "home" in early June. None of the original migrants will ever return to Mexico.

Visiting these fir forests within the Monarch Butterfly Biosphere Reserve, west of Mexico City, was, and still is, strictly controlled and you need a guide. I was lucky to be invited to join a group of visiting VIPs one February, which is the best time to see them. It's a fairly steep climb down into the valley,and up again, but when you get there, the sight is astonishing. There are over 100 million of them, all folded up and stuck together, hanging from the branches of the firs in what look like gigantic black wasps' nests. Seeing them is truly something I will never forget.

North of the Border, Up San Antonio Way

Whilst our personal cars were mainly locally produced, the Embassy cars were American as we were able to take advantage of a diplomatic discount which made them cheaper to buy. Some of my colleagues opted to buy American also, but not many. The Ambassador's official car was an armour-plated Jaguar, but this was always breaking down as the armour-plating made it too heavy for the chassis. After I left I think they changed over to a Range Rover, which made much more sense.

About halfway through my tour, the Embassy needed a new Ford Mercury and as the Ambassador was away, I offered to drive it down from San Antonio to Mexico City. Roger and Gill

Woodward had just arrived at post (Roger was 2nd Sec Commercial) and they wanted to buy an American car too, so it was arranged that the three of us would fly up to San Antonio, stay two nights there, and then drive the two cars back to the DF, stopping the night at Monterrey and Zacatecas. I was to drive the Embassy saloon, with Roger and Gill driving their own estate car and relieving me every so often along the way. I was really excited to be doing this as I got on very well with Roger and Gill, so off we set on the evening flight from the Benito Suarez airport to San Antonio, in the heart of Texas.

The next day we completed all the necessary paperwork at the Dealership fairly quickly, and had time to visit The Alamo, a Spanish mission and fortress built by the Roman Catholic missionaries in the mid-1700's. It fascinated me, and our guide was excellent. It was much smaller than I had expected, which surprised me, and was wedged between two modern buildings, but it was unmistakable nevertheless. After a bit of shopping, we treated ourselves to a great meal at a restaurant on River Walk on the banks of the San Antonio River, before heading back to the hotel to pack up in readiness for our early start the next morning.

We set off around 7 am as we had 156 miles to cover to the US/ Mexico border crossing at Laredo, and a further 140 miles to Monterrey after we had completed all the formalities. We always drove in convoy, me leading most of the way, which worked fine. At the border we went through the Diplomatic Channel, and after only an hour or so's delay, we were on our way on the long drive south.

Nowadays there are *autopistas* (motorways) to get around Mexico, but when I was there there were very few. Our roads were single lane, straight, never-ending it seemed, bumpy and lonely. We rarely passed through a village or settlement, and petrol stations were non-existent so we had to make sure we had a full tank and spare cans, as well as lots of drinking water and emergency rations. Bearing in mind we were running these cars in, we also travelled much of the way with crossed fingers!

We spent the night in a pleasant hotel on the outskirts of Monterrey, and again set off early to cover the 287 miles to Zacatecas. I seem to remember getting out of Monterrey was a bit of a nightmare (no sat-navs in those days), but at last we found ourselves on the right road and "put our feet down". Little happened. Same old cactus and Joshua trees, dust, mountains, lack of anyone, until in the evening we arrived at our destination. It was a lovely town and, as we were staying near the centre, we did manage a quick walk round the main square before dinner. Then early to bed again for the last stage of our marathon trip.

It's 382 miles from Zacatecas to Mexico City. Again, there now looks to be a new motorway between the two, but not for us, and I have to confess it did seem a long way. We were climbing all the way to reach the 7,000 ft at which the DF lies, and at times the cars struggled a bit, and so did I. We could have chosen to go from Monterrey via San Luis Potosí to the DF, which was slightly shorter, but Roger and Gill wanted to see Zacatecas, which was fine by me, so that's the way we went. We arrived back late evening and I have to confess I slept most of the next day, which was a Saturday. But it was one of the most memorable journeys I have ever made, and I wouldn't have missed it for the world.

The US/Mexico border crossing at Laredo

Above: With Roger and Gill: Taking a break on the long and lonely road to Monterrey.
Those cactus are deadly, and so are rattlesnakes.
You didn't stray far, or linger long, on these occasions!

Below: Packing up again to leave Monterrey

Above: The Churrigueresque style Cathedral of Zacatecas

Below: El Palacio de Gobierno (Municipal Offices)
in the Plaza de Armas, Zacatecas

The Social Side of the Embassy

We were never short of things to do in the DF. Eating out was fabulous, and as the Embassy was in the heart of the very trendy Zona Rosa area, with its boutiques and elegant restaurants and bars, groups of us would often walk across the road and have lunch there, or in the evenings head off to another favourite haunt in the lesser known *barrios* where I had many memorable meals. We had drinks parties at each other's houses - some official entertaining, some not - and whilst we didn't mix that much with the Americans, even though their large Embassy was just across the road from ours, we saw a lot of the Aussies, New Zealanders and Canadians.

One of the areas I loved to visit most was the quiet, elegant suburb of Coyoacán, with San Ángel next door. The *Conquistador,* Hernán Cortés, and his mistress, *La Malinche,* used to live here centuries ago, and there still remain many buildings and squares dating back to the 16th century. It was (and is) full of charm and atmosphere, and I spent many happy hours just wandering around, appreciating the architecture.

It is here, also, that León Trotsky lived, with Frida Kahlo and Diego Rivera, until he was assassinated on 20 August 1940 by Ramón Mercader, who pierced his skull with an icepick. There were, and still are, excellent museums dedicated to all three in Coyoacán.

The colourful craft markets held at weekends in the *Jardín Centenario in Coyoacán,* and the *Plaza San Jacinto* in San Ángel were irresistible too. You could buy exceedingly good paintings, both oils and watercolours, as I did, as well as pottery, jewellery and obsidian (polished black volcanic rock) sculptures. I had one of those too. Never one to miss an opportunity – me.

Our Embassy Guest Houses

Because of the dreadful air quality in the DF, it was vital to get away from the city as often as possible, and when I was there the

Embassy had a guest house in a small village called Yautepec, to the south of the DF between Tepoztlán and picturesque Cuernavaca. We could book up to go there, paying a nominal amount, and could take visitors too. I liked it. Although it was rather spartan and the kitchen facilities weren't great, it did have a large pool and nice gardens, and it didn't take long to get into Cuernavaca. Invariably I enjoyed my stays at Yautepec, except when I found a shed snakeskin of a poisonous variety at the bottom of the garden. Fortunately I never did meet its owner! Snakes seem to follow me around the world, somehow – just like the puddings.

Now, sadly, Cuernavaca (literally "cow's horn") is in the clutches of the drugs cartels and people are afraid to go out of their homes. How times have changed.

Towards the end of my stay, we gave up the Yautepec house and rented a more modern, comfortable one at a place called Huastepec, to the south-west of the DF. I was over the moon: at the bottom of the garden was a golf course. Couldn't be better. What a shame I was about to leave Mexico! I only managed to go there a few times, but I would pay a green fee and happily play the course. Sometimes, if it was evening and there didn't seem to be anyone about, I would go through our fence onto the 6th fairway and have a few practice shots and putts on the green there. Whatever I did, I was in my element. This was the place for me.

Sport in Mexico

Tennis

This seemed to be the place for tennis too, and so I joined a Country Club at Satelite, an area to the north of the city, which had excellent courts and a good social side. The members were mostly ex-pats, and I made some good friends there. As I wrote to Mum and Dad:

"Tennis is going great guns here. My pro is a bagful of energy, whilst I'm still trying to find my altitude legs and get used to decompressed balls which fly through the air at something approaching Concorde speed. Consequently most of mine go out of the court! But we're winning slowly and my acquired bad habits are beginning to disappear.

"Maybe I'll make next year's Davis Cup team. Next week it's the turn of the Aussies v Mexico. I'm desperately trying to charm our colleagues from Down Under to get a ticket. Well they invited me to the Aussie National Day Reception, and I do send a regular supply of British sausages (made specially by a British lady here) to the Aussie Ambassador each week as he is very partial to them. So, if no ticket is forthcoming, no more sausages!"

I did get a ticket, and the Ambassador happily continued to munch his way through many more packets.

Golf

In Mexico City I couldn't afford to join a club, nor was it possible for me to do so as they were very exclusive. The Ambassador could have been a member, but he didn't play golf and his membership was not transferable, so our Security Officer, Syd Richardson (a former Band Master with the Royal Marines, who was the only other golfer in the Embassy), his wife Jen (who used to come along for the ride), and I used to drive an hour or so into mountains west of the DF, along tortuous roads but through spectacular scenery, to Ixtapan de La Sal, a small village where there was a spa hotel and a short 9-hole course. Syd and I paid our green fee, arranged a caddy, and off we went, meeting up with Jen for a delicious late lunch in the hotel afterwards. Happy times! It wasn't a particularly demanding course, and Syd used to tease me about my "lazy 8" which was all I needed normally to reach the green on the par 3's.

I kept in touch with Syd and Jen until very recently, when Syd died and Jen moved away. Again, such happy memories of our fun times together.

Our Embassy Guest Houses:

Above: Yautepec.
Below: Two photos of Huastepec, with the golf course at the bottom of the garden.

Food for Thought

As if snakes hadn't been bad enough in the Philippines, try something a bit bigger - ALLIGATORS. These were another golfing hazard I had to contend with, particularly at the course at Ixtapa, a very pleasant town just along the coast from Acapulco, where I would play if I was down that way.

The course there is lush, tropical and relatively flat, with challenging lakes. I was keen to play it as often as I could, and so if I had a few days break when the Ambassador was off travelling again, I'd load my clubs into the car and drive the 10 hours down there on my own (no-one else was free to come usually), staying in a small hotel near the beach.

Again, it was hot and humid, but at least there was a welcome sea breeze to cool me off a bit. I'd pay my green fee, be allocated a caddy, and off I went. The first time I was there I was doing quite well until I came to one of the lakes with a raised tee beside it. There was a big sign on the tee, which you couldn't help but notice. I stared at it with a certain amount of apprehension. *"Beware of the Alligators"*. No-one had told me about this. Perhaps I should get my green fee back. But, undaunted, I approached the tee and was preparing to drive over the lake when instinct made me glance down, straight into the steely eyes of an alligator basking in the sun on the other side of the slope of the tee. It seemed he was eyeing up this prospective lunch with great relish. I froze and dropped the club, but by this time, luckily, my caddy had caught up with me.

"Esta bien, señorita" he said, grinning. *"Acaba de comer"*. ("It's OK. He's just eaten."). Who, I'm not quite sure. Someone in one of the flights in front of me, no doubt, as I did seem to be going round the course at a cracking pace all of a sudden! Anyway, I had no intention of being dessert, so I teed off quickly. I had no wish to meet the rest of the family, either, and so didn't feel like going to look for my ball which I had shanked into the lake. I

gave that hole a miss, and some of the subsequent ones with water. It turned out to be a very short course!

Back home, I've tried to continue with my golf, but, hating the cold and being busy with weddings in the summer, I don't get to play that much now. However, I do chuckle at the memories of those rounds of golf long-ago. Life seems pretty tame on the course these days!

The signs on the course at Ixtapa.
It's enough to put anyone off their game!

Medical Matters

Keeping well and coping with strange environments is an important part of living abroad. If I'm ill, I can't work, and the Ambassador is decidely unhappy, so it's up to me to keep as fit as I can. Before I went to Mexico, I had to make sure all my vaccinations were up to date, and have new ones if not, but sometimes problems at Post just creep up on you and you have to deal with them as best you can.

A Night With a Star, Under the Stars

Sometimes, though not often, there were advantages to being ill, and in Mexico City this turned out to be the case.

I hadn't felt well for a little while, nothing drastic, but one degree under, so I went to Dr Drijansky, our Embassy Doctor, who immediately referred me to an eminent gynaecologist, Dr Guillermo Rocha del Valle, who felt it was advisable that I should have a hysterectomy. Agreement had to be sought from Personnel Department in London, who looked at all my medical notes that had been sent to them and agreed that I could have the operation at the ABC (American British Cowdray) Hospital in the DF.

It was 31 October 1988, the night before I was due to go into the hospital for my operation. I had been invited by Harry Clements, the very nice, single, head of Unilever in Mexico, to accompany him to a rather special concert given by Placido Domingo at the Pyramids of Teotihuacán, outside Mexico City. Harry often invited me to dinners or functions where a partner was needed, and occasionally he would ask me to join him for a round of golf as he was a member of the most prestigious and very exclusive club in DF. Harry and I got on very well, but we were just good friends.

On this particular occasion, it was a Charity Concert. Full evening dress was required, which meant I had to borrow a fur coat as, being outside at night and at altitude, it would be freezing cold, which it was. Harry brought a cashmere rug for us both, but my feet fared rather less well!

Harry had paid US$300 each for our tickets, but this meant we had front row seats, which was fabulous, and that we would attend the private dinner with the Maestro afterwards. The concert was special in that it was the first (and as far as I know, only) concert sung entirely in Nahuatl, the ancient Aztec dialect. How Placido managed it, I'll never know. We didn't understand a word, of course, but outside under the stars, with the ancient Pyramids towering above us, it was absolutely magical. I will never forget that evening.

The concert ended at about 11 pm and those of us invited to the dinner made our way the short distance to the gardens of a convent nearby, where sumptuous tables were laid. Lanterns were hung in the trees and it was like fairyland, despite the cold. There must have been about fifty of us and it was an intimate, but supremely enjoyable, affair.

Placido came to each table and spent time chatting to us. What a thoroughly charming man. Service was not of the quickest, and dessert came at around 4 am, but it didn't seem to matter. I was lost in the sheer wonder of it all.

I got back home at around 6 am, packed up my things and waited for Alan Smith, our Admin Officer, who had kindly offered to take me to hospital to check in before 10 am. It was now 1 November, *Día de los Muertos* (Day of the Dead) in the Latin world. Not terribly auspicious, I thought, but never mind. I had such wonderful memories of the night before that would keep me going.

My surgeon, Dr Rocha, was superb, as was Dr Drijansky. I couldn't have asked for better care and they both looked after me exceedingly well during my whole time in Mexico. I was in the ABC for a week, and was off work, much to the Ambassador's chagrin, for five weeks, not long really - considering. A "floater" PA covered for me whilst I was on sick leave; and I only told Mum after the operation so as not to worry her.

"Licence to Kill"

Prior to all this, however, something quite unexpected had happened. I'd been working away one afternoon (the Ambassador was out) when I answered a telephone call.

"Good afternoon. This is Timothy Dalton here".

I nearly dropped the phone. At this time, they were filming "Licence to Kill" in Mexico City and he needed our advice on a certain matter. I was able to help, and he invited me down to watch the filming at the Churrubusco Studios to the south of the DF. I leapt at the chance – well, who wouldn't? He's absolutely gorgeous, I have to say, and we got to chat quite often. I supplied him with real English tea bags which we got from Hong Kong (which I had, and he'd run out of) and he gave me tins of baked beans, which we couldn't get, despite all the beans in Mexico, and he had. We set up quite an efficient bartering system between us which kept both of us going very nicely, thank you.

It was fascinating to watch the filming and I got to know some of the cast and the film crew quite well during that time. I helped them with medical or dental appointments with our Embassy medical team, when needed, and one weekend, when there was a break in filming, I took June Randall (Continuity), and George Frost (Make Up Supervisor) and his wife, down to our house at Yautepec for a bit of R & R. Tim preferred to rest and just chill out in DF, but the others loved it.

When it was time for me to go into hospital, Tim and the crew sent me an enormous bouquet of flowers, which sadly I wasn't able to see as flowers weren't permitted in the hospital (I never did know what happened to them).

Above: A night under the stars with Placido Domingo
Looking at the Pyramid of the Sun from the Pyramid of the Moon, Teotihuacán
(our seats were in the foreground of The Sun)

Below: Looking towards the Pyramid of the Sun along the Avenue of the Dead, Teotihuacán

Above: The Hospital ABC

Below: Saying goodbye to left, Dr Guillermo Rocha del Valle,
and right, Dr Ruben Drijansky

With Timothy Dalton during the filming of "Licence to Kill" in Mexico City – 1988
(One of my favourite photos!)

Then followed my convalescence. When I was well enough (but still not able to work), the crew sent a car to pick me up most days and take me to the studios, where Tim sat me down and got me lunch and a cup of tea when he was free. I did get a telling off from Robert Davi (Franz Sanchez, the villain) at one stage for inadvertently sitting in his Director's chair, but that didn't detract from the excitement and fascination of seeing the film take shape.

Whilst filming, there were some very, very funny incidents (sorry - trade secrets) which nearly caused me to burst my stitches on more than one occasion. I particularly loved the scene where they shot up the fish tanks. Water went everywhere, but the fish weren't real, of course! There were many practical jokers amongst the cast and crew as well. I was handed (by Tim, I think) a rather squidgy A5 size sealed envelope one day. Not trusting any of them, I opened it gingerly, only to find it was stuffed full of rubber maggots which had been in the drawer into which Bond had thrown one of the baddies in the aquarium scene. How I loved those maggots (yes, really) and I kept them for years! Friends thought I was mad, but they brought back such happy memories.

When it was a "wrap", I was sad to say goodbye to them all when they left. At the end of filming, the crew and cast were given the chance to buy their costumes if they wished (they don't do it now, I gather) and I was thrilled to be asked if I would like to buy something too. Still not quite in shape after my operation, I managed to squeeze myself, with great difficulty, into a gloriously sequined, very low cut, black fishtail evening dress as seen in the casino scene. I also bought Della Leiter's white lace wedding shoes. I kept both of these items for many years, but eventually, when I could no longer get into the dress, and didn't have cause to wear the shoes, they went to auction. I was sad to part with them, but it made sense.

Above: Some of the "Licence to Kill" cast and Production Team at the Residence.
The Ambassador is second on left, his daughter in front of him, and Angela
next to Tim. I really liked "Q" too. (I took the photo)

Below: The Centro Cultural Otomí, just north of the DF,
where the last scenes of the film were shot

I thought, once the crew and cast had gone, that I would never see them again. Little did I know that I would. I happened to be on mid-tour leave at the time of the première at Leicester Square and Iris Rose, Production Assistant, very kindly sent me an invitation to attend. I was over the moon, as you can imagine! I was able to take one guest but, not having an escort in the UK at that time, I wondered whom I could take. Neither Mum nor Dad wanted to go, and Sheila was occupied with her family so, as I was staying with Pam, I asked if she would like to come with me. She jumped at the chance, so we put on our finery and walked the red carpet. I only got a chance to smile at Tim as he was very much in demand, but I did catch up again briefly with my friends in the film crew. What a magical and memorable evening that was. To tread the red carpet, with all the crowds gathered (not to see me, of course) was so special. And it was really interesting to see the finished film at last, having seen the "mini-dramas" that it took to shoot some of the scenes. I have such happy memories every time I watch that film. I can even see my dress walking by!

Birthdays

Yes, the years tick by and one of the joys of having a birthday in the DF was that you were never stuck for where to go. My favourite place was Xochimilco, to the south of the city. Once a small lakeside village connected to the main town of Tenochtitlán, it's the only part of the DF still to have canals and *chinampas*, semi-floating vegetable and flower gardens made by covering aquatic roots with soil. Cándido and I got to know it well from our sorties to buy plants, but it was here also that you could hire a colourful boat, a *mariachi* band and a chap to punt you up and down the canals. When asked what I wanted to do for my birthday, I always said I would like to go to Xochimilco, so a big group of us would hire one of these boats, take some

My 45th birthday (surely not!) at Xochimilco

booze and food, and have a real knees-up. It got a bit noisy at times as there were dozens of other groups all doing the same thing, but it was fantastic fun and that only added to the atmosphere. It didn't cost a lot, but it was worth every peso.

Out and About Around Mexico

Apart from my mid-tour leave, I didn't leave Mexico in my three years there. I had no need as it's such a vast, diverse country with so much to see that there was more than enough to satisfy my appetite for travel. The only place I longed to visit was Cuba (which I have done twice since then), but when I applied to The Office for permission to visit, as we had to do because it is a Communist country, permission was denied.

No matter. Luckily for me, the Ambassador loved to travel too, which gave me a chance to take a few days leave at the same time, so I was able to visit most of the places I wanted to see, but not all. The one journey I didn't manage was a trip to the Copper Canyon as, unfortunately, when the opportunity arose, I couldn't get away.

However, I did fly down to Oaxaca to visit Monte Albán, the greatest of all the Zapotec cities. This southern civilization, further down the coast from Acapulco, was sandwiched between the Aztecs and the Mixtecs, and was noted for its jade handicrafts. This capital city lay at 1,315 ft above the Oaxaca Valley, on a mountain whose top had been levelled to create the site. This was a major feat of engineering at the time, and its location is stunning. From here I went to Huatulco, on the coast, but sadly there wasn't enough time to go into the neighbouring state of Chiapas.

Pam's Visit

Yet again, Pam's diaries have proved invaluable. She came out to stay with me from 6-25 July 1988 and, after a trip to the Pyramids at Teotihuacán, we headed off to Pátzcuaro via Morelia, staying at the Posada Don Vasco. After much shopping (what a surprise!), we toured the area before making our way back to the DF, where we discovered that the fridge had de-frosted and there had been no electricity for two days so we had no food. Nothing new there.

Our next trip was to Acapulco, via Taxco, which was a great place to buy silver, and we did! On through the mountains on a road that was both tortuous and dangerous (now there is a motorway which goes by a different route and only takes 8 hours), arriving in Acapulco in the evening at the Pierre Marques Hotel, where we stayed for three days. Being here brought back happy memories for both of us of our P & O days, and we reminisced a lot over the odd *marguerita* cocktail. I met our Consul, Derek Gore, again at Las Brisas; we went on a trip around the bay; explored a bit further afield; jewellery shopping; I played golf as Pam felt unwell for a time (the dreaded Montezuma's Revenge); and then back again on the ten hour journey up to the DF.

Next day, as it was Saturday, I suggested a trip down to the *Bazar Sábado* in San Angel for more shopping (how Pam was ever going to carry everything back, we didn't know). Then followed a few parties, after which it was time for her to fly home. As she was travelling on a BA Staff Travel ticket, she couldn't get on her first flight, came home and tried again next day. Success! We'd had a ball, though, and as always, I was so sorry to see her go.

On my own, amongst other places I visited San Miguel de Allende, Guanajuato and Veracruz, but didn't have time for Chichén Itzá, Tulum or Merida. Well, I couldn't do it all!

On my way back to the UK for my mid-tour leave, I decided to treat myself to four days in New Orleans as I love that city. Once there, I went on as many tours as I could and I also fulfilled my promise to Dad who, like me, was a great classical jazz fan, that

I'd go to Preservation Hall, which I did. It was the most fantastic concert and experience. I bought him a cassette (no CDs in those days), which Mum said he played endlessly, and he was thrilled to hear about it first-hand once I arrived home.

My New Ambassador

Three-quarters of the way through my tour, John Morgan left post and we welcomed his successor, Michael Simpson-Orlebar, with his Colombian wife, Rosita. I got on well with both though, like my colleagues, I did find the Ambassador rather withdrawn and uncommunicative at times. This Ambassador didn't travel as much as my previous one had done, so I was less able to get away for the odd break now and then. But I couldn't complain. I was very grateful, and counted myself very lucky to have seen all that I had seen.

Adiós, Mexico

I couldn't believe it when, in February 1991, my three years were up. The time had passed so quickly and there was still loads I wanted to do and see but, as with Chile, all good things must come to an end.

I'd been waiting for news of my next posting with great anticipation. The letter arrived about two months before my tour ended and as I knew Madrid was up for grabs, where I desperately wanted to go and for where I knew I was being considered, I opened the envelope with much excitement. Spain here I come!

I just stared at the destination. Hungary? What on earth would I want to go there for? They don't speak Spanish in Hungary, surely! But The Office moves in mysterious ways sometimes (well, most of the time actually), and they have a policy of not letting you stay too long in any one region in case you "go native". They obviously thought this was happening to me as I just couldn't get enough of South America. A change of scene is what you need, Gillian, and what better place to send you than to a former Communist country in the heart of Europe. My heart sank and I found it difficult to summon up any enthusiasm at all for my next "home". Once there, my opinion changed, but for now Budapest was what I'd been given, so I just had to get on with it.

As there was no possibility at all of me learning much Hungarian in two months since it's such a difficult language, and I didn't speak Russian either, I decided that, in order to make myself even remotely understood, I ought to learn a bit of German. I only had a smattering of it, but I enrolled at the Goethe Institute in Mexico City and began to learn German, in Spanish. This proved to be an interesting exercise as I kept getting muddled up between the two, but eventually I could hold a simple conversation in German, which I thought would at least get me round the large supermarkets if nothing else. Little was I to know that in Hungary at that time, there weren't any!

So, with little enthusiasm, I packed up all over again, waved goodbye to my baggage and planned my flight back home, again Club Class via KLM to Schipol, which I was beginning to know very well, then BA to Heathrow and on to Birmingham, where Mum and Dad would meet me. The Ambassador and Rosita, as well as my neighbours and friends, held super-enjoyable lunches or drinks parties for me, and I gave one myself for close friends which, if a little sad, turned out to be a really good "do". Even my hummingbirds came out in full force to say goodbye.

And so on February 25th 1991, I closed the door of my beautiful bungalow for the last time and bade a very tearful farewell to my faithful friend and helper, Cándido, who clung to me, tears streaming down his face too, saying *"no te vayas, Señorita Gill, no te vayas"* (don't go, Señorita Gill, don't go). It was so tough to leave him behind. Yet more goodbyes to my colleagues at the Embassy, and, at the airport, one final adiós to the home, city and country in which I had been so privileged to live and work, if only, in the general scheme of things, for a short time, but which I had come to love so much.

Visions and memories of Mexico will never leave me.

Time now to head for unfamiliar and slightly daunting pastures new.

Adiós - One last Time

Below: The Ambassador's farewell lunch for me at the Residence
(Ambassador in the foreground, Rosita at the other end).
I got to choose the guest list this time – my closest friends in Mexico

Above: My farewell lunch for my closest friends:
Erwan Fouere, EU Ambassador to Mexico; Mike and Jennifer Waddington
and Peter and Kay MacDonald

Below: My super neighbours' farewell party for me

Goodbye little house. I shall miss you.

PART ELEVEN

FROM COPENHAGEN TO BUDAPEST

I only had two weeks at home before I had to leave for Hungary.

There were moments, prior to my departure, when I thought I'd never see the light of day, and I couldn't have managed without Mum and Dad, who had come down to Wallington to give me a hand. Two weeks is not long to plan travel arrangements and sort out the mess my tenants had left. I had to mop up mould, replace ripped off wallpaper, buy new carpets, clear out the garage of the old fridge and washing machine they had left, and in addition, hound the bank for my currency; put in my order to the diplomatic suppliers, Peter Justesen in Denmark, for provisions I would need in Budapest as there was very little available at that time, and get packed up.

In amongst all this turmoil, I had to attend a week's computer course! I'd graduated to an electric typewriter by now, but had never been on a computer before, and I remember being nearly in tears when I was told to use the mouse. Mouse? What mouse? What on earth was that? I hadn't a clue, and the cursor went all over the place when I tried to use it. But I had to do the course to be able to function properly when I arrived at Post, so I gritted my teeth (again) and struggled on. If I could, I'd have bought a mouse trap and killed the …… thing!

And, of course, I needed a car. I was thrilled to be booked on a one-day course on the skid pan at Thruxton (shades of Daytona) in readiness for the harsh Hungarian winters, but I needed to sort out my own "wheels". This was solved by taking out yet another car loan and ordering a tax-free 1.6 GLX Ford Escort (the new design, much to my delight) from Dana Ford Forhandling A/S in Copenhagen. The only thing was - I had to collect it from there and drive it down to Budapest. No problem: I was becoming quite used to long journeys, and it would be interesting and, hopefully, fun.

At last, exhausted by these whirlwind two weeks, I was ready. I said goodbye again to Mum and Dad, but they were hoping to come out to stay with me in Budapest, so things didn't seem quite so bad this time.

Pam came to the rescue again as she said she'd drive down to Budapest with me, so on 18 March 1991 we set off for Harwich, complete with 156 kgs of baggage, to catch the *Princess of Scandinavia* to Esbjerg. We arrived there at 1.15 pm the next day, but our bags (well, mine really) were so slow coming off the ship and were still in Customs when they announced that our train for Copenhagen would be leaving in five minutes, that we missed it, and I ended up having to hire a Volvo Estate for over £100 and drive all the way to Copenhagen. Weary, we finally arrived there at 9 pm.

John Schroff, the car dealer, came to collect us from our hotel the next morning, and I spent nearly all that time sorting out the paperwork, paying for the car, filling out endless forms and acquiring temporary number plates. That done, he dropped us off in the centre of the city for some sightseeing, promising to return at 8.15 am the next day to take us to the garage to collect the car, which he did.

At 9.30 am we set off, armed with a vast number of maps and information, in my shiny new, dark blue Escort (left-hand drive of course, as all my cars had been) to catch the 12.10 pm ferry from Rodbyhavn to Puttingen. From there we motored to Grönnigen, where we spent the night at the very comfortable Hotel Rennschuh.

It was a long journey to Passau, on the German/Austrian border, the next day, so it meant an early start. We left Grönnigen in sunshine, but the further south we got the worse the weather became, until it was torrential rain, and we spent ages driving round and round Passau searching for the Hotel König, where we were to stay the night.

The next day was to be a day of rest, we decided, so we wandered around the lovely old town of Passau, went on a Three

Rivers boat trip and, according to Pam's diary, I got my hair cut there as I hadn't had time to do it before I left. I'd forgotten all about that, but I had to be decently coiffured to arrive in Budapest, that was for certain.

We set off again for Vienna, sailing through the Austrian border control with no problems at all, finally arriving at the Embassy to collect the keys to Julie and John Larden's flat, where we were to stay the night. John was Security Officer at our Embassy in Vienna and he and his wife were good friends of mine so, as they had gone back to the UK for a few days, they had kindly said we could stay at their place. Needing to stretch our legs by this time, we went on a long walk around the centre of Vienna, which I really enjoyed, and which I was to do quite often during the next three years.

After dropping the keys off at the Embassy, we sailed through the border with Hungary, again with no problem, arriving at the Embassy at lunchtime. After brief introductions, we then followed the Admin officer to my new flat so that we could unpack and spend a restful afternoon after our long journey.

Next day, 26 March, I managed with some difficulty to find my way down to the Embassy to meet everyone properly this time, dropping Pam off at Old Buda on the way so that she could explore that historic part of Budapest whilst I started work. She returned to the Embassy at lunchtime and I then went with her, and the Unclassified Diplomatic bags, to the airport, waved her off and returned to start my new life in Hungary.

Above: Pam and me, back at sea again!
Sailing from Harwich to Esbjerg

Below: Copenhagen: Excited at taking delivery of my new car

PART TWELVE

HUNGARY
1991-1994

Above: The British Embassy, Harminçad utca, Vörösmarty tér, Budapest
(with my car in the foreground).

Below: The stunning Residence at Lorántffy Zsuzsanna utca 7, Budapest II

Above: My new home (ground floor flat, right) owned by Ernö Rubik.
As you can see, I lived in a Rubik Cube!

Below: My street, Napvirag utca, in the Buda Hills, and my new car

A Definite Change of Scene

Once back in the UK, the more I thought about Hungary the more excited I became at this new challenge. It was a far cry from Aztec plumed head-dresses, the vibrant atmosphere of Acapulco, the opulence of Cancun, or the misery of the DF's rubbish dump cities and street children, but Hungary too was facing a great challenge of her own as she emerged from years of Communist domination. Perhaps we could both grow together – for a while at least – and learn from each other.

Pastures New

When I was there (1991-94), Budapest was a city of two million people, with stunning architecture, mainly on the Buda side of the Danube. The skyline was truly a sight to remember, particularly at night when a myriad of lights glistened on the water along the banks of that great river, and the Var (Castle District) was so tastefully floodlit. It was all very dreamlike and romantic. Of course, there were areas, mainly on the Pest side, of high rise, drab, communist style housing estates. But this was an elegant city filled with history and eager to re-establish itself as one of the world's greatest. I was so happy to have arrived.

Further afield, there was the vast expanse of the Puszta (the Great Plain), the Tokay wine-growing area, and a wealth of fascinating cities to explore. I have to confess that I found the Hungarian language (a mixture of Finnish and Turkish) very hard to get my tongue around, and throughout my tour I did miss not being able to converse even moderately well with the local population. But, somehow, I got by. At least the German I had learnt in Mexico had some use: I could tell people I couldn't speak Hungarian quite fluently!

As time went on, I became very settled here. At the bottom of Mum's "Tuppence Box", I've found my old letters and "Christmas Epistles" (that I still write) relating to Budapest, and it has been absolutely wonderful re-reading them and re-kindling old memories. In one I have written:

"Each time I cross one of Budapest's beautiful bridges, I'm drawn nearer to the heart of Hungary, her culture, her people, her countryside. At last my surroundings seem less alien and my ears a little more attuned to the Hungarian language, even though I still can't understand a word of it.

"There are definitely worse places to be than in Budapest, and I've therefore agreed to stay on for another tour of eighteen months, taking me to April 1994. The Ambassador thinks it's a good idea to remain for longer now that the option exists. In any case, there will be a change of Ambassador next summer, so for continuity reasons I have to stay on to see the new man in. It also gives me a much-needed period of stability, and saves the Foreign Office and the taxpayer money, so the decision seems to satisfy everyone."

I should confess here that I incurred the Ambassador's slight displeasure in asking London if I could stay before I'd talked it through properly with him first. I realise now that I was wrong to have done so. Sorry. But he agreed, and we were soon back on an even keel.

The Political Situation

The early 1990's was a fascinating time to be in Hungary. When I arrived in March 1991, the Soviet troops were just beginning their withdrawal from the country, finally leaving on 19 June 1991. There had been around 100,000 military and civilian personnel stationed in Hungary. Now, at last, there were none.

The first free parliamentary election was held in May 1990, and a coalition, under Prime Minister József Antall, was formed between the Hungarian Democratic Forum (MDF), the Independent Smallholders' Party (FKGP) and the Christian

Democrats People's Party (KDNP). Antall died in December 1993 and Margaret Thatcher came to his funeral. He was replaced by Péter Boross.

Without the relative stability and security that the Communist years had afforded, living standards began to decline as a new market economy developed. Prices rose dramatically and unemployment soared as the old, unprofitable businesses closed down. People were no longer assured of a job, inflation soared to 35%, and the Forint devalued. It was still not yet a convertible currency, which meant that foreigners had to pay for travel tickets etc in hard currency. Therefore, a proportion of our salary was in sterling in case we wanted to visit neighbouring countries and needed, for example, Austrian Schillings or Czechoslovak Crowns, which we couldn't buy with Forints. Violence and burglary also increased as people tried to make ends meet.

As inevitably happens in these situations, since day to day living conditions are the yardstick by which the performance of a government is measured, the coalition became very unpopular. New elections were to be held in 1994 (the term of office being only for four years), but it was hard to see how a new team could improve on what the present one was doing.

The Embassy

The Embassy occupied a former bank, built in 1911, and was the most impressive of all the Embassies I had worked in. The magnificent main staircase was solid marble, polished to a high degree over the years, and the original brass-work was everywhere: the lights, around the heavy doors, even in the Ambassador's personal loo, where there were some very odd contraptions for which I had difficulty fathoming out their use, but didn't like to enquire. It was centrally situated near the banks of the Danube on the Pest side, just off Vörösmarty tér.

Unfortunately, it was also right next door to the renowned and irresistible patisserie, Gerbeaud, which I used to sneak into when I thought no-one was around. Did I feel guilty? Not at all, though I had to be careful not to end up looking like a Russian weight-lifter!

This was also, for me, the first Post where there was a Commissary in the former bank vaults. This was run most efficiently by the "Dippy Wives" and stocked miracle items such as Branston Pickle, decent cheese, baked beans, HP sauce, pork and beef sausages, all of which you couldn't buy in Hungary when I arrived, although they were slowly appearing by the time I left in 1994. Most of the items came from the NAAFI in Germany, and the perishables from Kings Barn in the UK. Because of freight costs, they were more expensive than in the UK, but we didn't mind. We were just glad to have such creature comforts to augment our diets.

The Ambassador was on UK leave when I arrived, so I had time to attend to all the complicated administrative tasks necessary on arrival: Visas, ID card, car certificate etc. When he came back to post, what a change from one or two of my previous bosses. As I wrote in my Epistle to friends:

"The Ambassador is a real sweetheart and we have established a good working relationship right from the start. His wife, Prim, is a lovely lady too. He is kind, unpretentious, extremely young-looking, and considerate to a fault. I even received a lovely bouquet of flowers on my birthday. Best of all, we can have a laugh. He is very particular about appearances – to an exaggerated degree sometimes – but since I tend to be the same, as my mother will tell you, we understand each other perfectly. Finally, after twelve years, I now feel I have someone I can work well for. At last, Personnel, we are getting somewhere."

My colleagues and the locally employed staff were equally welcoming. There was a Deputy Head of Mission here, Howard

Above: UK-based Embassy staff at The Queen's Birthday Party (QBP),
at the Residence, 1993 (I'm second row from front, five in)

Below: A very cold, lonely and poignant Remembrance Service
at the small Commonwealth War Graves Cemetery outside Budapest

Pearce, also single, whom I liked, and I got on well with his PA, Carol, even though she was quite a bit younger. Our joint office was between the Ambassador's and Howard's, but there was little time for either of us to gossip. There was a very happy atmosphere in the Embassy, and we had a lot of good times together.

The Ambassador's and Embassy's main goals were to bolster this fledgling democracy, seek out commercial contracts and generally help Hungary on her way. To this end, we had a fairly large Commercial Department, and two Defence Attachés.

We were always busy, but as time went on and Hungary began to open up to the outside world, we were inundated with VIP visitors which kept us even more on our toes: Edward Heath, Betty Boothroyd, John Major, not to mention a host of Royals (more of that later). It was fascinating and extremely satisfying work.

The Rubik Cube

It had been agreed that I wouldn't take over my predecessor's flat which was in a beautiful area up on the Var. Chosen by the Ambassador, initially it had been ideal, but this area was fast becoming a popular tourist destination and having to live with constant streams of people, exhaust fumes from all the coaches and cars right outside the windows, the bars and all-night clubs, was not conducive to a peaceful existence for anyone, particularly like me who thrived on peace and quiet at home. Our single Security Officer, Tony, however, was more than happy to move into it as it was much nearer the Embassy, so he went there, and I occupied the flat allocated to him.

I was slightly apprehensive as I followed a colleague round all the back streets, up "The Snake" (not another one!), along Törökvesz to my new home, Napvirag utca 17/1/4, up in the Buda Hills at the end of the No 11 bus route. I despaired of ever finding my way back down again, but with street guides and maps by my side, I did in no time.

The flat was a private hiring as opposed to one in one of the old, bug-ridden Hungarian Government-owned compounds, and was owned by none other than Ernó Rubik, of Cube fame. The flat was indeed square, and I used to announce with great authority that I lived in a Rubik Cube. He visited quite often to see how the flat, and I, were getting along. Quiet, unassuming and camera-shy, he looked like an absent-minded professor (he probably was) in rather tatty jeans and sweater, and he just smiled each time he came when I had to confess that I still couldn't do his Cube (but he never showed me how to do it, and I still can't get it right).

There were four flats in the Cube, and I occupied the ground floor right hand one (the one above me was boarded up for some reason). My neighbours seemed pleasant: the Horvaths – parents and teenage son - next to me; the family Szabo – parents and two early teenage girls – underneath; they also had the garden. I did initially detect envy and resentment (sadly common amongst Hungarians – a legacy of the "dark years") that a single female should own a new car, never mind that I had had to take out a loan to pay for it, and be housed in solitary splendour when families had to squash into the same area. But I worked hard to overcome these feelings, and by the time I left we were best friends and they gave me a super, "en famille" farewell party.

It was a pleasant flat, not over-large, with a small galley kitchen leading to an L-shaped lounge/diner. There was one double bedroom, a tiny single room (not as much spare accommodation as I had hoped for), and an "unusually tiled" brown bathroom and separate loo.

It wasn't without its problems though. The gas water heater exploded with a tremendous roar one Sunday morning, soaking everything in sight; the leaking bathroom tap used to flood the bathroom frequently; and I had trouble getting the car down the steep slope into the underground garage. The manoeuvring space was absurdly small, and my car kept hitting the concrete lip at the top of the slope, which was not ideal. I rang Ernó. Here's a man who can solve the problem quite easily, I thought. He did. He hired a chap to hack away at the concrete sill so that now the car only scraped on the metal bit which the gate fitted into. Wish I had a brain like that!

But for all this, the best feature by far was the lovely balcony, bordered by deep concrete window boxes which I kept well stocked with tulips, pansies, daffodils, geraniums, miniature

Living in the Rubik Cube
(November, July, and summer view)

azaleas in the spring and summer, but as it was much colder up here in the hills than down in the city, we had a lot of snow in winter so nothing grew.

Typical, though. When in Mexico I had begged Admin to let me have some garden furniture for my large patio, but they didn't so I had to buy my own. Now, on a much smaller balcony, I had two lots, which was a bit of a squash. Perhaps before I retire, I thought, like golf, I would have everything right at the same time.

As I love gardening, I also asked my neighbours if I could plant up the two concrete beds at the front of the property, which were just weeds. They were astounded that I wanted to do this, but readily agreed, though in true Hungarian fashion, only the family said how nice it all looked. I think Communism had robbed people of any pride in themselves or their surroundings, which was so sad.

It was much cooler up here in the Buda Hills, which was great in the scorching hot summers, but was distinctly unfunny in the winters. It was often minus 21°F, and was so icy that I couldn't get the car up the slope, so I would put on my moon boots and ski wear, neatly pack a change of clothes in my rucksack, and trudge along to the bus stop for the No 11 bus, which was normally able to run. One of the few plusses of forty years of Communist rule was that Budapest had an excellent transport system – buses, Metro, trolleys and the HEV tram system. What was so good was that where one ended, the other started. Truly joined-up: UK take note. So, I could catch the No 11 bus to Batthanyi tér, and immediately get onto the Metro to the main hub, Deak tér, near to the Embassy. Simple, huh!

Then there was the saga of the dustbins. A few days after my arrival a roster was pushed under my door, in Hungarian, on which I appeared (I was the only familiar word on the sheet). I scratched my head and spent an age pouring over the dictionary trying to figure it out. I couldn't, so I went to ask the Horvath's what I had volunteered for. Both sets of neighbours spoke some English, so they were able to tell me that we had to take it in turns on a Tuesday and Friday to get up at 6 am and pull the five heavy bins up the steep slope and out onto the street as, with all the break-ins, the gates had to be locked and the dustmen couldn't get in. I did my first stint, with much huffing and puffing, on my birthday, but it didn't take me long to gauge that Fridays were better than Tuesdays when, after a weekend of gardening rubbish, the bins were much heavier. I don't think they ever twigged why I kept asking to swap my duty to a Friday. I came to the conclusion that I would have made the world's worst Communist!

Trials and Tribulations in the Diplomatic Service

Baggage

My heavy baggage spent three months sitting in Mexico after an oversight with the agents (I wonder whether the fork lift truck driver tipped them?), but at last it arrived. All that time I'd been living with the basic Embassy "float" – one cup, one saucer, one plate etc. Pam came out on 7 June just at the time the crates turned up, and again was such a help in emptying thirty odd boxes, although that was not at all what she had come for. However, we did it in record time and still managed to do a lot of sightseeing - up on the Var; to Szentendre; on the Danube to Vác; to Esztergom, Visegrad and the Danube Bend. We hoped for a spot of thermal bathing at the Helia Hotel, but, typical, they were shut due to a technical problem.

Pam left on 12 June, kindly being taken to the airport by the Ambassador's driver, who was going there to pick him up.

My Lovely Car

As is always the way, after four days my "mechanical delight" decided to expire. Not once, but every time I slowed down. Definitely not good when you're driving to work in a line of traffic. Unfortunately, the new Ford agency wasn't yet able to undertake repairs, so this meant I had to go to Brück-an-der-Leitha, in Austria, to get it fixed. The Ambassador was very understanding. "Of course you can't go around like this", he said. "Take a day's leave to get it fixed". More to the point, I suspect, was that as I had Diplomatic number plates, it made it look as if the British Embassy was staffed by incompetents who couldn't even master the rudiments of driving. So I grabbed my passport, hastily packed an overnight bag, telephoned the garage to let them know I was coming, left Budapest after work on a Thursday night, drove 3½ hours to Brück and camped out for the night at a little hostelry just up the road from the garage.

I was waiting outside the garage at 7 am. The mechanics spoke no English, and my three months at the Goethe Institute in Mexico hadn't quite equipped me with the skills to wrestle with a fuel injection system. There then followed a series of exchanges between the mechanic and me, broadly as follows, and detailed in my Epistle:

"Das Problem?" "Mein Auto ist krank (sick)." "Warum (why)?" Hmm, I thought you might ask me that. I then had to go into "charade mode", simulating going ever so slow, then stopping. "Kaput." "Das ist nicht sehr gut". Indeed. Sorry, we can't fix it: you'll have to go to Vienna. But I can't go to Vienna as I have to be back in Budapest tonight, so I'll just stay here until you can do it. "Gott in Himmel." Not one of <u>those</u> females, please. Perhaps if we ignore her, she'll go away. No chance, I'm afraid, Herr Direktor. Tenacity is the mainstay of my character. I'm in the Foreign Office you know, and it's a prime requisite (I didn't actually know how to say this in German, but it's true).

So there I remained until the Direktor, Herr Braun, took pity on me and agreed to do it. But it couldn't be done that day, even though I wanted it "schnell-isimo", and they only worked till mid-day on a Friday. Come back at lunchtime tomorrow and we'll review the situation, he said. Disconsolately, I trudged back to the hotel, asked if I could stay another night, and then headed off to see if I could find a supermarket where I could buy two floor mops, a window-cleaning device, a door mat and other indispensable items not available in Budapest.

I returned to the garage next day. All fixed, Herr Braun assured me. It needed a key electronic part that had broken, but we managed to obtain one. I thanked him profusely. That will be €90.00 please. But it's under Warranty, so I don't have to pay. There then followed yet more "discussion", and when it became obvious that I wasn't going to be allowed to leave without handing the money over, wearing my "Queen Victoria look", I wrote out my first Eurocheque. Back in Budapest, there then followed a further saga with Dana Forhandling in Copenhagen, who didn't want to know, and Ford Europe, who didn't know me from Eve, but soon would. Come back Nissan, I thought. I love you! Happily, I got reimbursed in the end.

One small point I hadn't realized. Unleaded petrol was not

common in Hungary, even less so in the rest of Eastern Europe. Pumps for unleaded were few and far between, so I had to carry a full spare can and plan my journeys carefully.

The "CSEM"

Life was never quite the same after your first visit to your friendly neighbourhood *csemege*, or mini-supermarket (*csem* for short). It heralded my first encounter with that élite battalion, the First Hussars Shoppers Brigade, and the battle was fierce. The weapon: the dreaded yellow shopping basket. Without one, your chances of survival, let alone victory, were nil. There were no trolleys, and even if the *csem* was only half full, if you didn't have your regulation basket you had to wait your turn outside, in the freezing cold, till you could pounce on the next shopper who was unloading their paid-for items into their own bag and snatch theirs. Usually, I hadn't even finished unloading my items before the basket was snatched from me and my goods ended up in a heap on the floor.

Once equipped with THE BASKET, you had to launch yourself into the fray. Hungarians see no-one and walk straight into you whereas in Mexico, being tall, moving around had posed no problem. Here, no doubt due to a surfeit of dumplings, pancakes, strudel and cream, the Hungarians presented a formidable obstacle and I fared rather badly. Obviously, I needed to work out a battle plan, and resolved to have a word with our Defence Attachés as to the best course of action. We never did come up with a foolproof plan.

Shopping in General

Under the former Communist régime, people earned the same whether they worked or not. This had been a great incentive-destroyer, and had sadly created a sullen, rude and unhelpful workforce. I remember being left shaken and speechless by the attitude of the hairdresser, and the shop assistant who continued to paint her nails whilst I stood waiting. I didn't much like having packages hurled at me either. Old habits die hard, I supposed, but it was obvious that attitudes had to change rapidly if Hungary wanted to take its place in the modern world and attract the tourists it so desperately needed.

The Sporting Scene

Golf

Hungary turned out to be one of my more memorable Postings for golf, in more ways than one. At last I was in a country where I could afford to join a golf club. Forget the US$20,000 a share in Mexico City. Here I became a very active, fully paid-up member of the Kek Duna (Blue Danube) Golf Club for the princely sum of US$122.00 per annum. This was, in fact, the only course in Hungary at that time - 9 holes and somewhat basic – so it was Hobson's choice really. It was about half an hour's drive out of Budapest, on Szentendre Island in the middle of the Danube. Forget snakes and alligators: this was the only course where I needed an injection against ticks before I could play. Being in the middle of the river, we were plagued with them. It was challenging, as in winter before the river froze, the fairways were rock hard and often sheet ice, so you were in danger of breaking a wrist if you struck the ground too hard. We played on them until the course was shut down in November. It opened again in April, and in summer, it was like a furnace and we were plagued by mosquitos as well as ticks. The sandy fairways were really bumpy, but in the end you got to know where the bumps were and tried not to aim straight for them. I never complained though: it was better than nothing and I enjoyed every minute there.

It was at the Club that I met Lola Ryan, from the American Embassy, an avid golfer like me, who was to become my best friend in Hungary. We were kindred spirits, and could be found most weekends on the course or, in winter, out and about sightseeing. Lola was the one to beat in our Club competitions, but our rivalry was always friendly and fun. I entered as many tournaments as I could, and I remember my partner in my first tournament was the Korean Cultural Attaché. We came third, and thoroughly enjoyed our two-day event. I also won the Ladies Club Championship (the Kiss Lajos Memorial Cup, after one of the founding fathers of golf in Hungary) and, after a hard-fought round against Lola, I eventually became the Hungarian Ladies Open Champion in 1991.

When Lola and I joined, the Club was under new management. There had been few entrepreneurial opportunities in Hungary during the Communist years, but Danny Hajnal, the new owner, was an exception, dabbling in property I understand (like Ernó). He devoted a lot of time to the Club and was keen to attract members who were either Diplomats, or members of the business community, especially the Koreans and Japanese. Few Hungarians played at that time, which in a way was just as well. We lived in hope that Danny could instill some discipline into them as they had absolutely no idea of golfing etiquette (actually I can think of some Japanese who don't either). Also, Lola and I prayed that we might at some stage have at least one level Ladies' tee. And that we might even get some grass on the greens. He said he'd work on it which, in all fairness, he did!

By Royal Appointment

As I said, Hungary for me became a memorable country for golf, and the following is taken from the letter I wrote to Mum and Dad after Prince Andrew's visit in October 1992.

"As the Ambassador doesn't play golf (though he is an excellent tennis player), he asked if I would look after Prince Andrew, who was visiting Hungary as part of the Defence College Staff delegation (one of a string of military visits now that the Cold War had ended) and wanted to play golf. I met HRH first

at the Ambassador's lunchtime reception for Embassy staff, then dashed home to change and gobble a sandwich before being whisked off to Szentendre in a Mercedes stretch-limmo with the Duke, his detective (Steve), our Security Officer, (Dave Hart), "H's" (as he was called) good friend Angus and "Hungarian Boris". A car full of yet more "heavies" followed close behind. The heavens opened on the way, and I must admit none of us looked forward much to a round in the pouring rain, but miraculously it cleared up just as we drove into the car park. From then on, the sun shone down upon us - obviously by Royal Command.

"I was playing with Dave as "H" had unilaterally decided it should be Staff College v Embassy, obviously thinking that against a team with a female player, it would be a walk-over. I must confess it began to look that way on the first hole. I was so nervous I played like a drain, shanking my first two shots into the woods on either side of the fairway. "Please let the ground swallow me up," I prayed silently to He who had made the sun shine so brightly. "H's" eyes rolled up to the top of his head, then shone with glee. But comfort was at hand in the form of dear Angus and Steve, who were both trying their best with hugs and words of encouragement to calm my nerves. It worked a treat. From that moment on, I never looked back (nor up, only down – golfers will appreciate that) and I won the last 5 holes outright. "H" was obviously not too happy at losing, but he was a good sport and we had a good time. It was irritating, though, when he kept saying "oh, lucky shot" when I hit a good one. Just because you're a Royal doesn't mean you're going to get away with that, I thought. "Not at all, Sir" I replied. "I meant to hit my ball there. You have to know how to play this course." End of "lucky" remarks. Also end of chance of an illustrious Damehood and early retirement!"

Above: Golf with HRH Prince Andrew at the Kek Duna Golf Club, Hungary, 1992.
Left to right: Dave Hart, our Security Officer, "H",
Danny Haynal (owner of the Club) and me

Below: Lola and me at a Kek Duna Golf Club reception

Tennis

Arranging tennis outings was rather difficult as most non-club courts were booked the year before for the following short summer season (peak out of work hours). I had thought I'd join the Phonograph Club (yes, a tennis club), but that proved to be too expensive and was very cliquish anyway, so I was told, so I had to content myself with playing where I could when I could.

Fortunately for the Embassy, the Ambassador and Prim were excellent tennis players and we had some fantastic days out on hired courts at Pasareti ut, where they thrashed us all roundly every time! One of our Second Secretaries, Danny Fearn, who was himself a very good player, even made one of his Work Objectives (we all had to have them) "To beat the Ambassador at tennis". He was never successful, but he never gave up. Nor did I. I was never successful at beating him either, but we did have some super games and the Ambassador and I made a formidable doubles team. These tournaments were always much looked forward to and were invariably followed by a delicious barbecue at the Residence. They beat work any day!

Swimming

Budapest had excellent swimming facilities, and many beautiful thermal baths, like the Gellért Hotel, and the Rudas Baths dating from the 1550 and covered in stunning mosaic tiles. Sadly, though, not all thermal baths were clean, and infections were common.

Also, depending which ones you were in, you had to take all your clothes off, as Gillian Phillips and I discovered when we first visited the Rudas. We were each given a small square of cloth with two tapes to tie somewhere, but we couldn't quite decide where. Eventually I sat on mine as the seat in the sauna was red hot, but I don't think that was the general idea! Some of the masseuses there were like gargantuan weight-lifters from the

Our Embassy tennis outings.

Above Left: My Ambassador: John Birch
Above Right: Me, with Prim (standing), DA's and wives

Below: Our British Embassy tennis tournament
(the Ambassador and Prim are back, right). Very happy times.

Russian Steppes, sporting St Trinian-style knickers hitched up to their more than ample bosoms, which in turn were encased in one of those old-fashioned bras with rings round the cups. You certainly didn't argue with them. Clothes off meant clothes off!

Winter Sports

Skiing was a favourite pastime amongst the UK-based at the Embassy, and during the winter months groups of us would often head over the border at weekends to Semmering in Austria to enjoy the facilities that resort had to offer. Many of my colleagues were excellent skiers, but I was hopeless: Woolwich dry ski slopes are no match for the baby slopes of Austria, so I just spent most of the time at the bottom, on my bottom, and waited till they all came down, by which time I was more than ready for a glass of Glühwein.

Skating in Budapest was also popular. It was so cold in winter that the *Vajdunyadhaz* Lake at Városliget (City Park), *Hösök Tére* (Heroes' Square), froze over and became an enormous ice rink, much frequented and enjoyed by the locals and us alike.

Leisure

There really was so much to do in Budapest: opera, ballet, symphony concerts, musicals, the circus, pop concerts, bars, restaurants. I went to see Pavarotti at the huge Sports Hall; John Nettles delivering a superb soliloquy from Twelfth Night; and at the other end of the spectrum, Paul Simon and Rod Stewart, both in the football stadium. We had a thriving Caledonian Society here too, so I could keep up my Scottish dancing.

I travelled far and wide sightseeing, discovering my own "Danube Beach" (the nearest I could get to the sea). And how could I possibly not indulge my passion for motor racing. The Hungarian Grand Prix was an absolute must, especially as Martin was racing. I also enjoyed our Embassy fishing trips in a tributary

Above: On the slopes at Semmering, Austria.
Don't be fooled. This was one of the few times I was upright!

Skating in winter at City Park on the Vajdunyadhaz Lake.

of the Danube; and sailed on Lake Balaton fairly often. I was spoilt for choice.

I also found out that the *Cadfael* television series was being filmed on waste ground behind the Föt Studios on the edge of Budapest, as most mediaeval buildings in the UK are in ruins and were unsuitable. Having so enjoyed watching *Licence to Kill*, I rang up the production team, explained who I was and asked if there was any chance that I could watch a bit of the filming one day. They were very obliging, and so off I went on two Saturdays, meeting Derek Jacobi, and thoroughly enjoying the experience. Being Ambassador's PA did have its advantages sometimes!

Leisure time in Hungary

Above: My trip to the seaside – a Danube beach

Above: Our Embassy table at the Burns Night Supper
Below: Parts of the set of *Cadfael* at the Föt Studios

Above: Our long weekends away fishing at Neuberg-an-der-Leitha

Below: Roger, with lunch

One aspect of my posting to Hungary that hadn't really been a problem before was security. Even though the Russians had left, I still had to be careful with whom I associated, and who I could and couldn't trust. I had one Hungarian boyfriend for a short time, but when I saw which way the wind was blowing, that relationship ended very quickly. I found it all rather disconcerting and sad.

However, we had each other in the Embassy. Apart from the skiing trips, we had long weekends away on fishing trips up in the mountains at Neuberg-an-der-Leitha, over the border in southern Austria, not far from Brück. We stayed in a small Gasthof there, amidst magnificent scenery and, generally, the weather was very good. We ladies went shopping at Murzsesschlag nearby for provisions, and the trout the men caught and we cooked on an open fire, were delicious. I also used to take advantage of these trips to get the car serviced at the Ford garage at Wiener Neustadt, not too far away. It did mean getting up at 5 am to be at the garage for 7.30 am, but I was always greeted with a hot cup of coffee, rolls and cheese, and was given a comfortable chair to settle down into whilst I waited. Take note, Brück!

Entertaining – From Tequila to Tokay

As I've said before, Budapest was a very social Post, with many official receptions and parties, usually within our Embassy, but with other friendly Embassies and the British ex-pat community in Budapest also.

My own space for entertaining was very limited. I could only seat six at my dining table, and the flat was small in comparison to my bungalow in Mexico, but I still managed to hold a few dinner parties. The Ambassador and Prim came to one, I remember, which was they said they enjoyed.

Royal Visitors

As Hungary was just beginning to open up to the world, it

seemed as if everyone wanted to visit, including members of the Royal Family. The Hungarians were very enthusiastic about such visits, even though they knew little about our "Royals", and we in turn were very privileged to have them. But it always meant a tremendous amount of work liaising with the Private Secretaries, arranging itineraries, planning everything down to the minutest detail and to the last second. I found it extremely interesting and, of course, we got to meet our Royal visitors ourselves. Most of them stayed at the Residence, which put a tremendous strain on Prim and the Butler, Istvan, and her household, but they always coped admirably.

Apart from Prince Andrew, our other visitors were The Prince of Wales and Princess Diana (separately as they had by this time split up), and Princess Michael of Kent, whom I was usually asked to accompany to the airport after her visit. She came frequently, as she had connections in Hungary.

But our most important visit was yet to come.

The State Visit (4-7 May 1993)

If we thought the other visits generated a lot of work, welcome to The State Visit, when Her Majesty The Queen and The Duke of Edinburgh were invited officially to Hungary by the Hungarian Government.

Planning started at least a year ahead and went into over-drive about six months before they arrived, when we never seemed to stop. Again, we spent most of our time liaising with everyone else, and both Carol and I were rushed off our feet.

When the time of their arrival came, the visit went incredibly well. Her Majesty and His Royal Highness, who were staying at the official Hungarian Guest House, were most warmly welcomed by President Arpad Göncz (who to me seemed like the epitome of an ideal grandfather) and the Prime Minister and Hungarian Officials. It was a landmark occasion, also, when Her

Majesty was asked to address the Hungarian Parliament, the first time ever that a member of the Royal Family had ever done so. I was very privileged to be allowed to attend Parliament and listen to that address. Such a far cry from those dark, oppressive days of Communism.

The Royal couple were then treated to a display of horsemanship and a barbecue at Bugacs, on the Puszta, which I know they thoroughly enjoyed, after which there was an official reception at the Embassy for Hungarian officials, VIPs, foreign Ambassadors, VIP ex-pats – in fact as many as we could possibly get into our newly refurbished (for the occasion), Embassy Hall. A small, private reception was also held at the Residence for Embassy staff and a few VIPs.

When it came time for them to leave, there was what is known as "Farewells", when those who have worked the hardest for their visit are "commanded" to attend a private audience at the Guest House with Her Majesty and His Royal Highness, and to receive a small gift.

They had been well briefed in advance as to whom they would be receiving, and I was over the moon when I received such an invitation. Hats and gloves were "advised", and it was a nerve-wracking wait to be called. At last it was my turn. I was escorted into the room by the Equerry, formally introduced, and then he withdrew.

I'd spent much time practicing my curtsey, which I think I did elegantly. Her Majesty held out her hand (you never offer yours), which I shook gently, and presented me with a lovely signed photograph of them both. I then curtsied to High Royal Highness and shook his hand also. The Queen then makes the opening remarks (it's a long time ago now, and I think it would be in order for me to repeat, more or less, what she said):

"Thank you so much for all the hard work you have done for our visit. I hope you will be able to have a short break."

I replied: "It's been a great privilege to be able to have done so, Your Majesty" (nodding to HRH too). Then it's for me to make the next remark.

"Actually, I'm driving home tomorrow for a few days with my family."

"You're driving?", the Duke asked.

"Yes, Sir."

The State Visit to Hungary, May 1993

Her Majesty addressing the Hungarian Parliament.
As President Göncz noted: The Queen was the first of her line
to visit Hungary since Richard the Lionheart.
(I'm far right, in the balcony, with the cerise coloured hat)

Above: Enjoying a display of horsemanship at Bugacs

Below: Leaving the Embassy with the Ambassador,
now Sir John Birch, having just received his Knighthood

Waiting our turn at "Farewells"

EIIR

On the occasion of the Visit of Her Majesty Queen Elizabeth II
and
His Royal Highness The Prince Philip, Duke of Edinburgh
The British Ambassador
is commanded by The Queen to invite

Miss Gillian Angrave

to a Reception to be held at the Ambassador's Residence,
Loróntffy Zsuzsanna utca 7, Budapest II
on Wednesday, 5th May, 1993 at 11.45 a.m.

R.S.V.P. Budapest 266-1552

"How long will that take you?"

"Two and a half days."

At which point HRH turned to The Queen and said: "There you are. I told you it was too far to bring the horses."

I nodded wisely, not having a clue as to how horses travel. Time then for another curtsey to them both, by which time the Equerry had reappeared to escort me from the room, clutching my precious photograph. I will never forget that occasion, as you can imagine.

At the end of the "Farewells", the Ambassador was Knighted. This was a private ceremony, with only Prim present, but we were thrilled, and proud for them both. Having a State Visit is a tremendous strain and, like us, they had worked so very hard. We all felt it was well deserved.

After the Queen and Prince Philip had left, we heaved a sigh of relief, and retired to the Residence for a thank-you drink. Time, then, for me to go home and pack in readiness for my two-and-a-half day drive home. Without horses!

Left: The Ambassador meeting Princess Diana at the airport (we were there too)
Right: At the Opera. Princess Diana with President and Mrs Göncz
(also Ken Wharfe, Detective, and Lady-in-Waiting)

I also attended that opera occasion, wearing my James Bond dress (shame you couldn't see it full length - the fishtail was lovely!) With my Hungarian escort for the evening, Zoltán

My Own VIP Visitors

Of course, I was absolutely thrilled when Mum and Dad came out to stay for twelve days in September 1992. This was the first time they had been able to visit me at Post as South America had been too expensive and too far away to travel to, but we made the most of our time together. I couldn't have all the time off, but they were very happy wandering around on their own with maps and instructions. The Ambassador very kindly gave a lunch for us at the Residence, which they much enjoyed, though Dad was somewhat shy and in awe of the occasion. At the weekend I took them to Szentendre, Esztergom, Visegrád and the Danube Bend, which they loved.

My friend, Lorna Best, from my Philippines days, was over in Europe, so she came to stay for a few days, as did my dear friend Erwan (from Mexico), now EU Ambassador to Slovenia

Pam came out twice more, the last time with Tricia from 4-10

August 1993. I was so pleased to see them, and though it was a bit of a squeeze, we all fitted into the Cube - more or less.

They arrived on a Wednesday, and I had to work on the Thursday, but they were happy to wander around on their own. I got the Friday off and we visited the citadel at Visegrád and continued to the beautiful Basilica at Esztergom where the largest single canvas painting in the world, Titian's *Assumption of the Virgin*, now hangs. I've seen, and written about, the original many times, which is in the Santa Maria Gloriosa dei Frari in Venice. We toured the Lake Balaton area, visited Kecskemet, followed in The Queen's footsteps to Bugacs for a display of horsemanship, and ended with a trip on the Danube. It was wonderful to be able to show them just a small piece of Hungary, and we had the time of our lives.

At last, now I was nearer Europe, I was able to offer my friends and family hospitality in return. It felt good.

With Mum and Dad at the Danube Bend

Above: Lunch with the Ambassador at the Residence

Below: With Pam and Tricia at Fisherman's Bastion on the Var

The thrilling horsemanship display at Bugacs

"Tripping" Around Eastern Europe"

Because of the unleaded petrol (or lack of it) situation in Eastern Europe, I was a bit stuck as to where I could take the car. With my spare can of petrol, just in case, I managed to go around Hungary without too many problems. Travelling into Austria was fine, so I went a few times to Vienna, which was only two hours or so from Budapest on the new motorway, as well as to Salzburg, the ski slopes and on the fishing trips with my colleagues. Other excursions included driving down to Slovenia via Zagreb in Croatia; and a few days in Prague (I flew there). I also had a quick trip down to Belgrade, but not in my car.

Just over the border into Slovakia was do-able too, as it only took about an hour from Budapest. There, I found an excellent Bohemian crystal outlet where I could keep adding to my wine, tumbler, liqueur and whisky glass set as and when I had the money and opportunity to do so. The design was beautiful, and I kept it, virtually intact, for many years until I auctioned it off as I no longer used it

The longer I stayed in Hungary, the more unleaded petrol was becoming available and the easier it was to travel further afield, but that definitely did not include Romania, Serbia and, to a lesser extent, Poland. In order to travel to those countries, I needed to team up with colleagues, which I did for two unforgettable, eye-opening excursions in particular.

The Painted Monasteries, Romania: 8-11 October 1992

Liz Ibbotson (wife of our DA), Sheila MacTaggart, our Admin Officer, Debbie Goldthorpe, our 2nd Sec Commercial, and I got on very well in the Embassy. We were of a similar age, and were definitely keen on travelling, so, arranging our leave accordingly, we decided to take off to Romania for four days in Debbie's right-hand drive Vauxhall Cavalier to visit the Painted Monasteries of Bucovina, in the north-eastern part of the country. These churches, masterpieces of Byzantine art, are unique, and their murals represent complete cycles of religious events. Considering they are external walls in a harsh climate, the colours are quite unbelievable.

It was a bit of a squash in the car, but we managed to get everything in, including a few emergency rations and a spare can of petrol, just in case. As Debbie's car ran on leaded, we felt this wouldn't be a problem. Really? We were in for a shock.

We set off early as we had a long journey ahead of us, our destination that day being the Hotel Castel Dracula in Bistrita, up in the mountains, which was also a centre for skiing in winter. But first we had to get there. We crossed the Hungarian/Romanian border near Szeged with a fair amount of hassle, and it soon became obvious that our journey would be "monitored". We headed for Cluj Napoca, 460 kms away, taking it in turns to do the driving, but on the way we needed to stop for petrol.

I don't think any of us was prepared for the situation in Romania. In comparison with Hungary, it was backward and hostile, the people sullen and suspicious. I doubt whether, away from the towns and cities, they had ever seen a foreigner before, let alone four females travelling together. We came to the only petrol station we had seen in miles, to find a queue at least two miles long by the look of it. What should we do? If we got on the end of the queue, it would take us days, so since we had diplomatic plates, we plucked up courage and went to the front. There was nearly a riot and we suffered much abuse: for me, it brought back the nightmare of Guatemala, which I most definitely didn't want to re-visit. It was only the begrudging intervention of the police, there to control the crowds, that saved us from serious physical harm. We all felt so bad, and so terribly sad. If this is what it had been like under Communism, and Ceausescu as well, what a horrendous time the Romanians must have had.

We filled up the car and the can, and got out of there as quickly as we could, insults being hurled at us every few yards. But the police had obviously radioed ahead, so we were stopped frequently *en route* to Cluj, which delayed us a lot. From there we had to sort out the map and find our way to Bistrita, another two hours further on.

After ten hours of travelling, we arrived at dusk at Dracula's Castel which, reading the Trip Advisor reviews now, bears no resemblance whatsoever to what we found in 1993. We had originally intended this to be our base for the next two nights, but one night was enough. That first night I shared with Debbie. What a room! There was no plug, or pipe from the washbasin, so the trickle of water that there was went all over the floor (we'd forgotten to bring plugs with us – a must in communist countries). The wardrobe door, with an enormous Dracula design on it, fell off. The beds were rock hard, and the sheets were former damask tablecloths. The facilities – well, basic. The worst thing was, though, that there was very little to eat, which we were to find during our whole stay in Romania. I've never felt so hungry in my whole life as I did when I got back to Budapest, and my heart went out to the city dwellers in particular. There were no supermarkets, only their equivalent of the *csem*, but whereas in Hungary there had been a small selection of items, here there was nothing but bare shelves with perhaps the odd tin on them. It was to prove a big problem for us, as was the petrol. From now on we couldn't risk stopping at petrol stations where there was, at each one, an equally long queue. Instead, we had to rely on the kindness of villagers to supply us with petrol of sorts, often from buckets, and at vast cost. It looked more like dishwater, but did smell vaguely of petrol so we kept our fingers crossed that the Cavalier didn't know the difference!

That evening we dined on bread, an oily sort of soup with bits of pork floating in it, and one small biscuit. That was it. Breakfast was more bread, and one barely-boiled egg. Fortunately, we'd taken a jar of coffee, so we asked for boiling water, which was much frowned on. No milk.

We couldn't wait to get away and head up to Suceava, where we decided we would stay the next night and which was nearer to the Monasteries anyway. As we hadn't booked anything, we drove around until we found a very basic small hotel, which was adequate - just.

The Grant Family

On the way up to Suceava, we couldn't believe our eyes when we came across a Romany gypsy style caravan with a WWF Panda placard on the back. We overtook it slowly, but when the occupants saw we had British diplomatic plates, they waved at us to stop, which we did, allowing them to catch up.

This was the amazing Grant family and I've kept the 30 December 1997 article about them that appeared in the Sunday Times when they returned eventually to the UK. David and Kate Grant, and their children Torcuil, 17, Eilidh, 16, and Fiona 13, came from the Orkneys. In 1990 they decided to sell their house and travel the world in their caravan, becoming the first people to circumnavigate the world in a horse-drawn vehicle. From the article, it seems that during their 12,360 mile trip, they endured much hardship, danger, illness and political upheaval, but when we came across them they had only just started out on their adventure. We spent half an hour or so chatting to them, but we had our own journey to make and so, sadly, wished them lots of luck, an interesting and safe journey, and said goodbye. I wonder what became of that family?

The Monasteries

The Monasteries, twenty miles or so from Suceava, were more than we could ever have hoped for. The weather was fine, and the sun glinted on the painted walls, enhancing their colour. We only managed to visit three, Moldovita, Sucevita and Voronet , but each one was breathtaking in its beauty and just seeing them was worth all the aggravation and hassle we were encountering.

We lived on bread most of the time, with an apple now and then bought in one of the small villages nearby, augmented by a tin of sardines or tuna which we had had the foresight to bring with us. The nuns living near the Monasteries were kind and on one occasion gave us a biscuit and piece of cake which they had to spare.

After two days it was time to start our journey back. Change of plan meant that we made our way to Timisoara instead of back to Bistrita, a long journey but which then left us reasonably near the Hungarian border. We found a small hotel in the centre

My trip to the Painted Monasteries

Above: The spooky Hotel Castel Dracula at Bistrita

Below: The amazing Grant Family

Above: *En route* to Suceava. The reality of living in the country in Romania.
Life was still very basic

Below: The last vestiges of Communism

The Painted Monasteries

Above: Sucevita

Below: Voronet

Above: Trying to eke out our meagre rations

Below: What do four ladies do when they are together? They go SHOPPING!

and at last enjoyed a meal of sorts of bread and scrambled eggs. Never have eggs tasted so good. Again, though, there was nothing in the shops

Our journey back to Budapest proved uneventful, and everyone was eager to know how we got on. Did we have some stories to tell! It had been an eye-opener for me, but I don't think any of us would have missed it for the world. But first we had to eat!

My Trip to Poland

(Again, taken from my Epistle sent to Mum and Dad)

The [same] four of us set off again, this time on a trip to Poland from 14-17 November 1993, leaving Budapest at 6 am via Vác to Sahy, the border crossing into south-eastern Czechoslovakia. From there, it was a wonderful drive through the magnificent Tatra Mountains to the Polish border at Chyzne, where we did all our money changing, then on to Krakow, where we had booked at the newly refurbished Grand Hotel. I loved the old centre of Krakow (known at the Royal Tract), with its Main Market Square, the Cloth Hall, the Wawel Citadel and Cathedral, and the ancient streets. It was a beautiful autumn day, and this whole historical area, encircled by parks, was a delight to wander around. We walked and walked, then did a little shopping (what a surprise!) as everything was much cheaper here in Poland and there was a far better range of goods; food, clothes, handicrafts. The Hotel was excellent value for money too, and the staff were so pleasant - smiling, courteous, and helpful to a fault. What a change from Hungary. We all remarked on it.

We left Krakow at 11.30 am the next day to visit Oswiecim-Auschwitz-Birkenau. I dreaded going there, but felt I had to, just to understand. To say it was ghastly is an understatement and I don't propose to say more, except that it took me back to Chile, and a remote and somewhat secretive German colony near Valdivia known as Colonia Dignidad, where it was alleged that

The two faces of Poland

Above: Wawel Citadel and Cathedral, Krakow

Below: The entrance to Oswiecim-Auschwitz-Birkenau

Walther Rauff, the inventor of the portable gas oven, was being sheltered by the Pinochet Government, who refused requests for his extradition, and where he eventually died. I couldn't get away from Auschwitz quick enough.

It was then my turn to drive to Warsaw. Again, we were in Debbie's Cavalier, and I suddenly found myself in the midst of heavy traffic, mainly filthy coal lorries leaving Katowice and all heading our way. We'd been advised to take the longer Czestokowa/Katowice route, but it still took four hours to get to Warsaw and it was a tiresome and boring journey across the Silesian Plain, which was as flat as a pancake. It then took us an hour and a half to find the Embassy, which didn't help much either.

We were staying with another colleague, Louise, who had been the Accountant in Budapest on her previous posting. Her flat was small and depressing, but the four of us camped out as best we could whilst Louise went to stay with a friend.

The next day, Saturday, was cold but sunny and we went sightseeing round the newly reconstructed Jewish Quarter where, I remember, I bought a beautiful, large, antique leather hatbox. Why? Don't ask me! The atmosphere in this Quarter was happy and friendly, though what it had been like during the Communist regime, I hate to think.

We shopped again. Would there be room for us in the car, we wondered? Lunch at the Marriott Hotel seemed the thing to do, having dined the previous evening at Warsaw's most elegant and exclusive restaurant, the Swietoszek, for the sum of £11.00 a head. More walking, a trip to Billa, the Austrian supermarket chain which was here, to stock up on teabags, etc, then back to the Marriott for a superb buffet dinner.

We were up early on Sunday and were on the road again by 9.30 am. It was a long twelve-hour journey to Budapest in pouring rain, fog and sleet and I did the three-hour stint in the dark through the Czech mountains, which was quite a strain. We were held up for a time at the Czech/Hungarian border by intransigent lorry drivers, and finally made it back to Budapest at 10.15 pm, physically exhausted but mentally stimulated after our "holiday", amazed that we had managed to cram so much into such a short time – and into the car. Again, we had got on very well and had yet more tales to tell. But that was for the next day. Now all I wanted to do was sleep!

Farewell Budapest

Yet again, all good things come to an end (this seemed to be the story of my life with The Office, somehow) and at the end of 1994 it was time for me to return to London for another home posting.

I packed up, went to a fair number of farewell parties I remember, and with much sadness said goodbye to my colleagues, Ernó, and my neighbours.

By this time, I had sold my faithful little Escort and bought a metallic red, right-hand drive Rover from the newly-opened Rover dealership in Budapest. I packed it up with my television and a great deal of baggage, and drove for the last time over the Hungarian border to Passau, where again I stopped the night. On into Germany, via Regensburg, Nürnberg, passed the Hochenheim Grand Prix racing circuit until, after eleven hours driving, I knew I must force myself to stop. I was feeling pretty tired by this time having been held up with road works on the Autobahn, and with the strain of driving a right-hand drive car in a left-hand drive country, so I found a small hotel in a town just south of Frankfurt and bedded down for the night.

I was up early next day as I had to make Zeebrugge for the overnight sailing on P & O's *Pride of Rotterdam* to Hull, from where I would drive to Pontesbury to Mum and Dad. Frankfurt proved a headache as there was a diversion and I drove round and round the ring-road for an hour trying to find my way out (no sat nav, of course). The Duke was right: this was definitely

Above Left: The Hungarian Customs Officer signing
my baggage release papers. They inspect your baggage at home.

Above Right: Here we go again!

Below: Me, with the Hungarian Parliament building behind.

not a journey for horses! On into Belgium via Maastricht, by-passing Brussels and at last arriving at the port in good time to load the car and settle down. But imagine my delight when, whilst passing the Bureau and looking at the list of Officers, who should I see there as Purser, but my great P & O shipmate, Mike Staddon. I was flabbergasted. I poked my head round his door and the look on his face was priceless. "Good God. It's Swilly Gilly", he exclaimed. It was almost twenty years since we'd last seen each other, but it seemed like yesterday. We only had time for a quick drink as Mike was working, but he made sure I was well looked after, for which I was very appreciative.

Once back in the UK, on to Pontesbury for another joyous reunion with Mum and Dad, and for a brief rest before heading down to London to take up residence in my own flat, having given my tenants notice.

Time to prepare myself for the next two years or so of being back at home before yet another posting. Life was still exceedingly good!

Farewell Budapest
One last view of beautiful Budapest from the Gellert Hill

PART THIRTEEN

ON HOME SHORES ONCE MORE

CHAPTER ONE

A TESTING TIME

After two weeks leave with Mum and Dad, it was back down to London to sort out the flat before starting work. At least this time my tenants had left it in reasonable condition, so it wasn't long before everything was shipshape and I was able to enjoy it once again. My air freight arrived, then my heavy baggage, which meant a fair amount of head-scratching as to where I was going to put it all, but eventually even my baskets were in their place and at last I could relax. Amazingly, there was even space for me too.

At work, I became PA to an excellent boss, Anthony Layden, Head of Western European Department. It was an exceedingly satisfying and busy job, but there were very sad moments when we had to deal with the death of Princess Diana as it had occurred in France. It was a traumatic time for everyone, but particularly for the staff at the Embassy there. They had as much support as we could possibly give, but it was still tough.

Socially, I was able to catch up with friends, and take up other interests. I became a member of the Arthur Ransome Society, and Secretary of the Nancy Blackett Trust which looked after AR's 1931 Hillyard cutter. I loved it and was able to sail her a fair amount. I gained my Competent Crew Certificate, braving the Alderney Races and the shipping lanes of the English Channel at night as part of my exam, and I progressed to Day Skipper Theory, although with no boat of my own and only spasmodic trips in other people's, I wasn't able to do the Practical part. But at least I could steer, which was useful on my Solos sailing holidays around the Greek islands in the Ionian Sea!

389

I went off for outings with the Martin Brundle Supporters' Club, and really enjoyed the British Grand Prix, sadly, though, without Dad.

Time was flying by, but in 1995 dear Dad was diagnosed with Parkinsons disease. I went up to Pontesbury as often as I could at weekends to help Mum, but as time past we seemed to be losing him more and more until, in the end, he didn't recognize me at all. This was the hardest thing to bear. We had shared so much and now he just stared at me vacantly. On 28 May 1997, Dad died. Mum, Sheila and I had been at his bedside in Shrewsbury hospital, where he had pneumonia, just a few hours before. We had, in our hearts, already said our goodbyes, and had gone home to snatch a few hours sleep, ready to return early the next day, but he slipped away in his sleep during that night. I have a feeling he didn't want us to be there when he died, but Mum took it badly that she hadn't stayed with him till the end.

The next two weeks until after the funeral were a blur. I stayed with Mum as long as I could, but I had to get back to work, so I returned to London. My boss was exceedingly kind and supportive, and I did manage a short time away a week or so later, when I took Mum to a site near Barmouth to stay in a static caravan owned by the local Breathing Club at Pontesbury, of which Dad had been a member. They had both enjoyed many holidays with their own caravan in this area, and Mum seemed to gain some peace when she was there.

When I returned to London again, I was asked to go to see my Personnel Officer, who said The Office could now offer me Madrid at last. I was elated, but I knew I couldn't go. I needed to stay in the UK with Mum and support her all I could. She and Dad had sacrificed so much for me throughout all my years of travel, and now it was my turn. So, although it broke my heart, I turned it down and asked if I could remain in London until my retirement in 2005, to which they reluctantly agreed.

Then on 19 March 1999 another tragedy hit our family. Sheila's husband, Len, died suddenly aged 50. Now she had the task of bringing up two teenage sons on her own, but we rallied round as best we could and, as I've said before, she did a fantastic job and they were and are a credit to her.

As I was now going to remain in London, I became PA to the Assistant Under-Secretary of State dealing with Wider Europe: in turn, John de Fonblanque, Stephen Wright, John Macgregor, and Linda Duffield. I loved the work: again, it was very busy but satisfying, and I got on well with all my bosses. I inherited a coffee mug with the inscription: "Behind every great boss, there's a really great secretary". This caused some mirth, occasionally a raised eye-brow, but it remained on my desk – "Lest we forget"!

Her majesty's garden party

EIIR

*The Lord Chamberlain is
commanded by Her Majesty to invite*

....

Miss Gillian Angrave

....

*to a Garden Party
at Buckingham Palace
on Tuesday, 16th July 2002 from 4 to 6 pm*

This card does not admit

INVESTOR IN PEOPLE

Foreign &
Commonwealth Office

7 April 2005

Ms Gillian Angrave
WLD
W111D

Human Resources Directorate
Old Admiralty Building
London SW1A 2PA

Telephone: (020) 7008 0579/80
Facsimile: (020) 7008 0581
E-mail: David.Warren@fco.gov.uk

Dear Gillian,

Your imminent retirement brings to an end your career of 29 years in the Diplomatic Service. I am writing on behalf of the Office to thank you for all your work during your time with us. You have made a great contribution to the work of the Office, and we shall be sorry to say goodbye.

After you joined the Service in 1976 you served in a variety of posts in the secretarial cadre at home and overseas, including Manila, Lima, Guatemala City, Santiago, Mexico City, and Budapest. For the last 10 years you have held senior PA posts in London.

You approached each job with impeccable professionalism, and justifiably took pride in setting the highest possible standards. Reliable, efficient, interested, and fastidious on detail, you took everything in your stride with enthusiasm and good humour. An engaging approachability and excellent skills as a thoughtful and supportive team player made you an enormously popular and valued colleague. You earned many accolades from your Reporting Officers – "a Rolls Royce service"; "outstandingly effective, polished and professional in the best traditions of the Service"; "a very friendly, calm and reliable presence at the centre of the Command " are typical examples. You will be greatly missed by colleagues and friends across the Service and I hope that you will keep in touch with them.

The Service relies enormously on the dedication, professionalism and flair of its members – qualities you have so amply demonstrated. As you look back over your career, I hope it is with a sense of achievement and pride in a job well done. You will be much missed. I wish you all the very best for a long and happy retirement.

With all good wishes,

Yours ever,

Jen

David Warren
Director, Human Resources

My Farewell letter from The Diplomatic Service, of which I am very proud

Twenty-Five Years with the Diplomatic Service

On 5 July 2001, I completed twenty-five years' of loyal service with the Foreign Office, and to mark the occasion, at a small reception on 3 December 2001 (it takes a little time for the Office to "catch up") given by my boss, John Macgregor, I was presented with a beautiful framed certificate in recognition of this achievement. I was thrilled, and it remains one of my prized possessions to this day. It had been an honour and a privilege to serve and, though exceedingly tough at times, a career I wouldn't have missed for the world.

Unknown to me, however, John had also put my name forward to be considered for an invitation to one of Her Majesty's Garden Parties at Buckingham Palace as a reward for my long service. This was approved, and I was overjoyed, and flabbergasted, when an invitation from the Lord Chamberlain landed on my doormat on 5 May, inviting me to attend on Tuesday 16th July, 2002. I immediately returned the RSVP and started worrying about a hat and what to wear, as one does.

It was a beautiful day. I'd been given special permission to bring the car and park it in the Quadrangle, so at least I hadn't had to struggle on the train with my outfit and my Polish hatbox (yes, it did have a use at last). I got changed after lunch, John wished me well, and off I went to the Palace. It was wonderful. The Queen and The Duke of Edinburgh passed nearby on one occasion, but more than anything I enjoyed meeting so many fascinating people, wandering around the beautiful gardens, and partaking of the delicate sandwiches and cakes that were served.

Life then returned to normal, but on 5 February 2003 (though the Death Certificate says 6th as that was when she was discovered) dear Mum died suddenly. I've already written about the circumstances, so I won't go over it again, but I was bereft. As [Sir]

Cliff writes in his autobiography: "You're never too old to be an orphan". This was exactly how I felt – abandoned and all alone.

But you just have to grit your teeth, dig deep and get on with things.

I'd already booked a holiday in April to the States – a few days with Pat and a few days in New York - so I decided to continue with my plans. It did me good, although New York was still struggling to come to terms with the Twin Towers disaster, and to see Ground Zero was a tremendous shock. I remember watching the horrific events unravelling with John on his small television in his office. We just stared at the screen in disbelief. It was overwhelmingly touching, when I arrived in New York, being approached by New Yorkers, shaking my hand and thanking me for still coming. We all have to stick together at times like this, and I think that's still true today. It would be a cruel and insensitive world if we didn't, although sometimes, with what seems to be happening these days, it makes you wonder.

As time marched on, the prospect of retirement began to loom large, so in January 2004 I moved from Wallington to near Chichester to prepare myself for this unwanted milestone event. I knew I didn't want to stay in London, and thought it would be a good idea to move house (again) and get settled in a new environment before I actually left The Office, which turned out to be the right decision.

After many weekends of just driving around East and West Sussex searching for an ideal location to live, I decided that the Chichester area was where I wanted to put down roots once I retired. It was and is a beautiful part of the country, near the sea, and I knew I would be happy here.

Although Sheila and the family were up north, all my friends were down south so, being on my own, it made more sense to stay here. However, I was determined to travel up to see the family as often as I could.

Retirement day was creeping ever nearer. I went on a Foreign Office pre-retirement course, the only single person there, and was amazed at how difficult the other attendees seemed to be finding the prospect of retirement too, especially the couples and the wives who now had their husbands to contend with, who thought all their time should be spent with them. Not so!

Eventually the dreaded day arrived: 16 April 2005, my 60th birthday. It was a Wednesday, but we had to go on our actual 60th birthday so there was no chance of stopping on until the Friday. Again, my boss held a leaving party for me, friends and colleagues came to say goodbye, and with a heavy heart I packed up my desk for the last time.

At 8.50 am on that Wednesday morning I walked through the arch into the Quadrangle, a proud member of Her Majesty's Diplomatic Service.

At 5 pm that evening I walked through that same arch again – a proud member of - nothing. A nobody. Like a mariner on a ship without a rudder, staring across a vast expanse of empty ocean with no land in sight. Ready for the breaker's yard, just like my beloved CANBERRA and ORIANA.

I went home and wept.

CHAPTER TWO

LIFE AFTER THE OFFICE

But, as I was about to discover, there was a fascinating life beyond retirement still to be lived.

My first two weeks or so as a retired person were tough. I felt cut adrift, with no idea of how I was going to fill all this spare time that I now had. And the worst irony of all was that now I had all this free time, Mum and Dad were no longer around to help me enjoy it. How I miss them still.

It didn't help, either, that I now found myself living next door to a very troublesome neighbour who, by her own admission, was jealous of me and resented me being there. Not much I could do about that, though I tried every which way to get on.

I knew I had to get out of this self-pitying mindset quickly so, after giving myself a good talking to, I set about sorting out the rest of my life.

One craft I'd always wanted to learn was bell-ringing. The memories will stay with me forever of one warm summer's evening, when I was about twelve and we were on a family picnic out in the countryside, hearing the haunting strains of bells, carried on the gentle breeze over the fields, ringing for Evensong at a church in a village nearby. I knew this was something I wanted to be part of as I'd always loved their sound, and their purpose in calling parishioners to worship. As a church-goer, having been christened and confirmed at St Peter's Church in Oadby all those years ago, it seemed the natural thing for me to do.

As soon as I moved down to where I live now, I'd wanted to become involved (and still am as a Lay Assistant) in my local church's activities. We have five bells at St Mary's, so I asked the bell-ringers if I could learn. Ideally, I should have been younger to take up the craft as it's not easy and is tough on the little grey cells, but they welcomed me with open arms. I had an excellent instructor in our Tower Captain, Ken Knight, who sadly passed away a short while ago, so that I'm now a fairly competent ringer, even though my repertoire will never be extensive.

We are a fantastic band of ringers at St Mary's, and have great fun together, as well as the more serious side of ringing for our Services, weddings, funerals and any other occasion that needs bells.

We endeavor to go on an outing each year to ring at other Towers in the County and on the Isle of Wight, and on one occasion we went up to the Whitechapel Bell Foundry in London (sadly no more) to watch the bells being cast, which was fascinating and gave me, certainly, a greater sense of pride and appreciation of what we have learned to do.

I also belong to the Sussex Counties Association of Change Ringers, and have even rung at Canterbury Cathedral, though with an experienced ringer by my side. When I go up to Sheila's at Christmas, I ring on Christmas Day at her beautiful local church, St Wilfrid's. However, with a touch of arthritis in my hands these days, I'm having to curtail my ringing slightly, but I have no intentions of giving up.

Wanting to become more involved in my community, I also became a Governor of our local Primary School, spending lunchtimes listening to the older children read. Having never had much contact with children in the past, I found I enjoyed it, though I was a bit put off when one of the boys refused to come to me because I had "gold teeth" - my fillings, which are a legacy from my wonderful, British Council-trained dentist in Peru. I told the young lad that it was Inca gold, and explained who the Incas were, but that didn't seem to impress him in the slightest. He still didn't want to come. Funny things, children!

By now I was steering a straighter course and my life was falling into place nicely. Ever up for a challenge, in June 2005 just after I'd retired, I answered an advert in the Chichester Observer for a West Sussex County Council Usher for weddings. After an interview, I was offered the job, along with another lady, Val Wright (now a good friend of mine), who had just retired from the MOD. Our Superintendent decided she didn't want to lose either of us, so it was agreed we would job-share, which worked out well.

Which brings me to the present.

A Busy Life!

On board "Nancy Blackett" with Charlie Dimmock
when she visited us in Littlehampton

Bell ringing at Canterbury Cathedral with the Association

The Life of a Registrar

Not only am I still covered by the Official Secrets Act, I now find myself bound by the Data Protection Act as well, which prohibits me from going into details about my wedding ceremonies.

Again, I love my job and feel so privileged to be part of a couple's special day as they start their married life together. Not only do I enjoy meeting people on such happy occasions (usually), but I feel I have a purpose in life yet again. I now "belong", and I am part of a team. After two years as Ushers, Val and I were asked if we would like to transfer over and become Registrars ourselves. I jumped at the chance, as did Val. Having never been married myself, I now find I'm marrying other people. It's a funny old world sometimes.

My weddings keep me extremely busy, particularly during the summer months. I can hardly believe that I'll soon have reached fifteen years' service with the County Council, but I have no intentions of giving it up just yet. I work with an amazing set of colleagues – supportive and great fun - who without doubt keep me going. The stories we could tell, but we won't of course!

However, without giving away confidences, one particular ceremony comes to mind. I was privileged to conduct the marriage ceremony for a "celebrity" at one of our stately homes. It's a beautiful venue, the sun shone brightly on that day, and I recognised quite a few faces amongst the guests. The bride arrived looking stunning, as she always does. As usual, the groom was quite overcome. Everything went exceedingly well, and I was roundly thanked afterwards. And I knew that I had "arrived" at last when my left ear and part of my colourful-jacketed left shoulder appeared in "Hello" magazine. What it is to be famous!

Coincidentally, Sheila went down to London to see my bride in her show. When it had finished, she waited at the stage door to have a few words with her. "My sister conducted your wedding ceremony", Sheila said. "Ah, yes" replied the star. "It was a beautiful ceremony and she wore a lovely jacket." Must remember to wear that jacket more often!

As part of being a Registrar, one of the other aspects of my job is that I'm one of only two Registrars in Chichester who conduct the Citizenship Ceremonies. It seems that my years with The Office have equipped me well to do this, and I find it both rewarding and at times very emotional listening to the journeys some of our new Citizens have had to travel to reach this stage.

And I've moved - yet again! Whilst my life in general was very happy, on the home front it was not. Problems with my neighbour were getting worse, so much so that in 2010 I collapsed outside the Post Office one morning and was rushed to hospital with viral myocarditis caused by stress. In the end my brilliant medical team - GP and cardiologist – warned me that if I didn't take myself away from this awful situation soon, the consequences would be serious, even fatal. This was quite a sobering thought but, as much as I loved my little house, I knew I had to listen to their advice.

And so, in 2012, I packed up all over again and moved not too far away, to a townhouse on a very attractive, and well-maintained small development. As it's turned out, this has been an excellent move. I have fantastic neighbours once again, love my new home, have become a Director of our Residents Association Company, and a member of the Garden Committee. When not involved in weddings, I can often be found pottering around in my own little patio garden or tending eleven or so tubs! Never a dull moment.

And, as you can see, writing is also playing an important part in my life too. Ever since that day so many years ago when I won the National Schools Essay Competition, I've always found great enjoyment and satisfaction in putting pen to paper to share my thoughts and experiences, and this love of the written word seems to be getting stronger as the years roll by. I'm not so interested in writing fiction, but for me describing the places I've visited is a real joy. Throughout my life I've always been a good letter writer, and with my new found passion for photography, I now try to make my words come alive even more. So much so that, having fallen in love with that most magical of cities, Venice, as well as writing this book I've published three books charting my wanderings and discoveries in that "water wonderland" as well. I just don't seem able to stop, but long may the creative juices flow!

Travel is still, and always will be, in my blood. At 74, I may not be quite as agile as I used to be, but I'm not about to let that deter me. I shall keep going for a long as I can, and have a fire extinguisher handy to douse the flames on my over-heating computer as I recount it all. Mouse and I are now great friends!

I'm off on a cruise in December in "my kind of ship", that is a small one. We're sailing around the Caribbean, visiting some of those islands that I never managed to get to all those years ago with P & O. Even Antigua is on the list! Was I right to turn it down as my first posting, or was I not? I can't wait to find out.

And for the future, I've adopted a mantra to help me on my way:

"Live your life like a butterfly. Have a rest sometimes, but always remember to fly".

I hope the Monarch butterflies would approve.

The life of a registrar

Preparing for a wedding ceremony at Edes House, our historic and very elegant Grade I listed "head office" in Chichester.